T5-CWQ-852

SUMMARY OF GREGG NOTEHAND

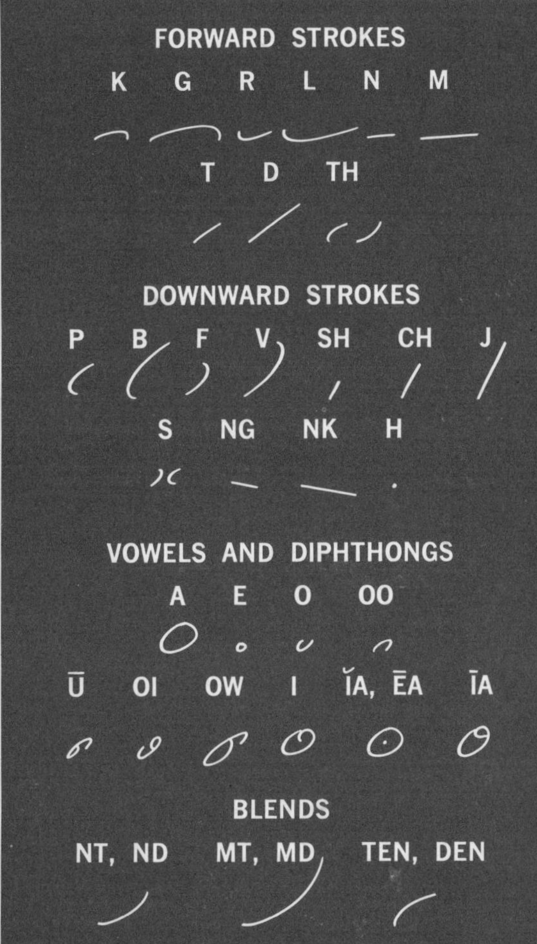
FORWARD STROKES
K G R L N M
T D TH
DOWNWARD STROKES
P B F V SH CH J
S NG NK H
VOWELS AND DIPHTHONGS
A E O OO
Ū OI OW I ĬA, ĒA ĪA
BLENDS
NT, ND MT, MD TEN, DEN

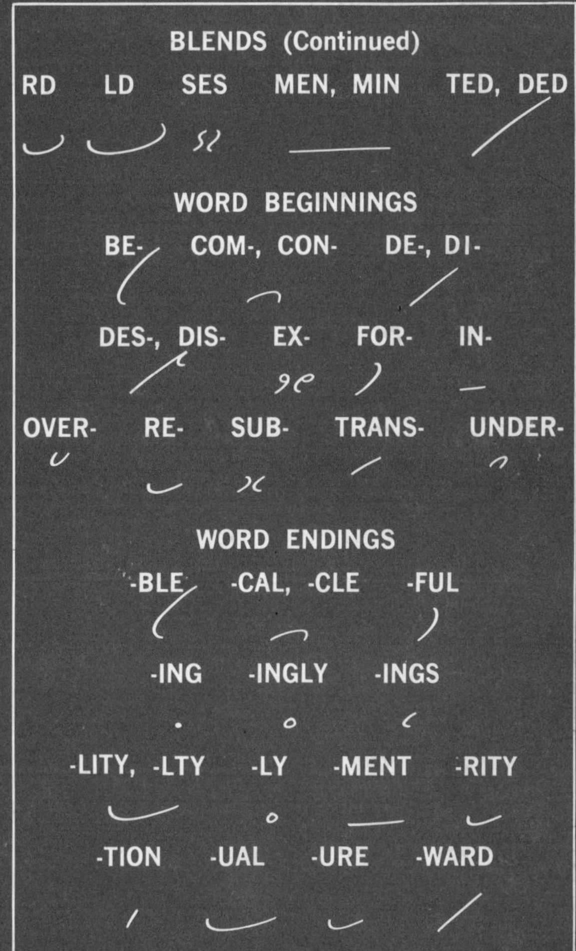
BLENDS (Continued)
RD LD SES MEN, MIN TED, DED
WORD BEGINNINGS
BE- COM-, CON- DE-, DI-
DES-, DIS- EX- FOR- IN-
OVER- RE- SUB- TRANS- UNDER-
WORD ENDINGS
-BLE -CAL, -CLE -FUL
-ING -INGLY -INGS
-LITY, -LTY -LY -MENT -RITY
-TION -UAL -URE -WARD

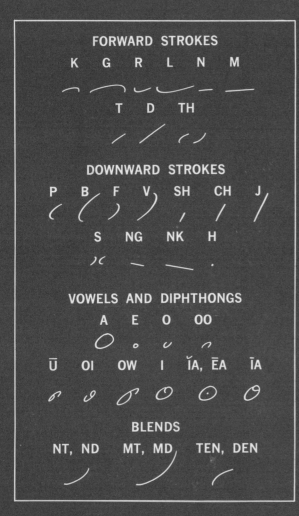

GREGG NOTEHAND

Louis A. Leslie

COAUTHOR DIAMOND JUBILEE SERIES OF GREGG SHORTHAND

Charles E. Zoubek

COAUTHOR DIAMOND JUBILEE SERIES OF GREGG SHORTHAND

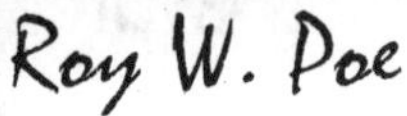

VICE PRESIDENT AND EDITORIAL DIRECTOR McGRAW-HILL BOOK COMPANY

Shorthand written by Charles Rader

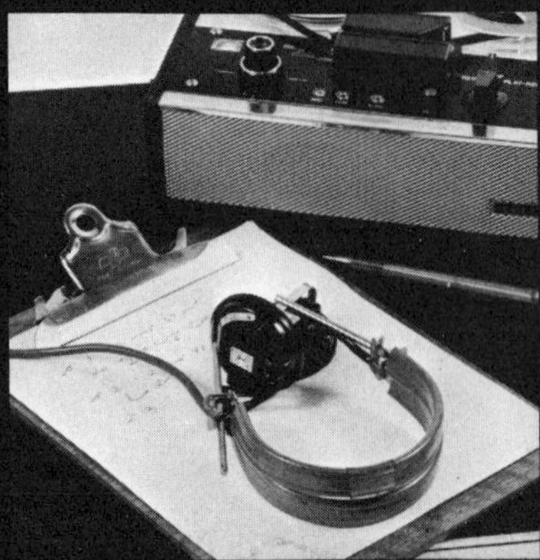

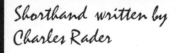

GREGG NOTEHAND

SECOND EDITION

James Deese

PROFESSOR OF PSYCHOLOGY

THE JOHNS HOPKINS UNIVERSITY

GREGG DIVISION □ McGRAW-HILL BOOK COMPANY

NEW YORK ST. LOUIS DALLAS SAN FRANCISCO
TORONTO LONDON SYDNEY

DESIGN BY BETTY BINNS

CREDITS

Cover Photographs: Martin Bough, FUNDAMENTAL PHOTOGRAPHS

Title-Page Photographs: Martin Bough, FUNDAMENTAL PHOTOGRAPHS

Unit-Opening Photographs: Martin Bough, FUNDAMENTAL PHOTOGRAPHS

Page 14: John Ashworth

Page 19: John Ashworth

Page 30: Nancy Rudolph

Page 63: Cornell Capa, Magnum

Page 92: General Dynamics

Page 103: Hanna Schreiber from Rapho Guillumette Pictures

Page 122: Roy Stevens, Ford Foundation

Page 135: National Urban League

Page 168: National Urban League

Page 177: Culver Pictures, Inc.

Page 199: Pierre Boulat, LIFE Magazine © Time Inc.

Page 220: Alfred Eisenstaedt, LIFE Magazine © Time Inc.

Page 231: Stan Wayman, LIFE Magazine © Time Inc.

Page 282: Hays from Monkmeyer

Page 295: Rowland Scherman, LIFE Magazine © Time Inc.

GREGG NOTEHAND, SECOND EDITION

Library of Congress Catalog Card Number 67-19903

6 7 8 9 DODO-68 7 6 5 4

ISBN 07-037331-0

Preface

The first edition of *Gregg Notehand* enjoyed immediate acceptance by schools and colleges throughout the country. As the first book written expressly to help students take more useful notes on their reading, lectures, and discussions, *Gregg Notehand* received newspaper notices in many cities. Administrators, teachers, parents—and students themselves—welcomed this pioneering effort to improve scholastic performance.

Schools that adopted *Gregg Notehand* found out very quickly that students did indeed take more effective notes and, as a result, learned better. Study after study showed that *Gregg Notehand* students enjoyed the course, improved their study habits, and became effective notemakers.

Objectives

The aims of the second edition of *Gregg Notehand* are the same as those of its predecessor: to provide instruction in notemaking processes and procedures and, at the same time, to develop a writing facility (Notehand) with which to make notes rapidly and easily.

Organization

The organization of the second edition differs from the first in a number of ways.

The book contains 70 units of instruction – designed to fit the typical one-semester curriculum. However, where the principles of notemaking and the principles of Notehand were formerly treated as separate skill-development sequences, they have now been largely integrated. Of the 70 units, 42 are organized so that both notemaking and Notehand principles are presented in the same unit.

Unit 1 is an introductory unit; it discusses the part that good notemaking plays in effective learning and how it enables the student to learn more faster and to retain what he learns longer.

Units 2-8 are devoted exclusively to the presentation of the most frequently used Notehand principles.

Beginning with Unit 9, a typical unit contains **1** a notemaking principle, followed by questions for discussion and an application; and, **2** a number of Notehand principles, accompanied by Reading and Writing Practice exercises that reinforce the learning of the Notehand principles of the unit.

New features

Many of the features of the first edition of *Gregg Notehand* that have proved effective have been retained. In addition, a number of new and helpful features have been added.

Notemaking principles

While the essential principles of notemaking have not been changed, the material has been completely reorganized and new examples provided. Three new principles have been introduced in the second edition:
1 *Using the Central Idea to Build Your Headings.* This new unit shows the student how he can select the central idea from reading or listening and adapt it as the main heading for his notes.
2 *Showing Contrasts and Comparisons.* In many notemaking situations the student is required to compare one set of data with another – for example, to compare the

American economic system with that of Great Britain. This new unit shows the notemaker how to record this information so that it will be of maximum usefulness in studying and reviewing for examinations.

3 *Definitions, Background Information, and Examples.* Some notemakers have difficulty in deciding where to put background information (events leading up to a presentation of facts, for example), definitions of important terms, and examples in their notes. Illustrations of recording such information, which does not lend itself to typical outline form, are provided.

Student activities

A greater number and variety of student activities in notemaking are provided in this second edition. These activities include questions on the content of the notemaking-principles material as well as practical notemaking exercises.

Notehand

Practice Material. No changes have been made in the Notehand principles in the second edition. However, much of the material in the Reading and Writing Practice exercises is new and more challenging. This new material deals with such subjects as psychology, literature, sociology, history, and others that the student is likely to study when he goes to college.

Other features

Practice Suggestions. To be sure that the student derives the greatest benefit from the time that he invests in Notehand, the authors have provided specific suggestions to guide him in every phase of his practice.

Key. The key to the Reading and Writing exercises and illustrations of notemaking techniques appears in type in the back of the book, thus enabling the student of *Gregg Notehand* to make the most rapid progress possible, especially in the early stages of learning.

Supporting materials

In addition to the textbook, a workbook, an instructor's guide, and a set of tapes are available.

The workbook

The workbook, *Practice Drills and Notemaking Exercises,* has been expanded considerably. The workbook includes new practice drills on Notehand principles as well as a wide variety of exercises on notemaking.

Instructor's guide

The *Instructor's Guide for Gregg Notehand,* Second Edition, contains suggestions for organizing and teaching the course, lists of source materials (books, audiovisual aids, etc.), suggestions on testing and grading the student's work, and supplementary notemaking exercises.

Gregg notemaking tapes

Gregg Notemaking Tapes enable the teacher to add interest and enrichment to the course.

Acknowledgments

The authors are grateful to the teachers who ventured to pioneer in the teaching of *Gregg Notehand.* Many have shared with the authors the results of their experiences and offered helpful suggestions on the preparation of the second edition.

THE AUTHORS

Contents

PART ONE

1. Fundamental principles of notemaking, *9* ■ **2-8.** Notehand principles, *13* ■ **9.** Getting ready to study, *35* ■ **10.** Planning your study time, *39* ■ **11.** Select the right notebook for notemaking, *45* ■ **12.** Notemaking from reading, 50 ■ **13.** Rules for remembering what you read, 53 ■ **14.** Notehand recall, *57* ■ **15.** Finding the central idea in your reading, *61* ■ **16.** Finding the central idea in your reading (continued), *67* ■ **17.** Selecting related ideas, *70* ■ **18.** Using the central idea to build your headings, *74* ■ **19.** Read before you make notes, *79* ■ **20.** Notehand recall, *84* ■ **21.** Making notes in your own words, *88* ■ **22.** Brevity in making notes in your own words, *93* ■ **23.** Organizing notes in narrative summaries, *98* ■ **24.** Organizing notes in outline form, *104* ■ **25.** Leave wide margins, *110* ■ **26.** Notehand recall, *113* ■ **27.** Use longhand headings in your notes, *116* ■ **28.** Use signals for "must remember" items, *120* ■ **29.** Making verbatim notes, *126* ■ **30.** The notemaker is an active listener, *131* ■ **31.** Getting the most out of your listening, *136* ■ **32.** Writing names in your notes, *140* ■ **33.** Notehand recall, *146* ■ **34.** Rules for effective listening, *149* ■ **35.** Rules for effective listening (continued), *152* ■ **36.** Preserve difficult longhand spellings, *157* ■ **37.** Showing contrasts and comparisons in your notes, *160* ■ **38.** Definitions, background information, and examples, *166* ■ **39.** Notehand recall, *172* ■ **40.** Using notehand in original writing, *176* ■ **41.** Making rough drafts, *183* ■ **42.** Footnotes, *189* ■ **43.** Special uses of notehand in original writing, *194* ■ **44.** How to make notes for research papers, *200* ■ **45.** Getting ready to make notes from research, *206* ■ **46.** Making notes from research, *210* ■ **47.** Writing the research paper, *216* ■ **48.** Notehand recall, *221*

PART TWO

49. Reviewing and preparing for examinations, *226* ■ **50.** Making derived notes, *232* ■ **51.** Making notes of class discussions, *237* ■ **52.** Making notes of other meetings and discussions, *243* ■ **53.** Making notes as a recorder, *247* ■ **54.** Writing the minutes, *253* ■ **55.** Indexing your notes, *258* ■ **56.** Disposition of your notes, *263* ■ **57-70.** Notehand principles, *267* ■ Key to Gregg Notehand, *311* ■ Index to Gregg Notehand, *352*

PART
ONE

Unit 1

PRINCIPLES OF NOTEMAKING

Fundamental principles of notemaking

Throughout your school and college career—and later in your professional life and personal activities — you will have reason to make notes. You will listen to lectures; read from textbooks, magazines, and other printed materials; and you will hear speeches, conferences, discussions, and debates on current topics. You are probably already in the habit of carrying a small notebook with you in which to jot down things you want to remember.

Trying to learn and remember what you read and hear without making notes is like trying to plan for a long summer camping trip without a list of what you will need. Sure, you will remember many of the things that are important, but you might easily forget the matches, flashlight, and mosquito repellent! Making notes is important to everyone because memories are faulty — we simply forget.

Making good notes will help you in three important ways:

1 You will learn more and learn it faster.

2 You will remember more and remember it longer.

3 You will study and work more efficiently.

Learning more and faster

It is a well-known fact that you learn more and you learn faster by *doing*—that is, actively participating with your mind while you are trying to learn. In fact, the degree to which learning takes place is in direct proportion to the extent to which you actively participate mentally in the process. The very process of making notes as you listen, read, or observe stimulates and guides your mental participation in the activity. The process of making notes actually *forces* you to participate actively. You can't help but learn more and learn it faster.

Remembering more and longer

The act of making notes will also help you to remember more of what you learn and remember it longer. Active mental participation helps fix important ideas and facts in your mind so that they become a part of you. As a result, you can remember them better. Good notes serve as a "memory storehouse" for you, that is, a reference source (just as does a dictionary or an encyclopedia) for the review and recall of facts and information. In addition, the notes trigger your memory of other facts, information, and ideas not recorded in your notes.

Learning and forgetting

It is virtually impossible to remember everything you learn. Herman V. Ebbinghaus, a famous German psychologist, proved this in his experimental studies of verbal learning and retention. Among other things, Ebbinghaus was interested in how much of what he personally had learned he could remember after various periods of time. By finding out how much he could remember a week after learning compared with, say, four hours after learning, Ebbinghaus was able to construct a "curve of forgetting"; that is, he could show by means of a curve graph when most forgetting takes place.

In his experiment Ebbinghaus learned that he did most of his forgetting *immediately after learning!* Thus, based on the results of Ebbinghaus's studies and other later studies, a psychological rule of considerable importance has been formulated: *We forget most of what we are going to forget immediately after we learn it.*

Relearning comes more quickly

After Ebbinghaus had measured how well he could remember, he resorted to a test, which is called the "savings method." Here the person whose memory is being tested relearns something he learned previously. The measure of retention is the difference in time it takes between original learning and relearning. Suppose, for example, Ebbinghaus took five minutes to learn a list of sixteen nonsense syllables. If, twenty-four hours later when he relearned the same list, he took only two minutes, he obtained a savings of three minutes, or 60 percent.

The significance of this experiment is that if you have learned something and then forgotten it, you can relearn it much more quickly than if you had to learn it "from scratch." In the relearning process good notes are especially useful. They contain only the essential facts and ideas and will save a great deal of time and effort in such relearning, as reviewing for an examination. After all, reviewing is essentially a process of relearning.

Studying and working more efficiently

The process of making notes induces active mental participation in studying, just as it does in any other form of learning activity. Every student needs a workable procedure for studying. Making notes is an important part of this procedure. What is more, participation by making notes helps you to organize your study effort.

In addition, the notes themselves provide material for subsequent study—the memory storehouse mentioned earlier. Naturally, the better the notes, the more useful they are in studying.

Notes may be made over a period of time or immediately preceding or at the time of studying. They may come from many sources—lectures, discussions, textbooks, experiments, library research, and so on. They can be used for reference and for review, or they may be used to get ready for examinations or in preparing papers and reports.

Notemaking is a combination of abilities

Notemaking consists of more than simply writing things down on paper. There are definite techniques to learn about notemaking. *What* you record and *how* you record it are important. You need to know how to listen with concentration, how to read effectively when studying, how to grasp and record essential ideas, how to outline as you make notes, how to make notes for research papers, and so on.

Good notemaking requires concentration, and you are not likely to give your full attention to a book or a speaker if you have to bend every effort to record the barest essentials, such as is the case with longhand. Thus, in addition to mastering the techniques for making notes, you need to master a simple shorthand system designed expressly for the purpose. That system is Gregg Notehand. Gregg Notehand is an adaptation of Gregg Shorthand which, as you probably know, is used by millions of men and women—stenographers, reporters, secretaries, and so on. But where Gregg Shorthand is designed primarily for taking dictation in the office and in the court and conference room, Gregg Notehand is designed for notemaking by students, executives, researchers, club and organization members, writers, and just average listeners and readers.

To think about and discuss

1 How does the process of making notes force you to participate mentally in the learning process?

2 What did Ebbinghaus discover as to when forgetting takes place?

3 What is the significance of Ebbinghaus's research based on the "savings method"?

4 How can a fast system of writing, such as Notehand, help you develop better concentration?

Turn now to the Application on page 12.

Application

On a sheet of paper, write the heading "Notemaking and Studying Inventory." Then list the following statements by number. Circle each statement "True" or "False" in the inventory. If your Gregg Notehand textbook is your personal property, you may record your answers on this page.

True False 1 **I do not have a plan for studying; I study on a "hit-or-miss" basis.**

True False 2 **I have trouble getting down to work and sustaining my effort in studying.**

True False 3 **I find it so hard to concentrate on what I am reading that I get very little out of it.**

True False 4 **When I make notes from reading, I always copy the author's words just as he wrote them.**

True False 5 **When I make notes, I put down too much; and later I have difficulty in sifting the important from the unimportant.**

True False 6 **My notes are too brief—they don't make sense to me when I come back to them for study and review.**

True False 7 **My notes lack organization and continuity; I can't seem to relate similar topics.**

True False 8 **The personality, voice, and mannerisms of speakers frequently disturb me and hinder my concentration.**

True False 9 **I miss important things in lectures and discussions because I am too pushed in getting down notes on what has gone before.**

True False 10 **It's difficult for me to grasp and organize ideas and information conveyed by a speaker and make notes at the same time.**

True False 11 **I don't know what to put down when I am making notes from reading—that is, I can't find the important ideas.**

True False 12 **I don't know how to use my notes efficiently once I have made them.**

True False 13 **I am so pressed for time when making notes that I can't read them later—they're too sloppy.**

True False 14 **When writing a term paper or a report, I have difficulty knowing how to go about making notes and then using them in writing my paper.**

True False 15 **Composition is hard for me because it is so laborious and time-consuming to write and rewrite in longhand.**

True False 16 **I put off too long reviewing my notes and preparing for examinations.**

True False 17 **I find it virtually impossible to make useful notes when participating in or listening to group discussions.**

True False 18 **I do not know the best tools for notemaking in various situations—notebooks or cards or what.**

True False 19 **My mind wanders so much when I listen to a lecturer or speaker that I get very little out of what he says.**

True False 20 **Essay examinations are a problem for me because I can't quickly draft answers before writing them.**

Unit 2

PRINCIPLES OF NOTEHAND

Gregg Notehand is easy to learn—easier, actually, than longhand. Why? In longhand, there are many different ways of writing a given letter; in Gregg Notehand, there is only *one* way. For example, here are six different ways in which the longhand *f* may be expressed:

F f f F F F

In Gregg Notehand, there is only one way to express *f*, as you will learn later in this unit.

The facility with which you will eventually write Gregg Notehand will depend, of course, on how well and how regularly you practice. If you follow carefully the practice suggestions given in Units 2 and 3, your writing facility will develop rapidly; and with each unit your study of Gregg Notehand will become more and more fascinating.

1 **S-Z.** Perhaps the most frequent consonant in the English language is *s.* In Notehand, *s* is a very small downward curve resembling the longhand comma. Notice how the *s* is derived from the longhand form of *s.*

S

In longhand, *s* often has the sound of *z* as in *saves;* therefore, in Notehand the *s* stroke also represents the sound of *z.*

2 **A.** The Notehand *a* is a large circle. Once again, notice how *a* is derived from the longhand form.

A

3 **Silent letters omitted.** In the English language many words contain letters that are not pronounced. In Notehand these silent letters are omitted, and only those sounds in a word are written that are actually pronounced. For example, in the word *say,* the *y* would not be written because it is not pronounced; *say* would be written *s-a.* The word *face* would be written *f-a-s;* the final *e* would be omitted

because it is not pronounced, and the *c* would be represented by the *s* stroke because it is pronounced *s.*

What letters in the following words would not be written in Notehand because they are not pronounced?

day	**eat**	**main**
mean	**save**	**steam**

Check your answers with the key to Paragraph 3 in the back of this book.

4 **S-A words.** With the letters *s* and *a,* you can form two words.

say, *s-a* **ace,** *a-s*

Practice these words, following the suggestions in Paragraph 5.

5 **Practice procedures for word lists.** *You will learn the words in Paragraph 4 — and all the other words that are given to illustrate the Notehand principles you will study — more quickly and remember them longer if you will practice them in this way:*

1. With the type key exposed, pronounce and spell aloud — if possible — each word and Notehand outline in the list, thus: *say, s-a; ace, a-s.* By reading aloud you will be sure that you are concentrating on each word as you study it. Repeat this procedure with all the words in the list until you feel you can read the Notehand outlines without referring to the type key.

The student studies the word lists by placing a card or slip of paper over the key and reading the Notehand words aloud.

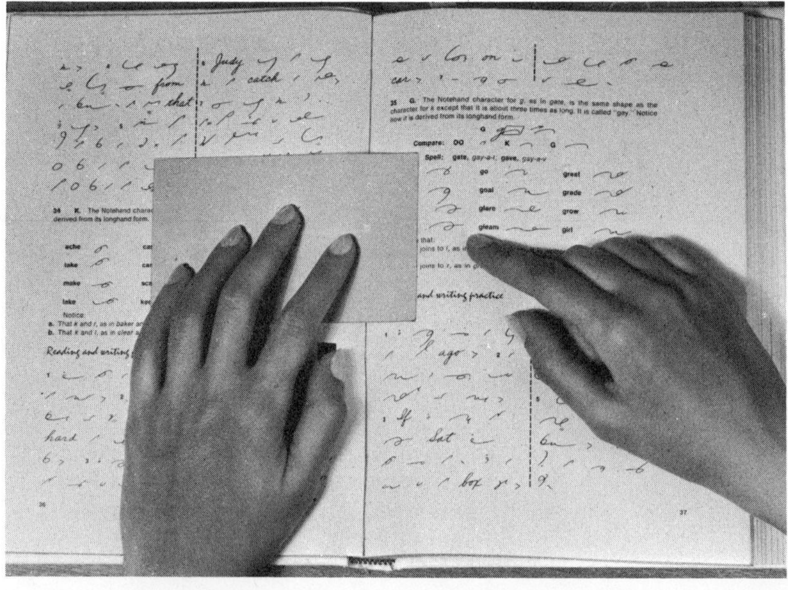

2. Cover up the type key with a card or slip of paper. Then spell and pronounce aloud, thus: *s-a,* say.

3. If the meaning of a Notehand outline does not come to you after you have spelled it, remove the card or slip of paper and refer to the type key. Do not spend more than a few seconds trying to decipher an outline. Reread the list of words in this way until you can read the entire list without referring to the type key.

4. In your notebook* write the entire list *once* in Notehand, saying each word aloud as you write it. Repeat this procedure two or three times until you feel you can write the words easily.

Caution: Under no circumstances write a full line or more of each word; this type of repetitious practice is not only monotonous, but it is also the least efficient way to learn the words.

6 **F.** The Notehand character for *f* is the same shape as *s* except that it is about three times as big. It is also written downward.

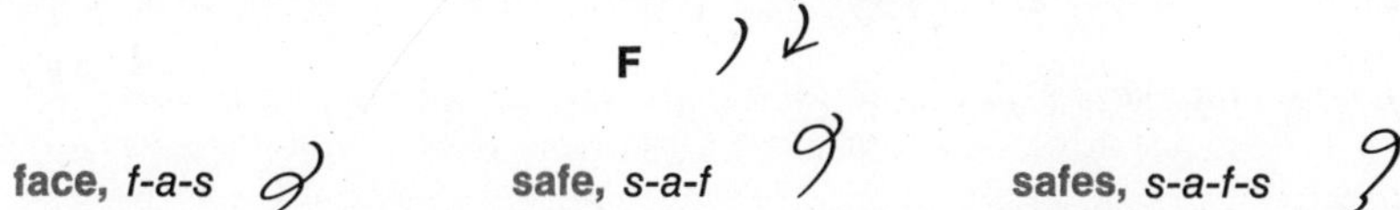

Notice that the *c* in *face* has the *s* sound and is, therefore, represented by *s.*

7 **V.** The Notehand character for *v* is the same shape as *f* except that it is about twice as big as *f.* It is also written downward.

Note the difference in the sizes of *s, f,* and *v.*

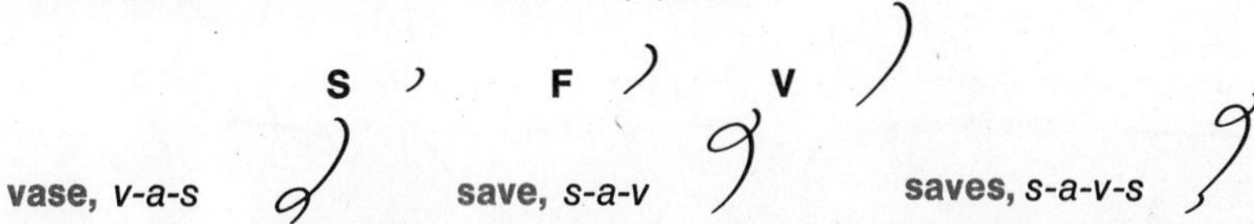

Notice that the final *s* in *saves* has the *z* sound, which is represented by the *s* stroke.

8 **E.** The Notehand stroke for *e* is a small circle. Notice how it is derived from the longhand *e.*

E

Always make the *e* circle small—tiny, in fact—and the *a* circle large.

Compare: **E** **A**

*A regular spiral-bound stenographic notebook will do nicely for your Notehand practice. The best writing instrument for your course in Notehand is a good ball-point pen. A ball point is easier to write with than a pencil; and the notes you make will be legible almost indefinitely, while pencil notes may become blurred and difficult to read.

see, *s-e* **fee,** *f-e* **ease,** *e-s*

sees, *s-e-s* **fees,** *f-e-s* **easy,** *e-s-e*

Notice that the *y* in *easy* is pronounced *e* and is, therefore, represented by the *e* circle.

Be sure to practice the *e* words as suggested in Paragraph 5.

9 **N.** The Notehand character for *n* is a very short forward straight line.

N

see, *s-e* **say,** *s-a* **knee,** *n-e*

seen, *s-e-n* **sane,** *s-a-n* **vain,** *v-a-n*

Notice that the *k* in *knee* is not written because it is not pronounced.

10 **M.** The Notehand character for *m* is a longer forward straight line, about three times as long as *n.*

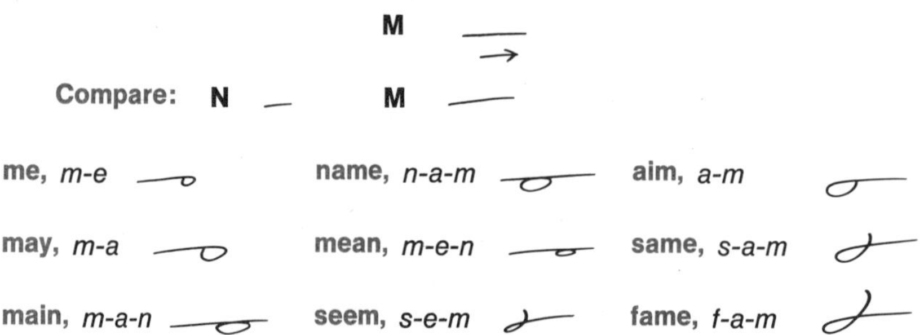

Remember, you will learn these words most effectively if you follow the practice procedures suggested in Paragraph 5.

Unit 3

PRINCIPLES OF NOTEHAND

11 **T.** The Notehand character for *t* is a very short upward straight line.

T

eat, *e-t* **tea,** *t-e* **team,** *t-e-m*

neat, *n-e-t* **stay,** *s-t-a* **tame,** *t-a-m*

seat, *s-e-t* **state,** *s-t-a-t* **stain,** *s-t-a-n*

12 **D.** The Notehand character *d* is a longer upward straight stroke, about three times as long as *t.*

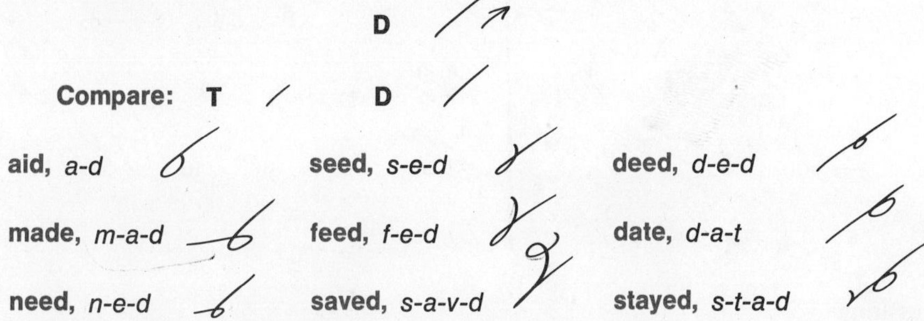

13 **Capitalization.** Capitalization is indicated by two short upward dashes underneath the item to be capitalized.

Dave **Fay** **Amy**

14 **Punctuation.** In Notehand the following marks of punctuation are used.

Period **Paragraph** **Parentheses**

Question **Dash** **Hyphen**

For all other punctuation marks, the regular longhand forms are used.

15

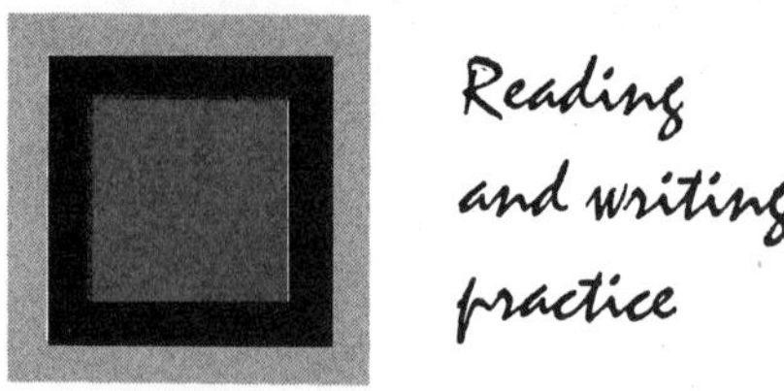

With the aid of a few longhand words, you can already read complete sentences. These sentences contain only the following Notehand characters, which you have studied thus far:

S A F V E N M T D

To get the most out of each Reading and Writing Practice, follow the procedure suggested in Paragraph 16.

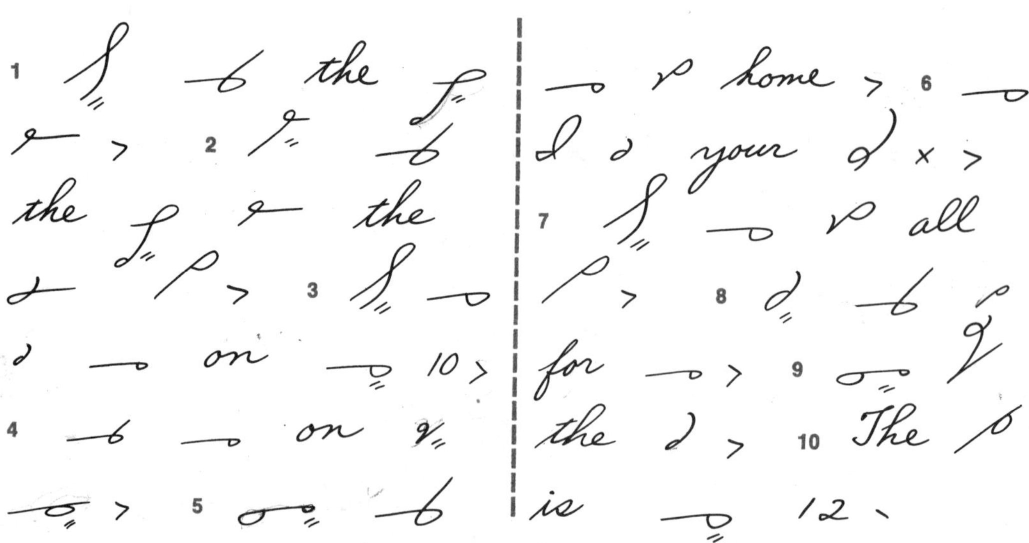

16 Suggestions

a. *For Reading the Reading and Writing Practice Exercises.*

1. Place your left index finger under the Notehand outline that you are about to read.

2. Place your right index finger on the type key to that Notehand outline. The key begins on page 311.

3. Read the Notehand, aloud if possible, until you come to an outline you cannot read. Spell the Notehand characters in the outline. If this spelling does not *immediately* give you the meaning, anchor your left index finger on that outline and turn to the key in the back, where your right index finger is resting near the point at which you are reading.

4. Determine the meaning of the outline that you cannot read, and then place your right index finger on it.

5. Turn back to the Notehand page from which you are reading, where your left index finger has kept your place for you, and continue reading.

This procedure is very important, as it will enable you to save much precious time that you might otherwise waste finding your place in the Reading and Writing Practice and in the key.

6. If time permits, read the Reading and Writing Practice a second time, perhaps even a third time.

You must keep in mind that during the early stages your reading may not be very rapid. That is only natural, as you are, in a sense, learning a new language. With faithful practice from day to day, however, your reading speed will increase rapidly.

b. *For Writing the Reading and Writing Practice Exercises.*

After you have read each Reading and Writing Practice, follow this procedure:

1. Read a convenient group of words aloud; then write that group in your notebook.

2. Keep your place in the Reading and Writing Practice with your left index finger if you are right-handed; with your right index finger if you are left-handed.

3. After you have made one complete copy of the Reading and Writing Practice, make a second copy if time permits. You will find that this second writing will go more smoothly than the first.

Of course, your early writing efforts will not be very rapid nor will your outlines look as pretty as those in the book. However, from day to day, as you use your Notehand in class and for your personal notes, your outlines will become noticeably smoother and more accurate.

The student refers to the key whenever he cannot read an outline. Notice how the left index finger is anchored on the place in the Notehand; the right index finger, on the corresponding place in the key.

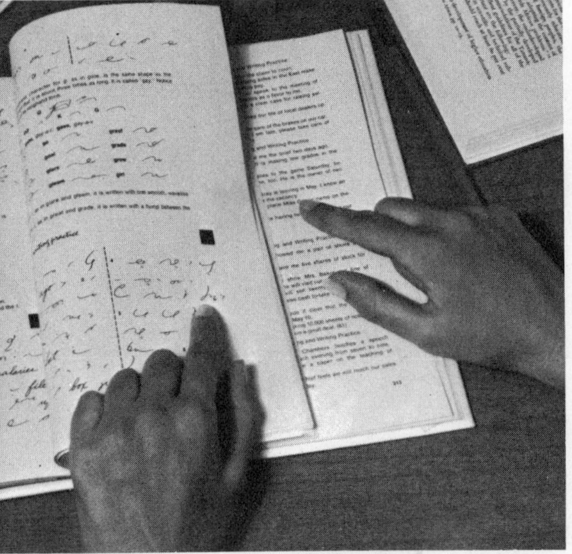

When copying, the student reads a convenient group of words aloud and then writes that group in his notebook. Notice how he keeps his place in the Notehand with his left index finger.

Unit 4

PRINCIPLES OF NOTEHAND

17 **O.** The Notehand character for *o* is a small, deep hook. Notice how it is derived from the longhand form.

o

no, *n-o*	**so,** *s-o*	**own,** *o-n*
toe, *t-o*	**phone,** *f-o-n*	**tone,** *t-o-n*
dough, *d-o*	**vote,** *v-o-t*	**stone,** *s-t-o-n*
snow, *s-n-o*	**note,** *n-o-t*	**dome,** *d-o-m*

Notice that in the words in the last column the *o* is turned on its side. This enables us to obtain an easier joining.

18 **R.** The Notehand character for *r* is a short forward curve. Notice how it is derived from its longhand form.

R

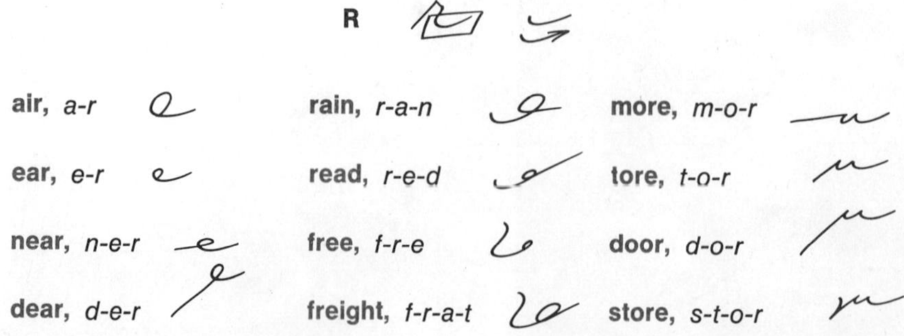

air, *a-r*	**rain,** *r-a-n*	**more,** *m-o-r*
ear, *e-r*	**read,** *r-e-d*	**tore,** *t-o-r*
near, *n-e-r*	**free,** *f-r-e*	**door,** *d-o-r*
dear, *d-e-r*	**freight,** *f-r-a-t*	**store,** *s-t-o-r*

Notice that *fr,* as in *free* and *freight,* is written with one smooth motion, without an angle between the *f* and the *r.*

19 **L.** The Notehand character for *l* is the same shape as the Notehand *r* except that it is about three times as long. Notice how it is derived from its longhand form.

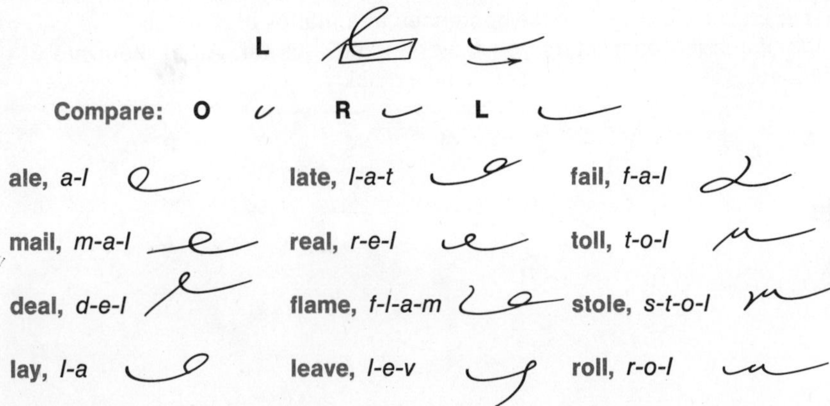

Notice that *fl,* as in *flame,* is written with one smooth motion, without an angle between the *f* and the *l.*

20 **Brief forms.** In the English language there are certain words that are used so frequently that we can save a great deal of writing time by providing abbreviations for them. This is a common practice in longhand—*Mr.* for *Mister, Ave.* for *Avenue, Sat.* for *Saturday.* In Notehand these abbreviations are called "brief forms." In your Notehand course you will study 42 brief forms for very common words. In this unit you will take up six of them.

Because of the frequency of these words, you will be wise to learn them well.

I ... **a, an** ... **for**

is ... **have** ... **am**

21 **Phrasing.** As you learned in Paragraph 20, we save writing time by providing abbreviations for common words. Another device for saving time is called "phrasing," or the writing of two or more words together as one outline. See how easily and quickly the following phrases can be written.

22

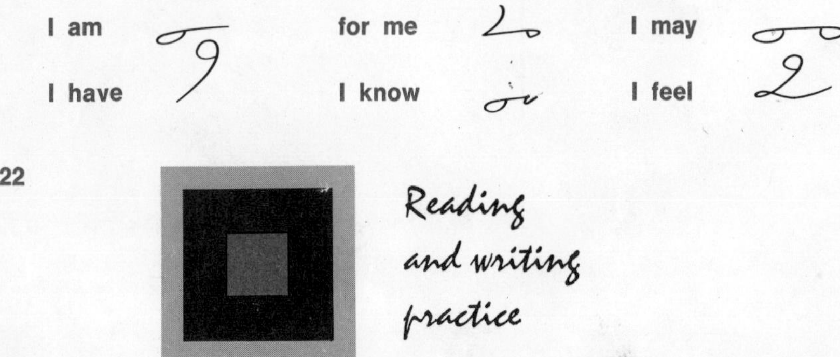

Your progress has been so rapid that in the sentences of the following Reading and Writing Practice only a few words are written in longhand. To be sure that you get the most benefit from this Reading and Writing Practice, take a moment to reread the suggestions given in Paragraph 16. If you use the key correctly, you will be able to complete your work with these sentences in a matter of minutes.

Here are the Notehand characters you have studied thus far. All of them are used in the sentences. Review these characters now quickly.

S A F V E N M T D

O R L

Unit 5

PRINCIPLES OF NOTEHAND

23 **H, -ing.** The letter *h* is simply a dot placed above the vowel. The letter *h,* with few exceptions, occurs at the beginning of a word.

Ing, which almost always occurs at the end of a word, is also expressed by a dot.

H

he · **hair** · **whole**

hay · **hate** · **heat**

heed · **here** · **horn**

-ing

Spell: hearing, *h-e-r-ing*

hearing · **heeding** · **rowing**

aiming · **reading** · **feeling**

trading · **rating** · **mailing**

24 **Omission of minor vowels.** Some words contain a vowel that is either omitted or slurred in ordinary speech. For example, *even* is pronounced *ev'n; motor, mot'r.* As these vowels are hardly heard in speech, they are not written in Notehand.

reader · **motoring** · **hasten**

nearer · **even** · **total**

dealer · **season** · **favor**

25

Reading and writing practice

You will notice that the number of words in longhand is getting smaller—a sign of the rapid progress you are making!

Reminder: See Paragraph 16 for practice suggestions.

Unit 6

PRINCIPLES OF NOTEHAND

26 Left S and Z. The first Notehand stroke you learned was the small downward curve for *s* and *z*. Because these sounds are so frequent, a second form has been provided to represent them—a "backward" comma, written downward. The use of the two forms for *s* and *z* makes it possible to obtain an easy joining in any combination of strokes. Use whichever *s* makes the easier joining in a word. For convenience, this stroke is called the "left *s*."

Left S

seal	**teams**	**fears**
sailing	**owns**	**seats**
meals	**days**	**seems**
eats	**stores**	**most**

Reading and writing practice

1 at of the

2 paving 4

4 on to

college

3 5

27 **P.** The Notehand character for *p* is the same shape as the left *s* except that it is about three times as long.

P

pay		hope		praise	
pair		opening		paper	
spare		paid		plate	
peel		rope		please	

Notice in the words in the third column how *p* joins to *r* or *l* with one smooth motion, without an angle between the *p* and the *r* or *l*.

Reading and writing practice

28 **B.** The Notehand character for *b* is the same shape as the character for *p* except that it is about twice as long.

B

Compare: **Left S** **P** **B**

bay		bone		brief	

base		obey		labor	
bearing		beat		blame	
boats		beans		label	

Notice in the words in the last column that *b* joins to *r* or *l* with one smooth motion, without an angle.

Reading and writing practice

1 first

2 on on Sat

3 order 1,500 1,200 cards 100 of

4

5

6

7

Unit 7

PRINCIPLES OF NOTEHAND

29 Brief forms. These six brief forms will come up again and again in all the writing that you will do. Practice them, following the procedure suggested in Paragraph 5, until you know them well.

it	of	will
in	are, our	*the

*The word *the* is represented by a short upward curve. This curve represents the sound of *th,* which you will study later.

Notice that the Notehand *r* stands for two words. Perhaps you have already discovered that a few Notehand characters represent more than one word. You will never have any difficulty selecting the correct word in a sentence; the sense of the sentence will always give you the answer.

30 Phrasing. The brief forms in Paragraph 29 enable us to form additional useful, timesaving phrases.

of the	in the	it will
of our	is the	it is
in our	I will	for it

The brief forms and phrases you studied in Paragraphs 29 and 30 are used many times in the sentences in the following Reading and Writing Practice to help impress them on your mind. If you follow faithfully the practice suggestions in Paragraph 16, you should be able to complete your work on this Reading and Writing Practice in 20 minutes or less. Can you do it?

Group A

1 … shape … 25 … 2 … car at … end … $450 … 3 … $50 … 4 … $50 …

Group B

5 … election … 6 … no … 4-1414 … 7 … car … old … 8 … take … $10 … worth …

Group C

9 … bought … 10 … 11 … that … 12 … end … off …

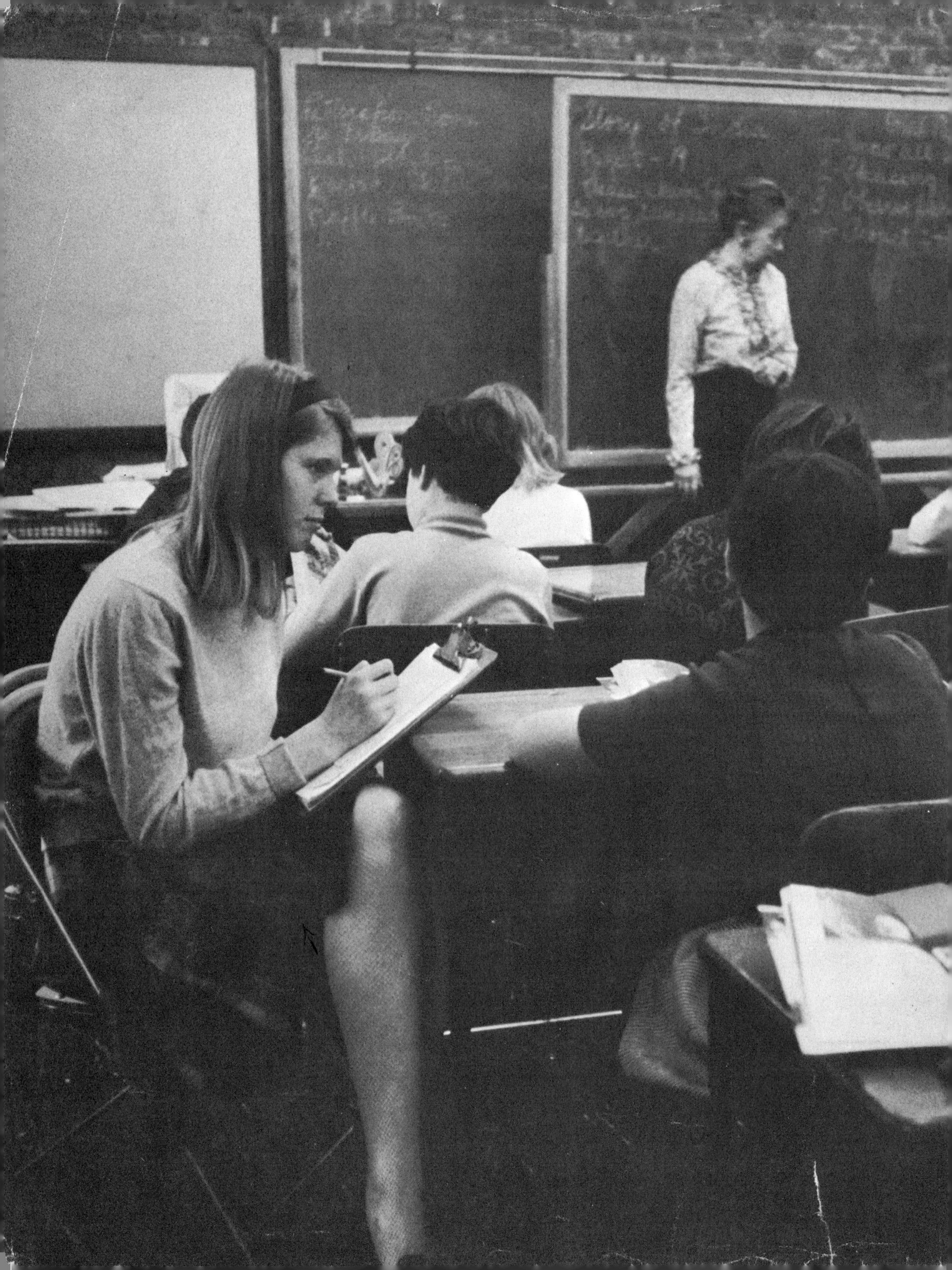

Unit 8

PRINCIPLES OF NOTEHAND
RECALL

There are no new alphabetic strokes for you to learn in this unit. You will simply review the strokes and principles you studied in Units 2-7. You will do this through a helpful recall chart and a Reading and Writing Practice consisting of complete sentences.

Here are the Notehand strokes you studied in Units 2-7. Review them quickly before you start your work on the recall chart and the Reading and Writing Practice.

F **V** **Comma S** **E** **A** **T** **N** **M** **D**

H **L** **R** **O** **B** **P** **Left S**

31 Recall chart. The following chart contains one or more illustrations of every alphabetic stroke you have studied in Units 2-7. Spell and say each word aloud as you practice it, thus: *s-a-v, save.* If the spelling does not immediately give you the meaning of the outline, refer to the key in the back of the book.

There are 108 words and phrases in the chart. Can you complete your first reading of the chart in 12 minutes or less? If you can, you are making good progress indeed!

Words

1						
2						
3						
4						
5						

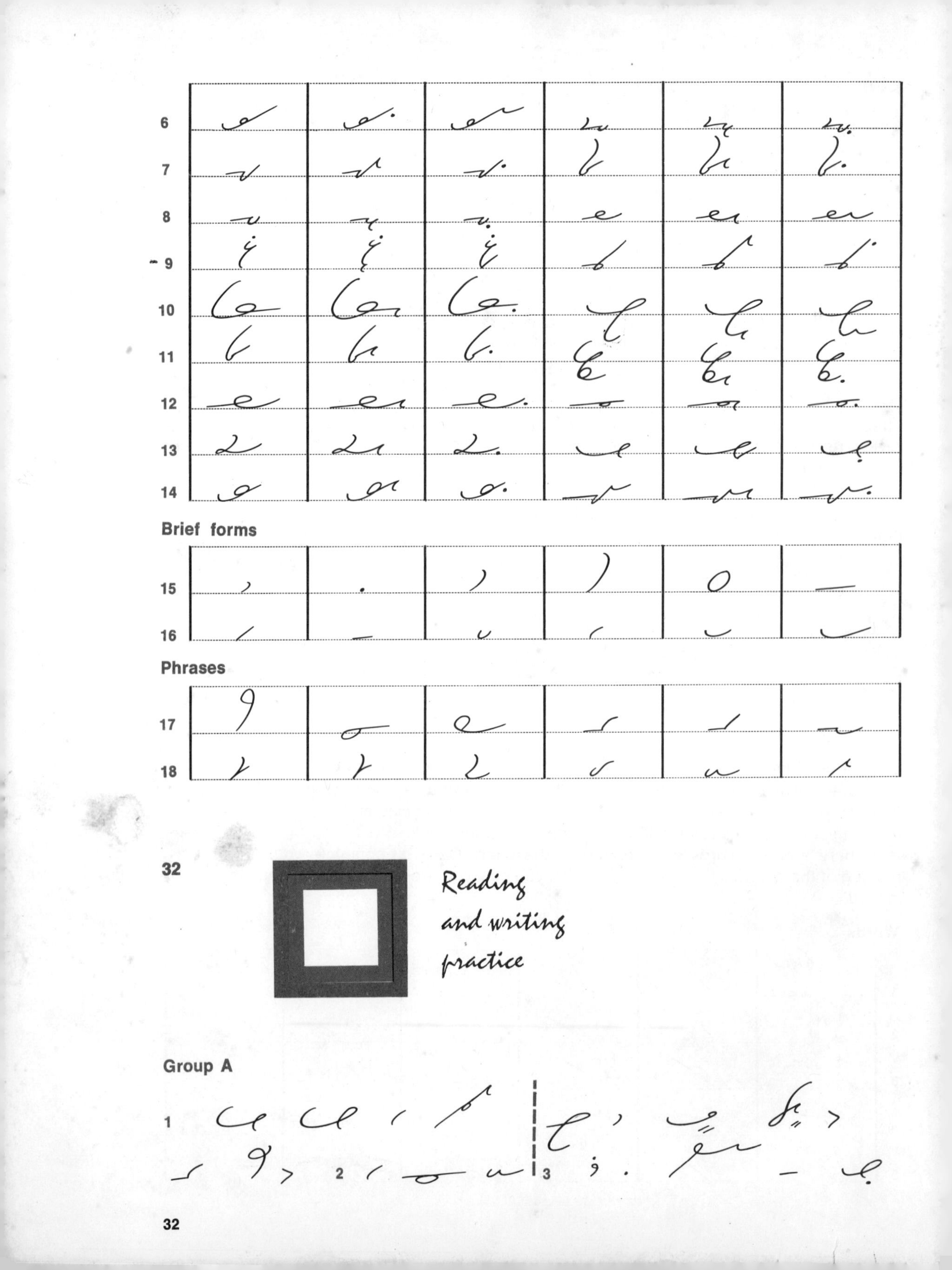

6

7

8

9

10

11

12

13

14

Brief forms

15

16

Phrases

17

18

32

Reading and writing practice

Group A

1

2

3

care 4 bought 5 $50

Group B

6 tho to Mon 9 7 living $100 room 10 8 Sat

Group C

11 at errors 12 14 15 13 to

Group D

16 18 $180 $180 19 price 17 to 20 job

Most-used Gregg Notehand forms

At this stage of your learning you will naturally have to write in longhand most of the words in any notes you make. If the longhand word comes to you more readily than the Gregg Notehand outline for the word, use the longhand.

You should, however, attempt to write as many words as you can in Gregg Notehand. Make a special effort in everything you write to use the Gregg Notehand forms for at least these words:

I	**the**	**a, an**	**of**	**in**
for	**it**	**is**	**have**	**will**

You have already learned all these words as brief forms. They were given special abbreviations in Gregg Notehand because of the high frequency with which they occur. They are called to your attention again here so that you may concentrate on them.

Suggestion: Write these ten Gregg Notehand outlines on a card and keep it before you whenever you are writing anything for your own use. Use the Gregg Notehand form every time you have occasion to write one of the words. Soon you will find yourself using these Gregg Notehand forms automatically.

Unit 9

PRINCIPLES OF NOTEMAKING

Getting ready to study

Studying is almost a full-time occupation for a high school or college student. And it doesn't stop upon graduation. Long after they have left school, many people continue to be students. They keep up with their businesses or professions by reading magazines, books, reports, and the like. The typical business executive, doctor, teacher, or lawyer today can't afford *not* to keep up to date on the latest developments in his field. In fact, education is a continuing process for almost everyone.

Knowing how to study efficiently is fundamental to making the most of one's educational experience. Many people have failed to benefit from much of their education because they never learned how to study. Let's consider some general techniques and procedures that will help you to study more efficiently.

Evaluate your goals and ambitions

First, take a look at yourself and see where you want to go. What do you want to achieve? Are your goals and ambitions worth the study effort required to reach them?

Whether or not you have established your long-range goals, you will have immediate goals, such as high school graduation or admission to the college of your choice or even college graduation. On the other hand, your goal may be admission to graduate study or to a professional school, such as a college of medicine, dentistry, or law. Effective study techniques will be invaluable to you in achieving these goals as well as personal-improvement goals. And they will be useful to you throughout your active life.

Studying is basically a matter of self-discipline. It takes time. It takes effort and concentration. It means sacrificing other activities that might be more pleasant and entertaining. But if you wish to accomplish your goals and ambitions, effective studying is worth any self-discipline.

Study in an environment that encourages concentration

Studying is most effective when it is done in an environment that offers quiet, privacy, and freedom from distractions—whether in the home, in school, or elsewhere. In these days of crowding, both at home and at school, it is not always possible to find the ideal environment for study. At any rate, make every effort to study in a place that offers as much quiet and freedom from distractions as possible.

Once you select a good place to study,

you should use it consistently rather than studying in a different place each day. When you study in the same place, you become adjusted to it as the "inner sanctum"—a place that means serious business.

It seems trite to say that you need good light and a comfortable temperature for your study, but these simple precautions are violated so often that they are worth repeating. Without a comfortable working environment, you simply can't do your best work.

So when you get down to the business of studying, go at the task seriously and do it in a place that is suitable for the purpose.

To think about and discuss

1 Think about your immediate and long-range goals and tell how effective study habits can help you to achieve them.

2 What is meant by "Study is basically a matter of self-discipline"?

3 What is the best environment for study?

4 Why should you study in the same place each time?

PRINCIPLES OF NOTEHAND

33 OO. The sound of $\overline{oo}$, as in *to,* is represented by a small hook. It is called the *oo* hook.

OO

Spell: **to,** *t-oo*

to, too, two	**true**	**soon**
who	**drew**	**pool**
whom	**room**	**noon**
do	**rule**	**move**

Notice that the *oo* hook is placed on its side in *noon* and *move.* The *oo* hook joins more easily to the end of *n* and *m* if it is placed on its side than if it were written in the normal manner.

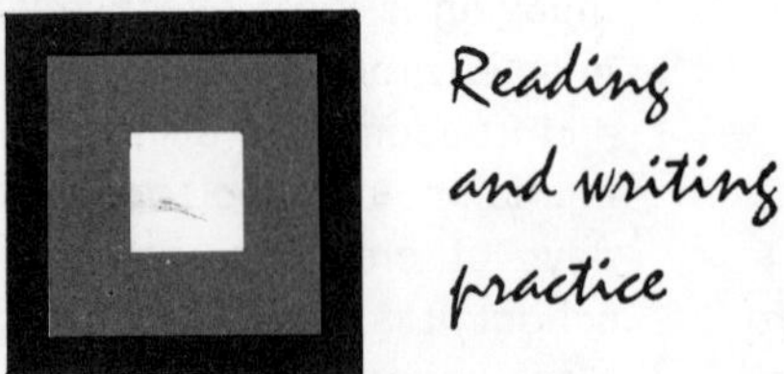

Reading and writing practice

1 repaired

2

3

4 from that 5

6 Judy catch 7 Hotel

34 **K.** The Notehand character for *k* is a short forward curve. Notice how it is derived from its longhand form.

K

ache	care	baker
take	came	cream
make	scale	clear
lake	keep	claim

Notice:

a. That *k* and *r*, as in *baker* and *cream*, join with one smooth, wavelike motion.

b. That *k* and *l*, as in *clear* and *claim*, join with a "hump" between the *k* and the *l*.

Reading and writing practice

1 2 hard his 3

as 4 salaries 5 file up 6

on

car 7

35 **G.** The Notehand character for *g,* as in *gate,* is the same shape as the character for *k* except that it is about three times as long. It is called "gay." Notice how it is derived from its longhand form.

G

Compare: **OO** **K** **G**

Spell: **gate,** *gay-a-t;* **gave,** *gay-a-v*

gate	**go**	**great**
gave	**goal**	**grade**
gain	**glare**	**grow**
game	**gleam**	**girl**

Notice that:

a. When *g* joins to *l,* as in *glare* and *gleam,* it is written with one smooth, wavelike motion.

b. When *g* joins to *r,* as in *great* and *grade,* it is written with a hump between the *g* and the *r.*

Reading and writing practice

1 ago 2

3 If Sat box

4

5 Miss on

6

Unit 10

PRINCIPLES OF NOTEMAKING

Planning your study time

Planning is important in everything you do—and studying is no exception. Most people study on a hit-or-miss basis, and the result is that too little time is given to study, the time that *is* given is not properly proportioned among the various subjects, and the efforts expended on study are largely wasted.

Make a schedule

A first step in planning your study is to prepare a *schedule for studying.* It might be as simple as a schedule of your current classes, recopied on a larger card to allow space for indicating study time. (See illustration below.)

You may even have to set aside some time on Sunday for study. Many college students think of Sunday as their best study time.

Be realistic

Don't plan more time for studying than you will actually use for the purpose. Allowing too much time may actually encourage poor study habits, for you will probably fritter away time and energy even though you have a schedule.

The right amount of time for studying will vary with the subject and with the student. Preparing a workable, realistic schedule requires your best judgment. Your objective is to study efficiently and effectively, and doing so isn't measured by *time* but by *results.* What you're after is getting the desired results as quickly and with as little effort as possible.

IME	MONDAY	TUESDAY	WEDNESDAY	THURSDAY	FRIDAY	SATURDAY
00-9:00	Biology	Biology	Biology	Biology	Biology	
00-10:00	Study Biology	Study Geometry	Study Biology	Study Geometry	Study Biology	English Theme
:00-11:00	Softball	History Report	Yearbook Committee	Softball	Camera Club	

Allocate your time

Some subjects will require more time than others. Allot to the study of each subject the amount of time required to do it well—enough time, but not too much.

Hardest subjects first

Schedule your toughest subjects for study first. If you put off your hardest subjects until last, you will dissipate your energy by worrying about the difficult task ahead. You will also run the risk of not allowing sufficient time for the difficult subjects.

The sooner the better

Study for a particular subject or an assignment promptly after the related instruction, such as a class meeting or lecture. Your mind is zeroed in on the subject, and you won't have to reacclimatize yourself to the topic, as you would if you picked the subject up later.

Establish a regular time

Set aside a regular time for studying—if possible, study at the same time each day. Getting into the habit of studying is half the battle; and if you think of your study schedule as being as inviolate as your class schedule, you'll find that study becomes automatic.

Relax, too

Allow some time in your study schedule for some relaxation. If you don't, you probably won't stick to your schedule.

Get down to work

No matter how good your intentions are or how well you have planned your schedule, results come only as you get down to work. Here is the real problem for most people. It is so easy to fritter away time!

Dribbling away time can be eliminated only by deliberate effort. If you are really a time waster, make your study periods short at the beginning. You will find it easier to get down to work if you know you have only half an hour or even fifteen minutes to go.

Make the time count

It is better to work hard for only fifteen minutes than to spend a couple of hours intermittently studying, daydreaming, studying, talking, studying, and entertaining yourself. Once you actually adjust to the hard fact of working when you study, you can make your scheduled study periods longer, with fewer breaks.

Be prepared to change your schedule

Be ready to change your study schedule from time to time. You will have themes, reports, speeches, and other assignments that you must budget for; and often you don't know from one day to the next what these assignments will be. Note in the schedule on page 39 that the student has set aside part of Saturday morning to work on an English theme.

Long-range assignments, such as term papers and research reports, should be scheduled well in advance of the deadline. These assignments should be planned to utilize longer stretches of time, such as weekends and vacations.

Good notemaking contributes to studying efficiently

Many factors contribute to effective studying: the individual's urge to achieve; his self-discipline; the environment for study, including equipment, materials, and supplies; the schedule for studying; and the habit of "getting down to work." Then there is notemaking—a tool of learning, a technique and procedure for studying, and a source of notes or materials for study.

The very process of making notes focuses attention on what is being studied, motivates and guides effort, and yields essential materials for further study and use.

Making notes in class discussions, in doing experiments, in listening to lectures, and so on, yields materials for studying. These materials, or *notes,* usually contain the essentials grasped from listening, from reading, from observing, and from other learning activities. The notes are particularly valuable in reviewing, relearning, preparing assignments, preparing for examinations, and preparing research papers.

Gregg Notehand will also be a great help to you in studying. Easier and quicker to use than longhand, it will save you time and effort, whether you're making notes, jotting down ideas, or writing a research paper or report.

To think about and discuss

1 Why is it best to schedule your toughest subjects for study first?

2 Should any time be allowed in your study schedule for relaxation?

3 How can you get rid of the habit of frittering away your study time?

4 How does good notemaking contribute to studying efficiency?

Application

Prepare a study schedule for the coming week, using a form similar to that on page 39. Such a form is included in the workbook that accompanies the textbook *(Practice Drills and Notemaking Exercises for Gregg Notehand).*

PRINCIPLES OF NOTEHAND

36 Sh. The Notehand character for the sound of *sh,* as in *she,* is a very short downward straight line. It is called "ish."

Sh

Spell: **she,** *ish-e;* **share,** *ish-a-r*

she	**shame**	**show**
share	**shape**	**shown**
shades	**shoes**	**showed**
shake	**sheep**	**showing**

Did you notice that the *oo* hook and the *s* in *shoes* join without an angle?

Reading and writing practice

37 Ch. The Notehand character for the sound of *ch,* as in *each,* is a downward straight stroke about three times as long as *sh.* It is called "chay."

Ch

Spell: **each,** *e-chay;* **reach,** *r-e-chay*

each	chain	cheer
reach	chairs	chamber
teach	speech	chose

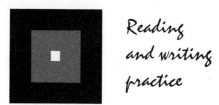

Reading and writing practice

we

3

5

at

on

4

38 **J.** The Notehand character for the sound of *j,* as in *age,* is a long downward straight stroke, somewhat longer than *ch.*

J

Compare: **Sh** **Ch** **J**

Spell: **age,** *a-jay;* **cage,** *k-a-jay*

age	**pages**	**jail**
cage	**stage**	**strange**
gauge	**raged**	**change**

Reading and writing practice

1

40 4

2

5

with

errors on 4

on 6

3 her

26 at

39 **Long I.** In Notehand, the sound of long *ī*, as in *my*, is represented by a broken circle.

I

my		sign		try	
might		file		time	
mine		light		dry	

Reading and writing practice

1 2 on town 3 at 50 ago

4 5 6 7 sells goods

Unit 11

PRINCIPLES OF NOTEMAKING

Select the right notebook for notemaking

Which kind of notebook is best for making notes? In some courses the instructor will specify the type he prefers, but usually the selection is left to the student. There are two types of notebooks that are commonly used by notemakers—the bound composition notebook and the loose-leaf ring binder.

Bound composition notebook

The typical bound composition notebook is about 8 by 10 inches. Some come with stitched bindings; others, with wire bindings. While either type of bound notebook will serve the purpose, the wire-bound notebook is somewhat easier to use because it lies flat when open. It is the more popular of the two types.

An advantage of the bound notebook, whether wire or stitched, is that the pages do not come loose. If you use a bound notebook, you will find it convenient to have a separate notebook for each subject. If you prefer not to have a notebook for each subject, it's a good idea to divide the subjects by index tabs.

Loose-leaf ring binder

The loose-leaf ring binder can be bought in several sizes, but the most popular holds regular 8½ by 11 sheets. Many students prefer this type of notebook because they can remove and reinsert pages easily and add new sheets whenever they want them.

The loose-leaf ring binder has the disadvantage that the holes in the paper pull loose, but the problem can be easily solved by using reinforcements. This precaution is recommended for pages on which important notes are recorded.

Most students keep the notes for all their subjects in one loose-leaf ring binder, separating the subjects by index tabs or tab divider sheets which are made of stiff paperboard. But if you are an avid notemaker,

Notebooks for making notes

you may still want a clearly labeled binder for each subject.

Number the pages

No matter what type of notebook you use, be sure to number the pages. Numbering the pages makes it easier to find things. In a bound notebook, number the pages consecutively throughout the book. If you use a loose-leaf ring binder in which you keep notes for several subjects, number the pages within each subject. Thus, if you find it necessary to add paper for a particular subject, you will not have to disturb the entire numbering plan.

In addition, you will also find it handy to date your notes.

To think about and discuss

1 Why do you think most students prefer loose-leaf ring binders for making notes?

2 Discuss methods of identifying the notebooks in which notes are kept. What might be included in your identification?

3 Would a stenographer's notebook be satisfactory for notemaking? Why or why not?

PRINCIPLES OF NOTEHAND

40 Ĕ. The tiny circle that represents the sound of ē, as in *heat,* also represents the sound of ĕ, as in *get.*

Spell: **get,** *gay-e-t;* **set,** *s-e-t*

get		**ever**		**check**	
set		**every**		**several**	
telling		**very**		**general**	
letter		**any**		***next**	

*In the word *next,* the *x* has the sound of *ks;* it is, therefore, represented by the Notehand characters *ks.*

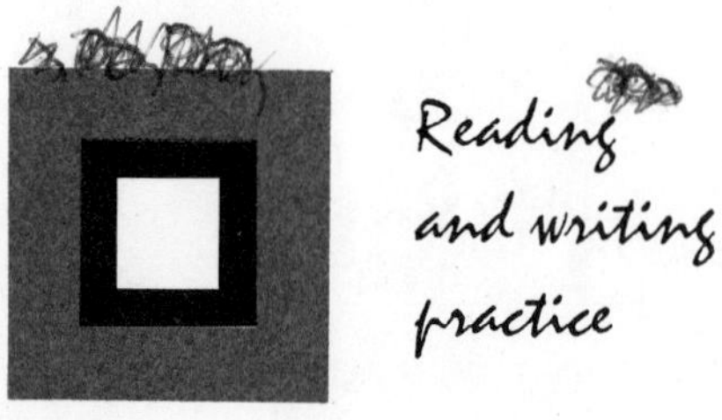

1 and you

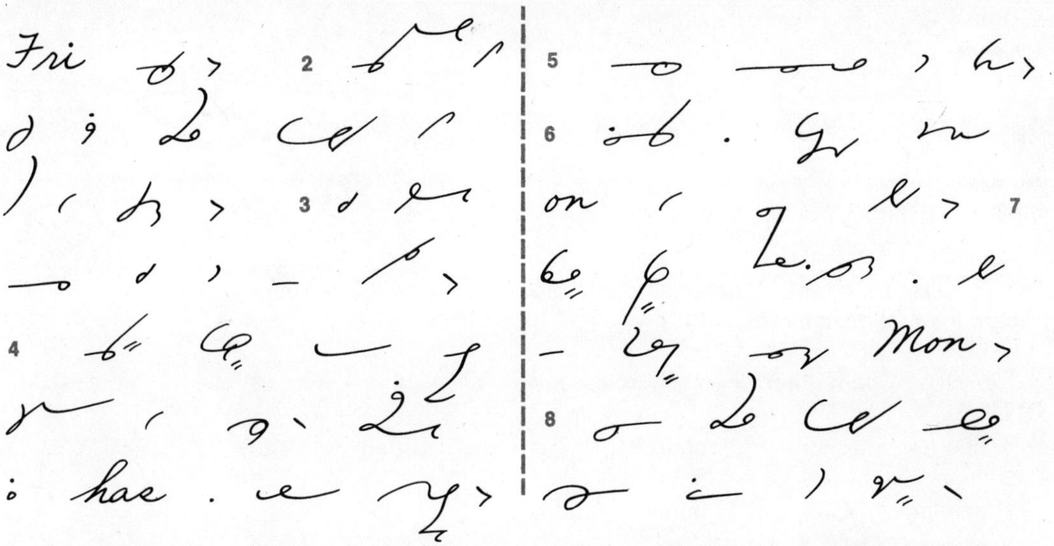

41 ĭ. The small circle also represents the sound of *ĭ,* as in *him.*

Spell: him, *h-e-m;* **his,** *h-e-s*

him	 give	 bid 
his	little	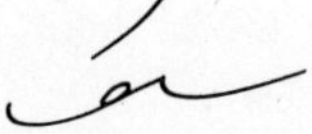 business 
if	miss	 mix 
bill	 did	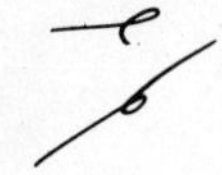 fix 

Notice that the *x* in *mix* and in *fix* is represented by *ks.*

Reading and writing practice

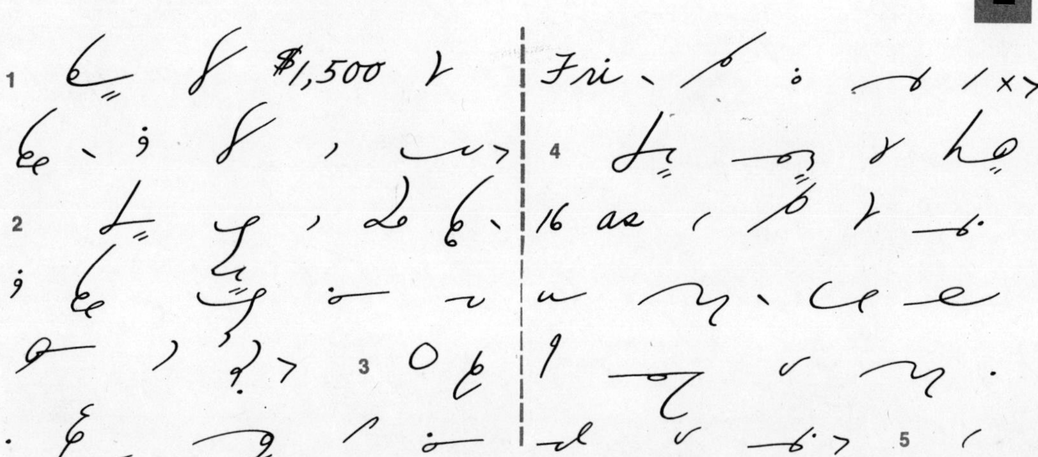

6 again 7 pass

42 Obscure vowel. The small circle also represents the obscure vowel sound heard in *her, firm, church.*

Spell: her, *h-e-r;* **church,** *chay-e-r-chay*

her	**church**	**urged**
serving	**nurse**	**major**
turn	**fur**	**firm**
term	**hurry**	**learn**

Reading and writing practice

1 10 6 before 2 3 4 Sept 8 5

Mon 6 7 Wed 5 6 absence

43 Past tense. As you no doubt have already noticed, in forming the past tense of a verb, we simply add the Notehand character for the sound that we hear in the past tense. In some words, the past tense has the sound of *t,* as in *baked (b-a-k-t);* in others, it has the sound of *d,* as in *saved (s-a-v-d).*

T

baked	**missed**	**mixed**
reached	**priced**	**faced**

D

saved	**changed**	**urged**
tried	**showed**	**stayed**

Reading and writing practice

1

2

3

4

via

Mon

5

6

not

7

with

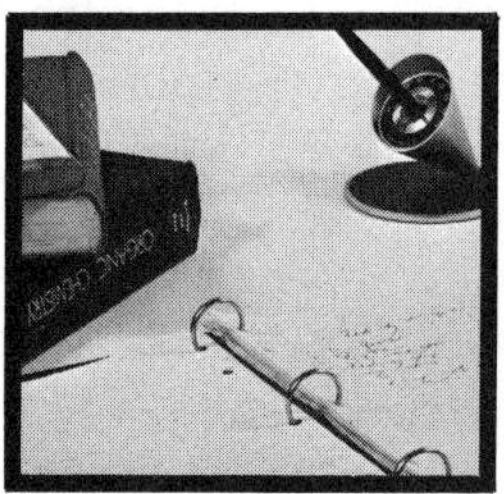

Unit 12

PRINCIPLES OF NOTEMAKING

Notemaking from reading

For many people, reading is the principal source of notes. To make good notes from your reading, you need to know how to read effectively.

Active participation in reading

You are more likely to understand and remember what you read if you actively participate in what you read. The degree to which you participate depends in part on your purpose in reading. Some kinds of material — such as the morning paper, a sports or fashion magazine, or a novel — you read primarily for general information, for enjoyment, or in the pursuit of some special interest. Such reading does not ordinarily require a high degree of participation and effort. But this is not the case when you read for educational purposes in school or for personal improvement. Such reading requires a high degree of active participation by the reader if he is to understand and remember what he reads.

Active participation in reading means, essentially, reciting to yourself mentally and in your own words the gist of what you read. Let's suppose you read the following two paragraphs:

Spring used to be an unhappy season. Along with the swallow's chirp, wails of anguish were heard throughout the land as people wrestled with their income tax blanks. They used to have to pay taxes for the previous year's income—which often had already been spent.

Now things are better. All through the year employers automatically withhold from each paycheck most of what we shall have to pay the government. This puts us all on a pay-as-you-go basis, so that by the end of the year, we are more or less all paid up, even if our pay checks have all been spent.

After reading these two paragraphs, stop and recite to yourself mentally and in your own words the gist of what you have read. The gist of the two paragraphs might be as follows:

People used to be unhappy in the spring because at that time they had to pay taxes on their previous year's income, which they often had already spent. Things are better today because employers automatically withhold a portion of the tax from each paycheck. Consequently, by the end of the year, most of our taxes are paid up, even though we have spent all that we received.

To think about and discuss

1 What does "active participation" in reading mean?

2 What does purpose have to do with the way in which you read?

Application

Read the following paragraph, and then summarize it mentally in your own words.

Nearly everyone had assumed that it would be a short war. But when a stalemate developed on the Western Front, it became clear that fighting might go on for months —perhaps even years—and the passions of most Americans cooled. Cases arose in which the Allies, too, paid scant attention to international law. Invoking dubious rules, the British stopped American ships on the high seas and took them into their ports to be searched for contraband. Nevertheless, most Americans regarded the Allies as morally right. The most common attitude, however, was a mixture of relief at not being involved and conviction that none of the issues in the conflict concerned America. At the outbreak of the war, President Wilson had felt it necessary to exhort his countrymen to remain impartial "in thought as well as in action."

PRINCIPLES OF NOTEHAND

44 **Brief forms**

shall	you	would
be, by	when	were

45 **Phrases**

I shall	to you	you have
I shall be	you are	I would
by the	you will	he would be
for you	you may	you would

Reading and writing practice

Your Reading and Writing Practice for this unit consists of a number of personal letters. You will notice that these letters are written almost completely in Notehand, with only an occasional word in longhand—a sign of the rapid progress you are making.

As you work with each Reading and Writing Practice, are you making proper use of the key in the back of the book? Remember, the key is not to be used as a "last resort" after you have struggled unsuccessfully to decipher an outline. The key will serve you most effectively if you refer to it the moment you cannot read an outline after having spelled it. Your key is a timesaver!

1

2

3

4

Unit 13

PRINCIPLES OF NOTEMAKING

Rules for remembering what you read

At first, you may find it difficult and awkward to recite to yourself mentally and in your own words what you read. But after you get accustomed to the process, you will find that you can do it more naturally. Even so, it will require some effort.

If you will observe the following rules conscientiously, you will be able to participate actively in what you are reading.

Survey what you are going to read

Glance over the material before actually reading it. Read only the main headings and the subheadings to get an idea of what the material is about. Look at the illustrations — photographs, charts, tables, diagrams, and the like. Read summaries and review questions. This survey will give you a perspective of the material and help you determine the important points to understand and remember.

Read actively

After you have read a paragraph — usually an author develops a single idea in a paragraph — recite to yourself mentally and in your own words the gist of what you have read. As you do this, emphasize particularly the main idea and the significant details. These are what you want to remember; by concentrating on them you will fix them in your mind.

Reread if necessary

Sometimes the material is hard to understand. If you don't understand something at the first reading, put it aside for a little while. Then come back to it later and read it again. If after several rereadings you still don't understand it, the chances are that you need some background improvement in order to grasp the ideas presented. For example, the author's vocabulary may be difficult or technical. In that case, skim through the pages you don't understand and make a list of all the words that are strange or unfamiliar. Then look them up in a dictionary, trying to establish their specific meaning in the context of the material you are reading.

Study examples and illustrations carefully

Examples and illustrations are prepared to help you understand and remember what you read.

An author often states or explains a principle and then follows with a specific example in which the principle is applied. For emphasis, this example is often printed in a style or size of type different from that used in the explanation. Do not pass over such examples; they will help you get a clearer picture of what the author is trying to say. In addition, study carefully all charts, drawings, graphs, tables, and other visual aids.

Review your reading

Even though you have read the material with a full and clear understanding, you will need to review from time to time. A quick skimming of the material may be adequate.

Reviewing should be done shortly after the material is first read. Otherwise, you may have to start "from scratch" again because you have forgotten so much of what you read.

How often you review will depend on the difficulty of the material, on its importance, and on such other considerations as preparing for examinations.

To think about and discuss

1 What is included in a preliminary survey of your reading?

2 What is the best procedure when you don't understand something you have read?

Application

Read the following paragraph and recite the gist of it to yourself in your own words.

The connection between word knowledge and success has been proved by scientific study. We have all wondered why one man with very little education has been able to advance to a high position while another man with, perhaps, a college degree has not been able to reach the top level of management. One of the answers is that the first man continued to educate himself by reading a great deal and by listening attentively to people from whom he could learn. In order to read and listen intelligently, this man had to understand the meanings of words.

PRINCIPLES OF NOTEHAND

46 **Ă.** In Unit 2 you learned that a large circle represents the sound of ā, as in *may.* This large circle also represents the sound of ă, as in *had.*

Spell: **had,** *h-a-d;* **has,** *h-a-s*

had	at	fast
has	agree	arrive
man	after	advice
can	matter	appear

Reading and writing practice

NO BUSINESS RUNS ITSELF

that run that run

47 **Ä.** The large circle also represents the sound of *ä*, as in *mark.*

Spell: **mark** *m-a-r-k*

mark car start

parked far part

large arm charge

Reading and writing practice

on Sat 10 5 10 up from 415

up

dull

dollars

48 **Th.** Two small upward curves represent the sound of *th.* (You are already familiar with one of them; it is the brief form for *the.*) Each of these strokes is called "ith." At this point you need not try to determine which *th* stroke to use in a given word; that will become clear to you as your study of Notehand progresses.

Over Th **Under Th**

Spell: **they,** *ith-a;* **though,** *ith-o*

Over Th

they	**then**	**bath**
that	**them**	**neither**
than	**these**	**teeth**

Under Th

though	**those**	**rather**
throw	**through**	**health**
thorough	**either**	**athlete**

Reading and writing practice

SAVING WITH A PURPOSE

Unit 14

PRINCIPLES OF NOTEHAND

RECALL

Unit 14 is a "breather"; it contains no new characters or principles for you to learn. By reading the recall chart that follows, you will review everything you have studied in Units 2-13. The material in the Reading and Writing Practice will help you expand your Notehand vocabulary further.

Before you begin your work on the recall chart and the Reading and Writing Practice, review quickly all the strokes you have studied so far.

Under Th **Over Th** **I** **J** **Ch** **Sh** **K**

G **OO** **Left S** **B** **P** **H** **L** **R** **O**

D **M** **T** **N** **Comma S** **V** **F** **E** **A**

49 **Recall chart.** This chart contains 108 words and phrases. Be sure to spell and say aloud each word as you practice it, but don't waste any time trying to decipher an outline that does not come to you immediately—refer to the key!

Time goal: 11 minutes.

Words

1

2

3

4

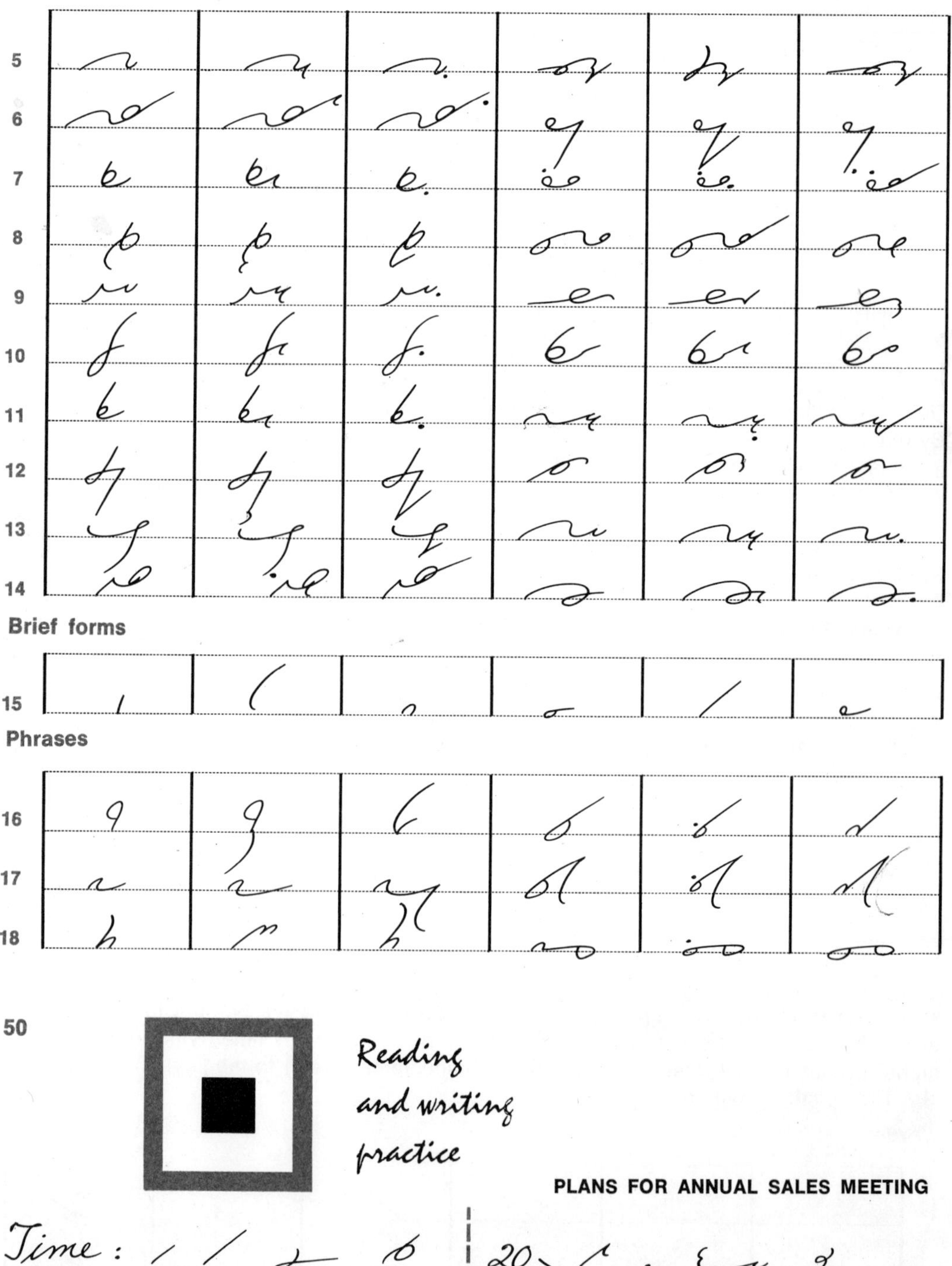

Brief forms

Phrases

50

Reading and writing practice

PLANS FOR ANNUAL SALES MEETING

Time: 20

10

Place:

from 9 5

on

Speakers: we

on

Expenses:

questions

$20.

Special Visits: An

12

and

and

how

Agenda:

Most-used Gregg Notehand forms

If in all your written work you have made a real effort to use the Gregg Notehand forms for the ten common words, as given in Unit 8, you are now ready to add another ten to your card.

to   **you**   **your**   **that**   **he**

as   **at**   **if**   **very**   **no**

Research shows that the ten words given here, plus the ten in Unit 8, make up almost one-third of all the writing you will ever do. Be sure to write these words in Notehand each time you have occasion to use them. Try to read them from your card a few times each day. Read them as rapidly as you can, sometimes forward, sometimes backward. The faster you can read them, the faster you will be able to write them.

Proportion drills

You probably will never be able to write Notehand outlines as beautiful as those in this book. But the outlines you write should be readable, and they will be readable if you try hard to maintain good proportion. Your *a* circles should be large; your *e* circles should be tiny. Your *n* stroke should be very short; your *m* stroke should be about three times as long; etc.

In a number of units you will find Proportion Drills that will help you develop and maintain good proportion. Practice them carefully. Here is the way you should practice:

1. Read through the entire drill to be sure you know the meaning of each outline.

2. Write each *line* once, striving to write each outline as *accurately* as you can rather than as *rapidly* as you can.

3. Finally, make a Notehand copy of the entire list of outlines, once again striving for good proportion.

Straight lines and circles

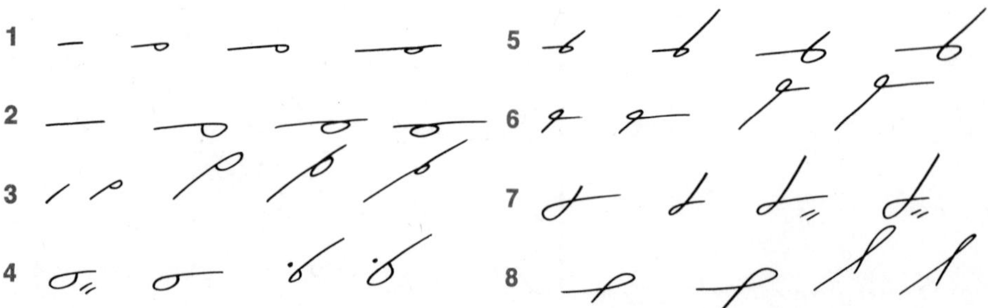

KEY

1 In, knee, me, mean. **2** Am, may, man, name. **3** It, tea, day, date, did. **4** Ann, aim, head, had. **5** Neat, need, mat, made. **6** Tin, team, dean, deem. **7** Shame, chin, Jim, Jane. **8** Mash, match, dash, ditch.

Unit 15

PRINCIPLES OF NOTEMAKING

Finding the central idea in your reading

In making notes from a segment of material you have read, your first job is to find the *central idea* in the passage. Finding the central idea involves recognizing the main or controlling idea. Most people who are good at selecting the central idea probably couldn't tell you how they do it. However, there are some general guides that will help you find the central idea.

There is usually only one idea per paragraph

You will remember this rule about only one central idea in each paragraph from your study of English grammar. This is particularly true if the paragraphs are short. For example:

> **Great literature is not limited to one country. Shakespeare (England), Goethe (Germany), Corneille and Racine (France), Dostoevski and Tolstoi (Russia), Ibsen (Scandinavia), Dante (Italy), and Cervantes (Spain) rank among the great immortals. In any compilation of a hundred great books, there are authors from all parts of the earth.**

Of course, you know that the central idea in this paragraph is that great literature comes from all parts of the world, not just from one country.

Look for key phrase or sentence

In finding the central idea, look for the phrase or sentence in the paragraph upon which everything else depends. It is the one thing in the paragraph that can stand alone; everything else is related to it. Let's take a look at this example:

> **The report that is most inviting in appearance has the best chance of being read. To make it inviting, the writer types it neatly on good white paper. He makes sure that erasures, if any, are undetectable. He keeps the right-hand margins as even as possible. He is careful to see that the type is clean. If the report is to be bound, he selects a cover that is eye-appealing.**

Notice in the example how everything in the paragraph relates to the central idea: The report that is most inviting in appearance has the best chance of being read. This statement stands alone, and the rest of the paragraph merely gives further explanations and examples. These explanations and examples are important, of course, in giving the reader an accurate picture of what the author is writing about and should not be ignored in notemaking.

First sentence often conveys central idea

Usually, the first sentence in the paragraph gives you the key to what the paragraph is about. More often than not, it *is* the central idea, as in the example on the next page.

George Washington was, by everyone's choice, the chairman of the Constitutional Convention. There simply could be no other; he was foremost in everyone's mind. There was no one less the politician and more the disinterested leader. He was a Virginian, to be sure, but was not identified with sectional interests. Even Ben Franklin, the Federation's elder statesman, lacked Washington's stature. Washington was the most eminent American of his day as well as the one most responsible for the formation of his country.

The key sentence in this paragraph is clearly the first one. The rest of the paragraph is given over to reasons why Washington was chosen as chairman.

Last sentence may convey central idea

Occasionally, the author deliberately buries the most important idea somewhere in the middle or at the end of the paragraph. This may be because the key idea has already been given in the heading; more often it is because the author feels he can make his central point better by first providing some dramatic background material. Can you find the central idea in the following paragraph?

The question of fall versus spring plowing is frequently debated. Such a question cannot be correctly answered without knowing what crop is to be grown. Plowing for spring-grain crops, which give their best yields when sown early, requires fall plowing to get maximum returns. If plowing is done in the spring, seeding of the crop is delayed and reduced yields result. In states where winter grains are grown, best yields have been obtained from plowing in the middle of July. Time of plowing is determined by the crop to be grown.

The theme of this paragraph is obviously centered around the statement "Time of plowing is determined by the crop to be grown." The central idea is the last sentence; everything else in the paragraph supports it.

Watch for two central ideas in a paragraph

Some paragraphs contain two or more central ideas, and the notemaker must find them. Notice the two central ideas in the following paragraph:

Credit is, from the point of view of the seller, simply confidence that a buyer will be willing and able to pay his bills when they become due. The seller gives evidence of his confidence by lending merchandise to the buyer. From the point of view of the buyer, credit is the power to obtain goods or services by giving a promise to pay money on demand or at a specified date in the future.

We won't argue the fact that this might have been better stated if it had been broken into two paragraphs — the first, a definition of credit from the viewpoint of the seller; the second, from the viewpoint of the buyer. But this is an actual paragraph from a textbook, and the fact remains that there are two central ideas. The notemaker must be on the alert for them and give them equal prominence in his notes.

To think about and discuss

1 What is a "central idea"?

2 Where is the central idea most often found in a paragraph?

Application

Read the following paragraph and find the central idea.

It is difficult to find the coherence in modern American art that one finds in, say, Greek art or Japanese art. While vast areas are unified politically or economically, there seems to be no corresponding artistic unity, except insofar as the old Indian tradition may be said to survive. The coming of the white man, with an ethos derived from a different environment and tradition, seems to have produced neither a cultural fusion of any enduring or comprehensive kind, nor a homogeneous transplantation. The general picture is one of broken strands and riotous individualism.

PRINCIPLES OF NOTEHAND

51 **Ŏ.** The small hook that represents the sound of ō, as in *low,* also represents the sound of ŏ, as in *hot.*

Spell: **hot,** *h-o-t*

hot	**sorry**	**often**
not	**copy**	**operate**
got	**stopped**	**on**
spot	**office**	**from**

Reading and writing practice

THE TONIC OF PRAISE

52 **Aw.** The *o* hook also represents the sound of *aw,* as in *law.*

Spell: **law,** *l-o;* **cause,** *k-o-s*

law		ought		all	
cause		taught		also	
fall		brought		call	
bought		broad		small	

Reading and writing practice

YOU CAN DO IT

"one"

we

up

53 Word ending -ly. The word ending *-ly* occurs in hundreds of English words. In Notehand, *-ly* is represented by the *e* circle.

Spell: badly, *b-a-d-lee*

badly	finally	readily
only	sincerely	easily
early	specially	daily

Notice, in the words in the third column, the joining of the *-ly* circle to words ending in a vowel, as in *readily* and *daily.*

Reading and writing practice

FOUR WAYS TO BE A HAPPIER PERSON

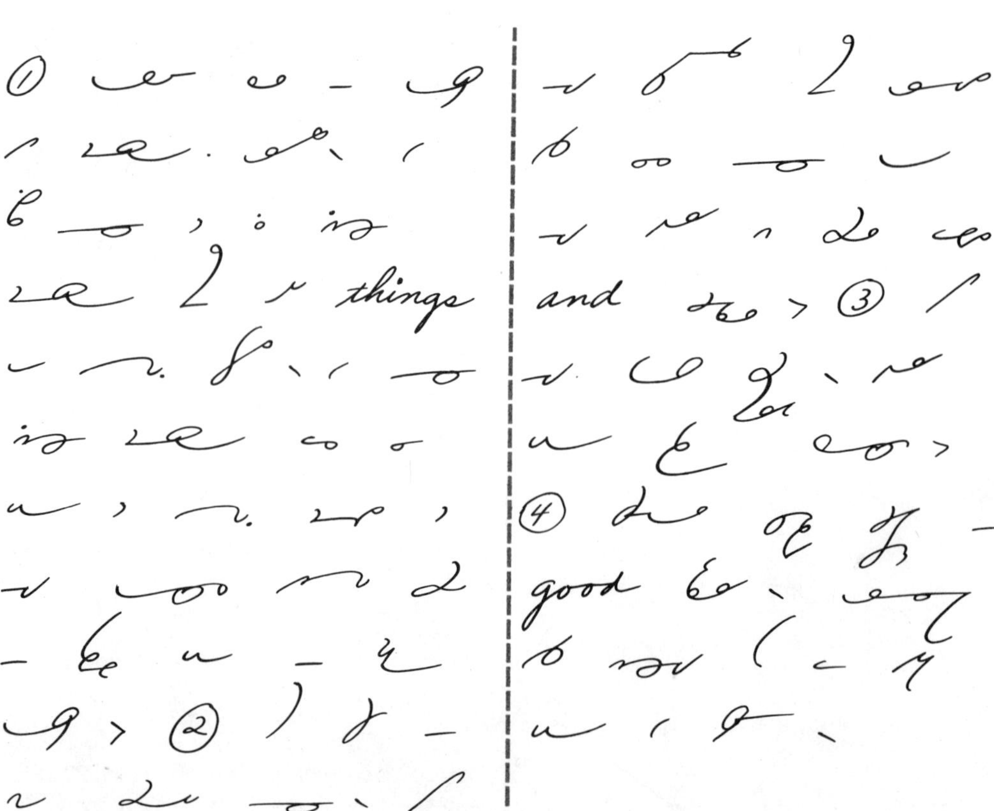

Unit 16

PRINCIPLES OF NOTEMAKING

Finding the central idea in your reading (continued)

In some paragraphs it is not easy to extract the central idea or a single statement that gives the key to the meaning of the paragraph. What is the central idea in the following?

The development of the radio placed a new burden upon presidential candidates. No longer could they escape the limelight by a "front-porch" campaign. The public wanted to hear them and, if possible, also to see them. Smith yielded to the new technique and toured the country extensively, speaking at various points before nationwide hookups. With radio broadcasting still in its infancy, he failed to make a good impression. He spoke from notes rather than from manuscript. While he was fascinating enough to the audience before him, he was often inaudible or inarticulate to the listeners. Moreover, his unusual accent and his occasional mispronunciations caused much unfavorable comment. Hoover, on the other hand, although a far less effective public speaker, poured what he had to say directly into the microphone; and it came out better than it went in. His pronunciation was no better than Smith's, but it was the kind that most Americans were themselves accustomed to use and so gave little offense.

The central idea is not stated precisely in this paragraph. Although it is hinted at in the first sentence, that sentence does not convey the entire idea the author is trying to put across. The notemaker, therefore, must phrase his own central idea. The author is telling you that in the Hoover-Smith presidential campaign, the radio, which had just been developed, worked to Smith's disadvantage and to Hoover's advantage. Stated in your own words, the central idea might be this: Development of the radio helped Hoover's campaign.

Let's take one more example.

Programming is a long and expensive process. For complex problems, it may take thousands of times as long to program a calculator as it does for the calculator to solve the problem. It took General Electric in Louisville twenty-five man-years of time to develop the program of over 200,000 instructions that its Univac needed to do the payroll for GE's 12,000 employees. Yet running off the payroll takes only two hours a day. Because programming now saves thousands of man-hours each month, it paid for itself. But this logic can't be applied to everything. The organization must make sure, before it decides to program something, that the hours saved in the future will compensate for the time and money spent in the programming. Obviously, one-time procedures, such as making a survey, shouldn't be programmed. The procedures to be programmed should be repetitive and frequent.

Is the central idea stated? You may be tempted to accept the first sentence as the central idea, yet it does not satisfactorily convey the theme. The last sentence is closer, but it needs elaboration too. The central idea may be stated as follows: It does not pay to put one-time, nonrepetitive jobs on a computer. Or: Complex, repetitive procedures can often be programmed economically.

Application

Find the central idea in the following paragraphs.

1 But the American marketer must take into account several things in packaging. One firm was unsuccessful in introducing its mayonnaise in Germany because the product was packaged in jars, and Germans usually buy salad dressing in tubes. Labels must be changed to identify the quantity of the contents in the metric system. Colors have different meaning in foreign nations. Red is popular in China but not in some African countries. White indicates mourning in China and Korea.

2 Probably no one has an imagination adequate to comprehend the vastness of the universe in the heavens revealed to the astronomer by his telescope. The earth is just a tiny speck in this vast universe. Some of the stars seen with the most powerful telescopes are so far away that it takes a billion years for the light they send out to reach us, traveling at the rate of more than 186,000 miles every second of that time. At the other extreme in size are molecules and atoms and their components. These are so small that the imagination is inadequate to comprehend their minute size.

PRINCIPLES OF NOTEHAND

54 Brief forms

with · their, there · this

what · was · about

55 Phrases

with the · what is · in this

with our · what are · on this

with this · what will · for this

there was · about the · there is

I was · about this · there are

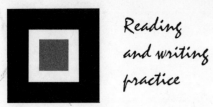

Reading and writing practice

TOM

PROOF

Unit 17

PRINCIPLES OF NOTEMAKING

Selecting related ideas

In making good notes from reading, you must be interested in more than the central idea, of course. You are also interested in facts, information, examples, and other ideas that explain, develop, and support the central idea. These essentials are really the "meat" of your notes.

To illustrate, let's take another look at the example that was given in the previous unit.

> **The development of the radio placed a new burden upon presidential candidates. No longer could they escape the limelight by a "front-porch" campaign. The public wanted to hear them and, if possible, also to see them. Smith yielded to the new technique and toured the country extensively, speaking at various points before nationwide hookups. With radio broadcasting still in its infancy, he failed to make a good impression. He spoke from notes rather than from manuscript. While he was fascinating enough to the audience before him, he was often inaudible or inarticulate to the listeners. Moreover, his unusual accent and his occasional mispronunciations caused much unfavorable comment. Hoover, on the other hand, although a far less effective public speaker, poured what he had to say directly into the microphone; and it came out better than it went in. His pronunciation was no better than Smith's, but it was the kind that most Americans were themselves accustomed to use and so gave little offense.**

For notemaking purposes your analysis of this paragraph might be as follows:

Central idea: Development of the radio helped Hoover's campaign.

Related ideas: Both Hoover and Smith used the radio widely in the campaign.

Smith made a poor impression because:

- He spoke from notes rather than a manuscript.
- He was often inaudible or inarticulate.
- His unusual accent and mispronunciations hurt him.

Hoover made the radio work for him:

- His words "came out better than they went in."
- His delivery was better than Smith's.
- His accent was what most Americans were accustomed to.

Using another illustration, let's look at the example you studied earlier on report writing.

> **The report that is most inviting in appearance has the best chance of being read. To make it inviting,**

the writer types it neatly on good white paper. He makes sure that erasures, if any, are undetectable. He keeps the right-hand margins as even as possible. He is careful to see that the type is clean. If the report is to be bound, he selects a cover that is eye-appealing.

For notemaking purposes your analysis of this paragraph might be as follows:

Central idea: Report with inviting appearance has best chance of being read.

Related ideas: Typed neatly on good paper.
Erasures, if any, undetectable.
Right-hand margins even.
Clean type.
Attractive cover, if bound.

Selecting the central idea and selecting related ideas, facts, information, examples, and so on, for notemaking requires recognition and judgment as to what is important and what is relatively unimportant. Whatever is pertinent should be included in your notes. Good notes are sufficiently complete but not too complete. They are just complete enough to serve your purposes effectively as tools for learning and performance.

To think about and discuss

1 What are "related ideas"?

2 Explain: Good notes are sufficiently complete but not too complete.

Application

Find the central idea and the related ideas in the following:

The most important component of a community health program is the health staff that makes it function. Many programs look promising on paper but are ineffective because of poor personnel. A functional program, one in which health needs are being met successfully, has sufficient competent personnel. Health officers, physicians, dentists, nurses, research workers, health educators, classroom teachers, hospital administrators, executive secretaries of voluntary agencies, social workers, and other health workers should possess skills that enable them to provide health services and an educational program that incorporates findings for the community.

PRINCIPLES OF NOTEHAND

56 **Oi.** The sound of *oi*, as in *boy*, is represented by [shorthand symbol].

Spell: **toy,** *t-oi*

toy	[shorthand]	**oil**	[shorthand]	**annoy**	[shorthand]
boy	[shorthand]	**soil**	[shorthand]	**noise**	[shorthand]
join	[shorthand]	**toil**	[shorthand]	**voice**	[shorthand]
enjoy	[shorthand]	**boil**	[shorthand]	**choice**	[shorthand]

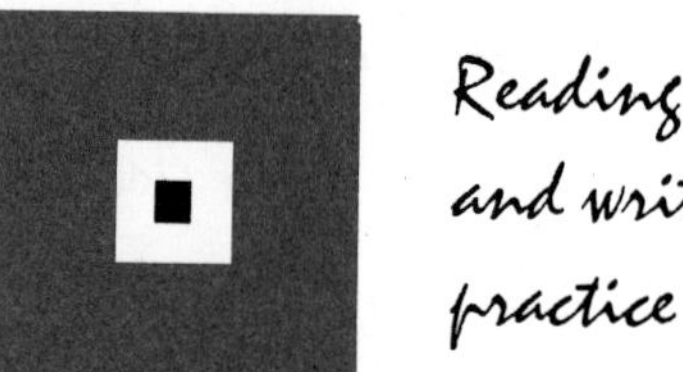

Reading and writing practice

57 Word ending -ure. The word ending *-ure,* as in *secure,* is represented by the Notehand *r.*

Spell: **secure,** *s-e-k-r*

secure	procure	picture
failure	figure	lecture
nature	feature	furniture
mature	featuring	procedure

Reading and writing practice

58 **Word ending -ual.** The word ending *-ual,* as in *actual,* is represented by the Notehand *l.* (Sometimes this ending is spelled *uel,* as in *Samuel,* or *ule,* as in *schedule.*)

Spell: **actual,** *a-k-t-l*

actual gradual equal

factual annual schedule

Reading and writing practice

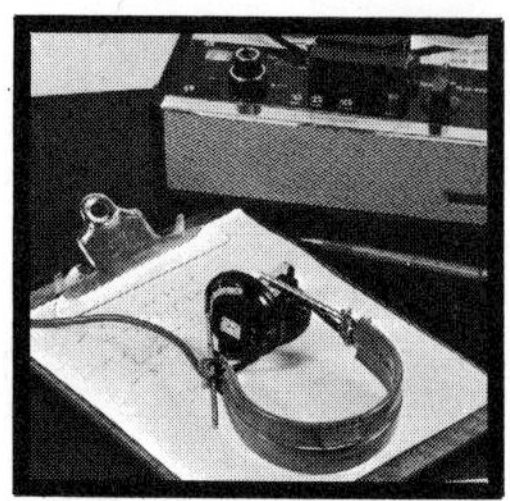

Unit 18

PRINCIPLES OF NOTEMAKING

Using the central idea to build your headings

Generally speaking, central ideas in your reading provide the clues for the major headings in your notes. For example:

> Through mass production, big business can take advantage of certain economies not available to small competitors. It can produce a huge volume of finished materials at a lower cost for each unit. Raw materials can be obtained at lower prices because they are purchased in larger quantities. Machines and labor-saving equipment can be purchased to reduce manufacturing costs. And by training workers to do efficiently one small fraction of a total job (specialization), increased production can be achieved.

The central idea is, of course, in the first sentence: Through mass production, big business can take advantage of certain economies not available to small competitors. Thus, the heading for your notes on this paragraph might be "Economies Achieved by Mass Production" or "Advantages of Mass Production."

Here is another example:

> Because we have what is known as a "free enterprise" system, it is sometimes assumed that all American businessmen make money. This goal, however, is not always realized. Free enterprise is not just a profit system; it is also one of heavy losses. In fact, more businesses fail than succeed. Statistics show that a third of all business undertakings fail in their first year. Another 15 percent fail in their second year. By the end of five years, nearly 70 percent of them are out of business.

As you can see, the central idea is not stated clearly in any one sentence, yet as you read the paragraph, you can quickly phrase your own: Not all businesses make a profit in a free enterprise system. How would you condense this idea as a heading in your notes? You might use this: "Free Enterprise Does Not Guarantee Profit." Or the heading might be simply "Business Failures," depending on the previous headings you have used and the general context in which the notes are being made.

As mentioned earlier, sometimes there are two or more central ideas in a paragraph. This is not very common, however, since the purpose of paragraphing is to separate big ideas. In most cases, one big idea predominates and the others support it or relate to it, for example:

> As you read earlier, monopoly is accomplished by eliminating competition, by adjusting production to prevent glutting the market, and by dictating prices. Economists distinguish between several types of monopoly. A "seller's monopoly" exists when those who sell a commodity control enough of the total supply so that they can create a scarcity by restricting sales. On the other hand, if there are only a few purchasers, like concerns that process vegetables, they can name their own prices. By restricting purchases they can also force prices down. This is called a "buyer's monopoly." When the government owns and manages an enterprise,

such as the Tennessee Valley Authority, it is called a "public monopoly," but when such utilities are operated by private persons or corporations through a franchise, they are "private monopolies."

While there are several definitions in the paragraph, there is only one big idea. Obviously, the author is discussing types of monopolies, and that becomes your major heading. Let's see how this excerpt might appear in the form of notes.

TYPES OF MONOPOLIES

Seller's Monopoly:	When sellers control supply and create a scarcity by restricting sales
Buyer's Monopoly:	When there are few purchasers (e.g., vegetable processors) who can name their own prices
Public Monopoly:	When government owns and operates an enterprise (TVA)
Private Monopoly:	When a person or corporation operates a utility through a franchise.

Application

Find the major heading for notemaking in the following:

1 The American Farm Bureau Federation, which is generally regarded as the spokesman for the nation's most successful commercial farmers, may include persons who joined for a host of reasons. Some may approve of the Federation's legislative program and may have joined in order to develop and support it. Others may have found it personally advantageous to join, but may disapprove of one or more points in the Federation program. A third group may have joined simply because they could not say "No" to the organizer, because they wanted to please a friend, in order to conform to neighborhood expectations, or for the sake of the group's social activities.

2 Price supports and Soil Bank are the basic programs for farm surpluses. The government also attempts to reduce these surpluses in other ways—through the school lunch program and through a 1954 act permitting gifts or sales to foreign nations under certain conditions.

15, 17, 18

PRINCIPLES OF NOTEHAND

59 **Word ending -tion.** The word ending *-tion* (sometimes spelled *-sion, cean,* or *-shion*) is represented by the Notehand *sh.*

Spell: nation, *n-a-shun*

nation	**selection**	**ocean**
action	**vacation**	**fashion**
section	**provision**	**occasion**

Reading and writing practice

VACATION

60 **Ŭ.** The hook that represents $\overline{oo}$, as in *to,* also represents the sound of ŭ heard in *but.*

Spell: **but,** *b-oo-t;* **up,** *oo-p*

but	product	touch
up	succeed	brush
does	us	must
other	just	number

Notice that:

a. In *us,* the *oo* hook and the *s* join without an angle.

b. In *must* and *number,* the *oo* hook is on its side.

Reading and writing practice

FIVE PRINCIPLES OF SELLING 

61 **ŏŏ.** The *oo* hook represents a third sound—the sound of ŏŏ heard in *book.*

Spell: **book,** *b-oo-k*

book		**looked**		**pushed**	
foot		**good**		**full**	
cooked		**took**		**pulling**	

Reading and writing practice

SPARE-TIME LEARNERS

Burchell

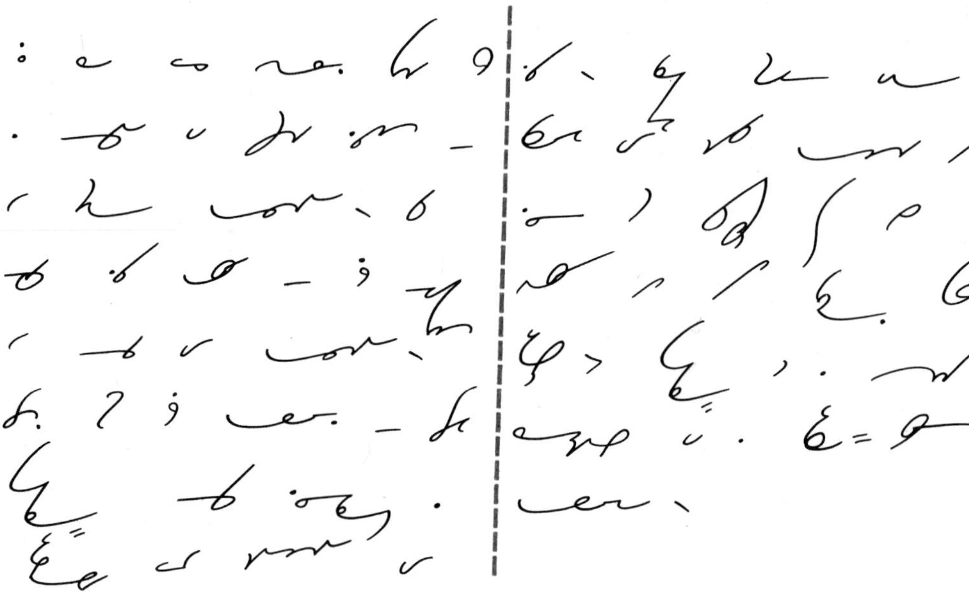

Unit 19

PRINCIPLES OF NOTEMAKING

Read before you make notes

After you have read a segment of material and have recited it to yourself in your own words, you are ready to make notes. It is very important that you know what you have read before putting anything down for two reasons:

1 If you begin to make notes before you understand thoroughly what you have read, you are likely to put down information that is irrelevant to the subject.

2 Sometimes the author does not express ideas in continuity. That is, he introduces a few of his main points, then digresses with side remarks and supporting data, and later takes up the main theme again. Knowing this before you put anything down will help you put points together in the right sequence.

Here is an example:

With the coming of the Industrial Revolution, the worker lost his tools and the power to make a finished product with his own hands. When mass production robbed him of his skills, it also chained him to a machine. Today, through labor organizations, the laborer has retrieved his self-respect and dignity of work. His living standards have risen. He works shorter hours and therefore has more time to enjoy a cultural and social life. Thus, where the laborer had been a victim of economic forces over which he had no control, by organizing into a collective group, he gained strength.

If you were reading the foregoing paragraph for the purpose of making notes, you would see that the information in the last sentence ties in with the first two sentences and really belongs with those ideas in your notes.

Let's see how the material would look as notes:

WHY WORKERS ORGANIZE

Background

1. Industrial Revolution took away worker's tools and his power to make things with his own hands.

2. Mass production robbed him of his skills, made him captive to a machine.

3. He became the victim of economic forces over which he had no control.

4. By organizing collectively, he gained strength.

How Organization Helped Labor

1. Through organizations, he has got back self-respect and dignity.

2. Living standards have risen.

3. Shorter hours, thus more time to enjoy cultural and social life.

You can see that if item 4 under "Background" were left until last, it would interfere with the list of ways organization helped labor.

Application

Prepare notes for the following excerpt, including a major heading, minor headings, and 1-2-3 enumerations under minor headings.

Efforts to conserve the recreation resources of national forests include planning of recreation developments in order best to serve the public and to make use of the scenic and sport resources, protection of developed areas from invasion by livestock, bringing water supplies to dry but attractive areas, requiring strict adherence to sanitary standards from those who have land under permit, assisting state officers in the enforcement of fish and game regulations, increasing the fish and other wild-animal resources, and resisting constant pressures to invade wilderness country with roads, reservoirs, airplane landing fields, and other developments. Various organizations are active in defending the recreation resources of the national forests, using the methods just enumerated.

PRINCIPLES OF NOTEHAND

62 **W.** *W* at the beginning of words is expressed by the *oo* hook.

Spell: **we,** *oo-e;* **way,** *oo-a*

we		**week**		**watch**	
way		**well**		**won, one**	
wait		**war**		**wall**	

Sw at the beginning of words is expressed by *s-oo.*

Spell: **swell,** *s-oo-e-l*

swell		**swim**		**sweet**	

Wh, as in *while,* is pronounced *hw.* As the *h* is pronounced first, it is written first.

Spell: **while,** *h-oo-ī-l*

while		**wheat**		**why**	
wheel		**whether**		**white**	

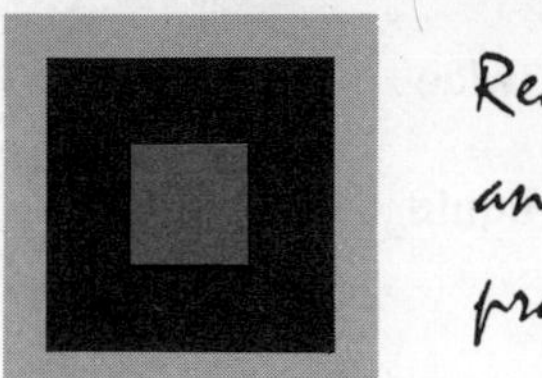

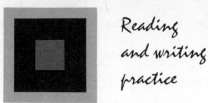

Reading and writing practice

BE CALM

(Concluded in Paragraph 63)

63 W in the body of a word. When the sound of *w* occurs in the body of a word, as in *always,* it is represented by a short dash underneath the vowel following the *w* sound. The dash is inserted after the rest of the outline has been written.

Spell: always, *o-l-oo-a-s;* **quite,** *k-oo-ī-t*

always   **quite**   **twin**

railway | quick | twice
roadway | quote | liquid

Reading and writing practice

BE CALM (Concluded)

Lincoln

Lincoln

Lincoln

64 **Ū.** The sound of ū, as in *use,* is written .

Spell: **use,** *ū-s;* **few,** *f-ū*

use | few | beauty
unit | view | tube

unite	fuel	value
utilize	pure	usual

Reading and writing practice

MEMORY

Unit 20

PRINCIPLES OF NOTEHAND

RECALL

Once again you will have a "breather" – you will have no new strokes to learn in this unit. You will review everything you studied thus far through the recall chart, and you will read and copy two interesting articles written entirely in Notehand.

65 **Recall chart.** Can you read the 108 items in this chart in 9 minutes or less? You can if you refer to your key the moment you cannot decipher an outline after you have spelled it.

Words

1						
2						
3						
4						
5						
6						
7						
8						
9						
10						
11						
12						

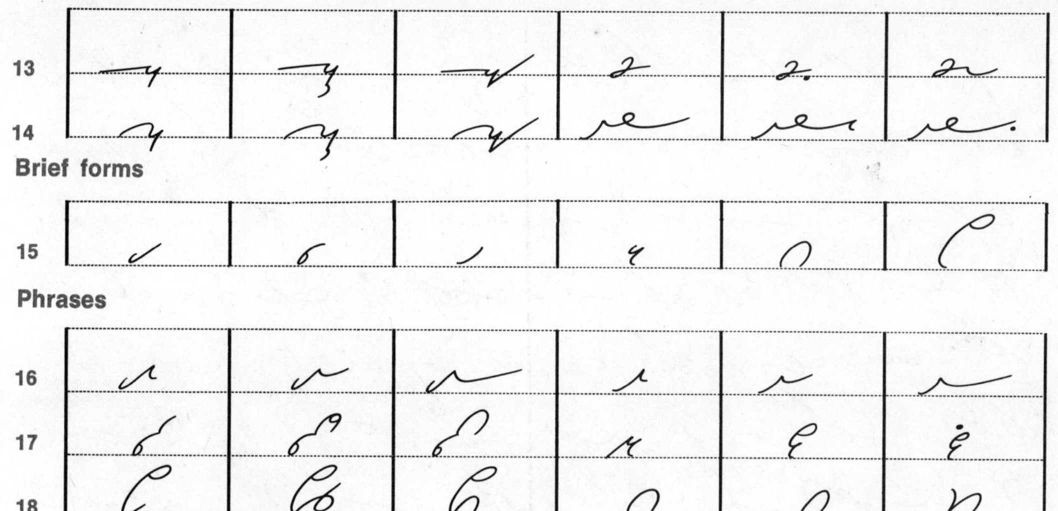

66

Reading and writing practice

FOLLOW THE LEADER

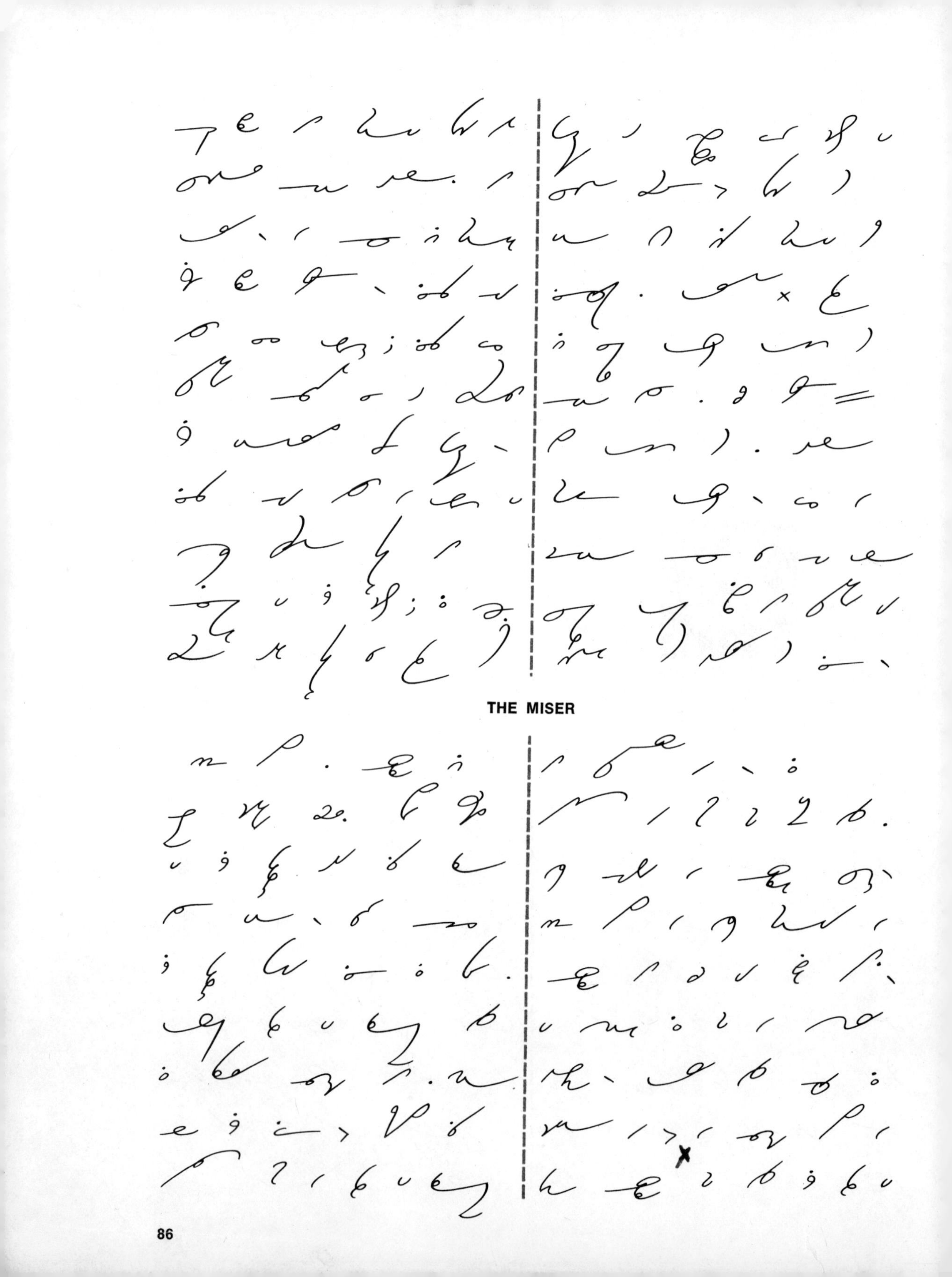

THE MISER

—*Adapted from Aesop's Fables*

Most-used Gregg Notehand forms

By this time you should have learned to use easily the twenty common words that were presented in Units eight and fourteen. Here are ten more of the most frequently used words in the English language. Add these to the Notehand forms that are already on your card. Remember to keep the card near you whenever you are writing and refer to it as often as necessary.

The ten additional words are:

all **this** **with** **but** **on**

was **from** **one** **about** **well**

Unit 21

PRINCIPLES OF NOTEMAKING

Making notes in your own words

When you make notes from reading, it is best to make them in your own words, except, of course, for statements you wish to recall exactly or to quote. Fortunately, making notes in your own words is but another application of effective reading.

How making notes in your own words will help you

Making notes in your own words will help you in five significant ways:

1 It will help you prepare more useful notes — notes that convey in your own vocabulary only the essentials of what you have read.

2 It will help you think for yourself. Making notes in your own words requires you to analyze, interpret, relate, and summarize what you read.

3 It will help you learn because it requires you to participate actively in what you read.

4 If will help you review. Notes made in your own words are a helpful source of material for reviewing. Ideas, facts, information, and examples that are put into your own words may help you recall the entire reasoning process that you followed in making the notes initially.

5 It will aid you in preparing for and taking examinations, not only by increasing your knowledge and understanding but also by helping you state answers in your own words. It will help you to relate ideas, facts, information, and examples. It will help you to approach examinations with confidence and to think creatively.

An example

Read the following paragraph for the purpose of putting into your own words the essential ideas that it contains.

> **Gluck himself had written a great many operas in the conventional Italian style of his day before he assumed the role of reformer, so that he knew whereof he spoke when he said that opera was in need of purification. Gluck tried above all to rationalize opera—to have it make more sense. In the older opera the singer was supreme, and the music served the singer; Gluck made the dramatic idea supreme and wrote music that served the purposes of the text. Each act was to be an entity in itself, not a nondescript collection of more or less effective arias. It was to be balanced and contrasted, with a flow and continuity that would give it coherence as an art form. The ballet, for example, was not to be a mere divertissement introduced for its own sake but an integral part of the dramatic idea of the work.**

The central idea in the foregoing paragraph is that Gluck assumed the role of a reformer in opera after having written many operas in conventional Italian style. The paragraph also contains several ideas related to the central idea. Put into your own words, the essential ideas of the paragraph might be as follows:

> **Gluck had written many operas in conventional Italian style. He thought opera should make sense; the drama was more important than the singer. Each act should be complete in itself and coherent. Ballet should be a real part of the story, not just something thrown in.**

As you will observe, the ideas have been selected, interpreted, and described briefly in words that in several instances are different from those in the original paragraph.

To think about and discuss

1 How will making notes in your own words help you?

2 Why do you think making notes in your own words will help you in taking an examination?

Application

In each of the following paragraphs (*a*) find the central idea or ideas and (*b*) condense the material in your own words for note-making purposes. Be brief, but not too brief.

1 High income makes it possible to obtain the recommended amounts of nutrients, but it does not ensure that these nutrients are provided. Studies have shown that some low-income families have met the needs while high-income groups have not. Certain nutrients are more likely to be related to income than are others. Vitamin C is the nutrient most closely related to income and thiamine the least. Higher income is closely related to purchase of good food sources of vitamin C, the citrus fruits in particular. Higher income families, on the other hand, tend to reduce the amounts of grains and pork, two of the best sources of thiamine.

2 The rise in our standard of living is not just a matter of the quantity of goods consumed. It is noticeable in the *kinds* of things consumed. Over the last fifty years, there has been a rapid increase in the consumption of durable goods. Today, consumers spend approximately 14 percent of their income for such durable goods as automatic washers and dryers, television sets, food freezers, power lawn mowers, dishwashers, and automobiles. The demand for services such as medical care, haircuts, dry cleaning, and transportation has also grown. At present, approximately 40 percent of consumer spending is for services.

PRINCIPLES OF NOTEHAND

67 Brief forms

***under**	**which**	**should**
***over**	**opportunity**	**could**

*The words *under* and *over* are written above the following Notehand character. They may also be used as prefix forms as in the following words:

underneath **underpaid** **oversight**

undertake overcame overlook

68 Phrases

under the I should which the

under that he should I could

Reading and writing practice

EASY PROFIT

"$125"

"$90"

10

$35

10

$35 and

$125

$35

$50

$50

4

5

$15

$75!

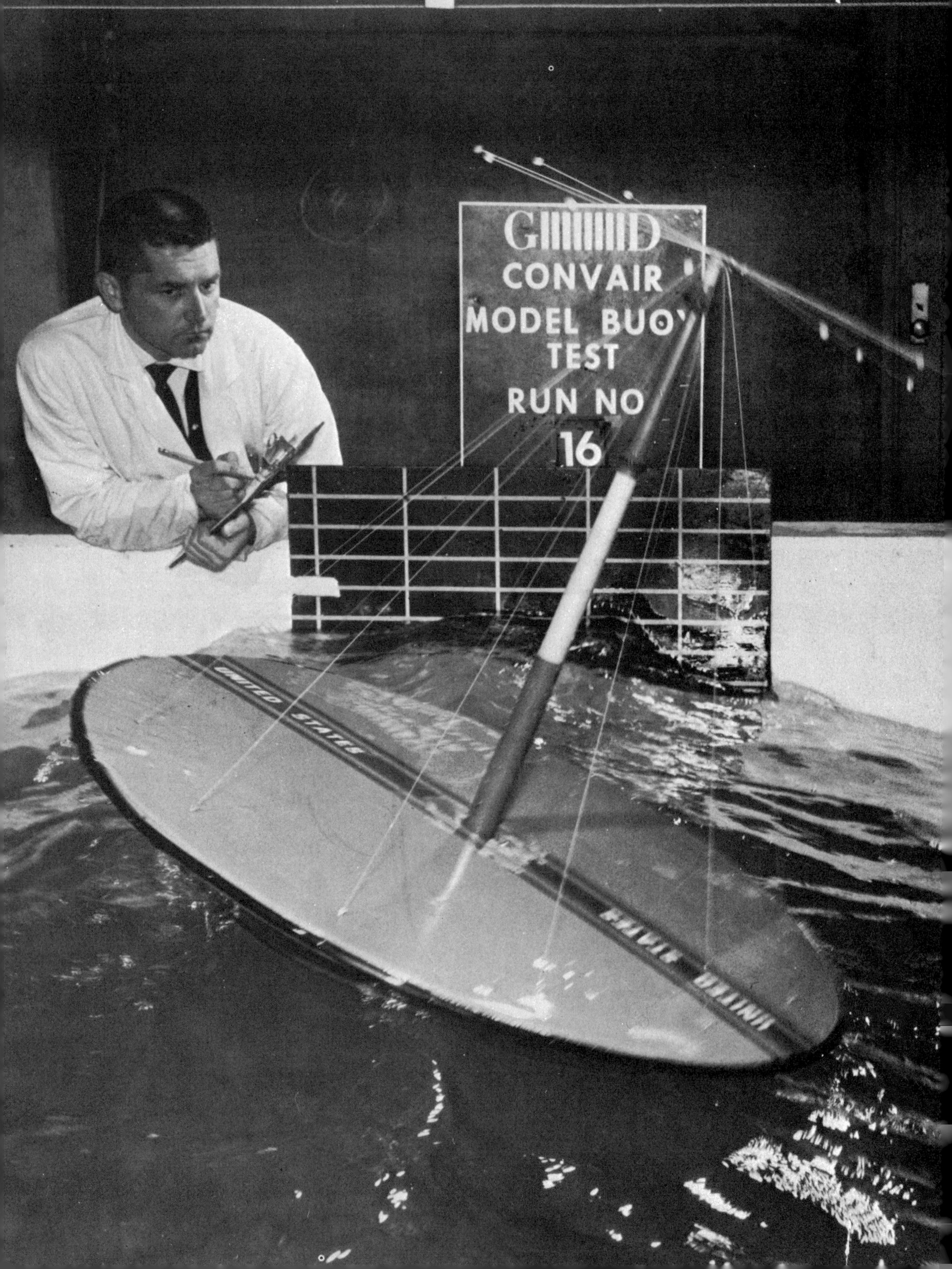

CONVAIR
MODEL BUOY
TEST
RUN NO
16
UNITED STATES

Unit 22

PRINCIPLES OF NOTEMAKING

Brevity in making notes in your own words

In making notes in your own words, strive to put down just enough — not too much or too little. The note that you make of each idea, fact, piece of information, or example should be brief and to the point, eliminating unnecessary words.

Nearly everything we read except telegrams has more words than are really necessary for comprehension. "Why, then," you may ask, "don't writers cut out the extra words?" Well, the extra words make the material easier to read and understand. Books and other types of literature would be very hard to read if they were written like telegrams. Also, extra words make it possible for an author to say things in more interesting and striking ways.

When you make notes, however, you should eliminate most of the extra words. Every unnecessary word you include requires time for the writing and later requires additional time for reading in using your notes. You must get down to the bare essentials. For example, read the following paragraph:

> **In all the pages of history, from the beginning of time, there is no blacker example of infamous treachery and inhuman cruelty than the campaign in which the Spaniards under Pizarro ravaged Peru and traitorously executed the Inca after extorting a vast treasure of gold as his ransom.**

Notice how much more interesting and colorful this paragraph is because of the use of such words and phrases as "in all the pages of history," "from the beginning of time," "blacker example," "infamous treachery," and "traitorously." Yet these words are not necessary in notes. As a matter of fact, your notes might simply read:

> **Spaniards under Pizarro were treacherous and cruel when they executed Inca after collecting ransom.**

Thus the fourteen-word note tells all that is necessary about the forty-eight-word paragraph. The brevity of the note has saved about two-thirds of the time that would have been required to write the paragraph in full.

Include useful little words

Brevity does not mean that you should write notes in telegraphic style from which useful little words like *and, to,* and *from* are omitted. Because of the ease with which these little words may be written in Gregg Notehand, they can be used without any appreciable loss of time. Furthermore, notice in the preceding illustration how much the inclusion of the word *and* helps the sense of the notes.

Words like *to* and *from* can be important in interpreting your notes long after they were written. This is not always the case, but it is important not to leave them out just because they are short words.

Don't be too brief

The effort to keep your notes brief must not be carried too far. Sometimes it may be quicker to write a slightly longer note than to take the time to decide how best to abbreviate it. In addition, notes must not be so brief that they are inadequate and difficult to use after they are made. Read the following paragraph:

> **Although medieval culture abounded in local, regional, and eventually national differences, the feudal upper classes throughout the West shared the way of life we call "chivalry." This term comes from "chevalier," the French word for knight. The chivalric code began as the simple creed of fighting men, and—like most things medieval—it came into full maturity during the thirteenth century.**

The central idea of the paragraph might be reworded in your own notes as follows:

> **Feudal upper classes shared way of life called "chivalry."**

For good notemaking purposes, however, this description of the central idea of the paragraph is too brief. It would be more useful if it were worded as follows:

> **Chivalry was a way of life for feudal upper classes in West. Originally a simple creed for fighting men (term comes from French word for knight), it came into full maturity during the thirteenth century.**

Notice, again, in this illustration the usefulness of such little words as *a, of, for, in,* and *from* in notemaking and especially in reading notes later.

To think about and discuss

1 Why do most of the things we read have excess words?

2 Is it desirable always to omit such "little" words as *to* and *from?*

Application

Condense the following paragraph into as few words as possible. Caution: Don't make your summary too skimpy—you want to be sure to preserve all the important points.

The length of the fashion cycle may vary considerably from one product to another. A style in houses or furniture may remain fashionable for many years, whereas styles in women's hats or shoes may be in fashion for only one season. Furthermore, the fashion cycle for a given type of product is considerably shorter today than it was years ago. Improved production processes, communications systems, and transportation methods have facilitated the introduction and rapid dissemination of styles. This does not mean that all parts of the national market accept and adopt a style with the same rapidity and eagerness. It may reach a given point in its fashion cycle a year later in Denver than in New York, and it may never be accepted as a fashion in some communities.

PRINCIPLES OF NOTEHAND

69 **Ow.** The sound of *ow,* as in *how,* is written ⸺. In writing *ow,* be sure to make the *a* circle large and the *oo* hook deep and narrow.

Spell: **how,** *h-ow*

how	doubt	proud
out	town	now
house	down	mouse
ounce	brown	mouth

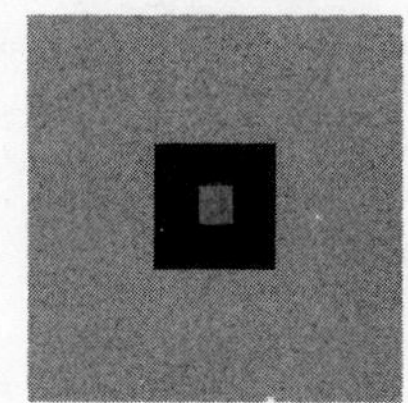

Reading and writing practice

TEMPER

70 **Omission of short U.** In the body of a word, the hook representing the sound of short *u*, as in *run*, is omitted before *n* or *m*.

Before N

run   gun   ton

sun   fun   lunch

Before M

come   summer   column

some   lumber   welcome

Reading and writing practice

DITHER

Watterson

H. W.

Unit 23

PRINCIPLES OF NOTEMAKING

Organizing notes in narrative summaries

Organizing your notes as you make them will help you get more out of your reading. Moreover, it will result in notes that are much more useful to you after they are made.

Notes may be organized in two basic forms: as narrative summaries of the essential ideas you have grasped from listening or reading or in outline form.

Narrative summaries are restatements in your own words of the essential ideas in what you are reading or listening to. The following is an example of a narrative summary.

Narrative summaries are especially useful in organizing notes:

1 In discussions and conferences.

2 When listening to a speaker whose remarks range over a number of topics and do not treat any one topic in depth.

3 In reading one or more reference sources for general information on a topic or a variety of topics.

Headings in narrative summaries

Providing frequent headings in narrative summaries will be helpful when you use the notes later. In the example below the headings are placed at the left with plenty of white space around them so that the eye can readily spot them.

JOHANN SEBASTIAN BACH

THE MAN

More than an intellectual musician. He was a lovable, warm-hearted man. Probably never danced, but enjoyed dance music. Had a cheerful heart, wrote cheerful music, such as his Gavotte in E Major and Minuet.

Bach had a deep and sincere piety. Loved the service of the church, for which he wrote great music.

COUNTERPOINT

Brought old church counterpoint to life.

Called his counterpoint tunes fugues.

In a fugue the melodies seem to chase each other. Musician's eye as well as his ear tells him the first tune begins with the left hand and proceeds for four measures. While left hand goes on with new theme, the right hand repeats first pattern. At measure 9, the right hand plays a new pattern, which the left hand immediately begins to imitate at measure 11, etc.

CANTATAS

Wrote over 200 cantatas. His Christmas oratorio is really a collection of six cantatas.

ORATORIOS

Bach was organist many years for German Protestant Church of St. Thomas. Here he wrote magnificent oratorios (church singing plays).

Called his oratorios Passions.

In his Passions, Bach used the language of the gospels of John, Mark, and Matthew.

B MINOR MASS

Among Bach's greatest works is the Mass in B Minor.

To think about and discuss

1 What are narrative summaries?

2 In what ways are narrative summaries useful in organizing notes?

3 Are headings desirable in narrative summaries?

Application Wed.

Make notes on the following in narrative form.

MAYOR-COUNCIL FORM OF GOVERNMENT

The large majority of our cities are governed by a mayor and a council. This type of city government is sometimes called the *federal plan* because it is modeled after the framework of our national government.

The mayor of a city is elected by popular vote, generally for a term which varies from two to four years. While his first duty is to enforce city ordinances, the mayor also carries out those administrative functions assigned to him by the charter. Usually he is given the power to veto ordinances passed by the council.

The administrative units of the city are operated by heads of departments, sometimes referred to as *commissioners.* These men are appointed by the mayor. The number of administrative departments varies with different cities, but they usually include such units as law, finance, safety, public works, and public welfare. In some instances, the mayor can remove his administrative heads at his pleasure. Quite often these officials form a cabinet which meets with the mayor to discuss problems of administration and to formulate policies.

The functions of the mayor and the council are separately listed in the charter. The mayor acts as executive head, while the council enacts ordinances. Several plans are used by American cities to select their councilmen. The majority of cities elect them at large, some elect them by wards, and others combine the two systems. In practice, councilmen are often chosen for a term of two years, although St. Louis, Boston, Philadelphia, and several other cities have four-year terms. The council passes on the budget, which is usually prepared by the finance officer and approved by the mayor. The council also makes the appropriations necessary to carry on the activities of the city.

PRINCIPLES OF NOTEHAND

71 **Ng.** The sound of *ng,* as in *sing,* is written ‿ .

Compare: **seen** **sing**

Spell: **ring,** *r-e-ing;* **long,** *l-o-ing;* **young,** *e-oo-ing*

ring	bring	single
rang	thing	young
wrong	sing	length
long	sang	strong

Reading and writing practice

ENRICO CARUSO

Met

Aida Carmen

72 Ngk. The sound of *ngk* (usually spelled *nk* in longhand), as in *sink,* is written —.

Compare: **seen** — **sing**

seem — **sink**

Spell: **link,** *l-e-ink;* ***thank,*** *ith-a-ink*

link	crank	think
thank	blank	rank
sank	blanket	drink
bank	ink	frank

Reading and writing practice

ABRAHAM LINCOLN

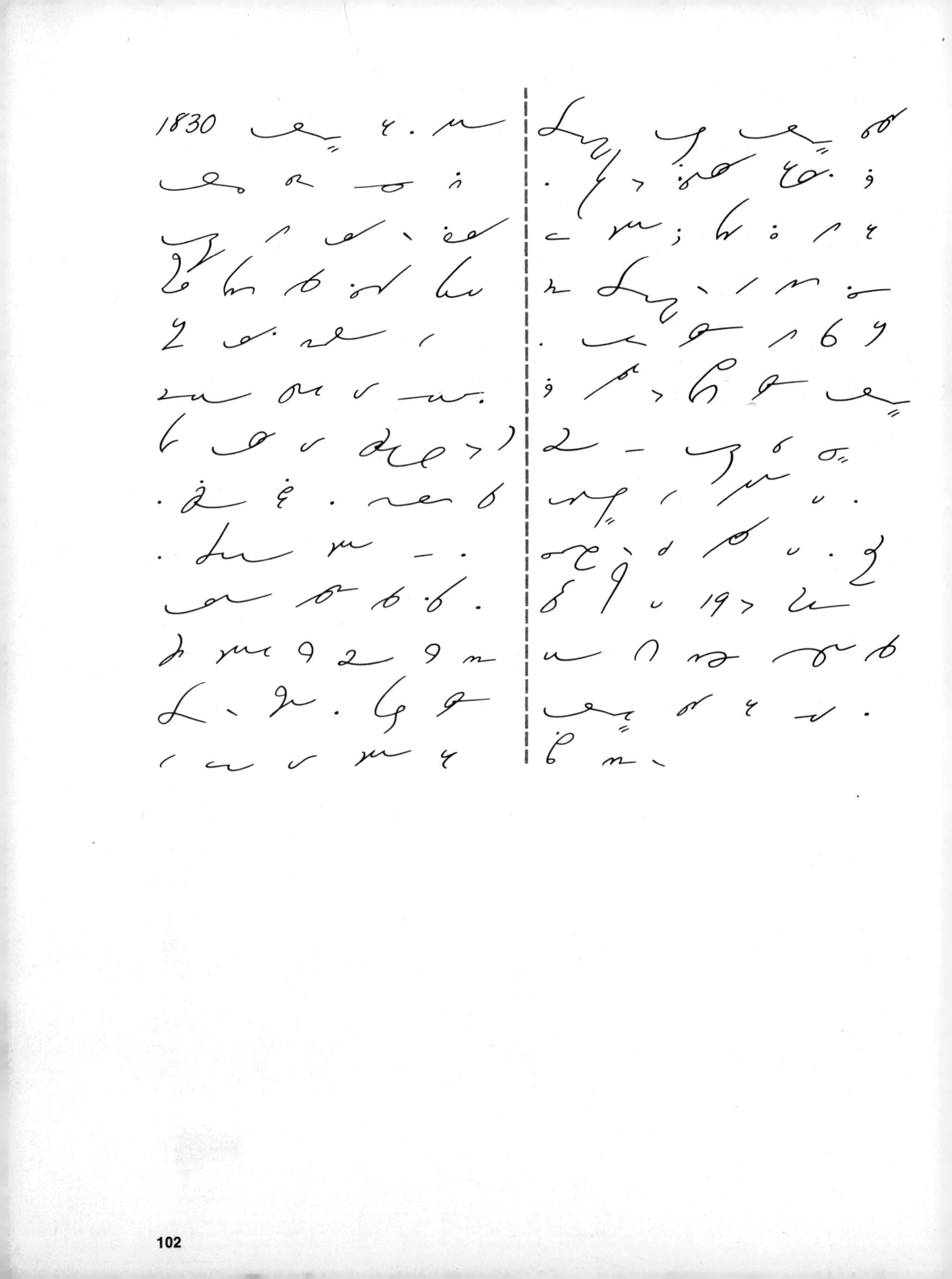

Unit 24

PRINCIPLES OF NOTEMAKING

Organizing notes in outline form

Organizing notes in outline form involves the use of main headings and subheadings. Main headings are used for items of primary importance, with subheadings for items of secondary importance. The degree of importance of the items and the relationship between them are shown by levels or ranks of headings. Thus essential ideas are main headings or subheadings, depending upon the level of their importance and their relationship.

Outline form is generally regarded as the most efficient form in which to organize notes. This is especially true in making notes *in depth,* that is, making notes that involve several levels of headings and subheadings and run to considerable length.

Organizing notes in outline form offers these advantages:

1 It will help you to think through carefully what you hear or read. It will help you select the essential ideas, facts, and information and to understand the relative importance and relationship.

2 It will help you to make useful notes — notes that can be used readily for studying, for review, and for reference.

3 It will help you save time both in making notes and in using them.

Informal and formal outlines

The two basic kinds of outlines are the informal and the formal. In the informal outline, simple indentions are used to indicate the relationship and relative importance of headings and subheadings. For some of your notemaking, the informal outline will do very well.

A more elaborate and often more efficient form for organizing notes is the formal outline. This uses a system of numbers and letters to indicate the importance and the relationship of headings and subheadings. The most commonly used system is as follows:

SUBJECT OR TOPIC (Not part of numbering system)

I. ....
  A. ....
    1. ....
      a. ....
        (1) ....
          (a) ....

Note that each succeeding level is indicated by a wider indention.

The outline on the following page illustrates the number-letter system.

Once you adopt a system of outlining for organizing a set of notes, use it consistently. Select your headings carefully. Indent subheadings consistently to show degrees of importance and relationship; that is, keep headings of equal importance at the same level. Watch the sequence of main headings and subheadings carefully so that each level develops and supports the next higher level.

Topic or sentence headings?

In outlining, headings may be in the form of topics (that is, brief phrases or single words) or complete sentences. Or a combination of the two forms may be used; that is, main headings may be in the form of

TRANSFER OF HEAT

I. Importance of transfer of heat
   - A. Life on earth dependent on radiation from the sun
     - 1. Plants receive radiation from the sun
     - 2. Energy from coal, oil, etc., largely from fossil plants
   - B. All man's sources of energy ultimately derived from radiation except atomic energy

II. Methods of transfer of heat
   - A. Conduction
     - 1. Definition: Transfer of heat between materials in contact
     - 2. Method: Molecules in motion on surface of "hot" object striking molecules on surface of "cool" object and imparting kinetic energy
       - a. Molecules do not pass from "hot" to "cool" object
       - b. Kinetic energy the "heat" that flows from one object to another
   - B. Convection
     - 1. Definition: Movement of molecules of gas
     - 2. Method: Kinetic energy of molecules increased
       - a. Causes gas to become less dense
       - b. Gas pushed upward by buoyant force of colder air
       - c. Hence the gas circulates
     - 3. Convection responsible for movement of winds, ocean currents, as well as heating from a "steam radiator"
   - C. Radiation
     - 1. Definition: Energy emitted by a body whose molecules are in state of kinetic energy
       - a. Radiation not transmitted by moving molecules
       - b. May be transmitted across a vacuum
     - 2. Types of radiation
       - a. Heat
       - b. Light
       - c. Electric waves
       - d. "X-radiation," etc.
     - 3. Factors that determine radiation
       - a. Energy radiated and absorbed by all bodies
       - b. Radiation determined by temperature (kinetic energy)
       - c. Type of material
         - (1) Some substances radiate more than others (platinum more than silver)
         - (2) Rough surface radiates more than smooth (because there is <u>more</u> surface when it is rough)

topics, and subheadings may be in the form of sentences.

There is no hard-and-fast rule for deciding when to use topics and when to use sentences. Topic headings are more concise and quicker to write. Sentence headings require more time and effort to construct. Sentence headings force the notemaker to think through more carefully what he reads or hears in order to make complete statements. The use that is to be made of the notes is also a consideration. For example, in outlining notes from the usual reading and listening, topics are more commonly used. In outlining notes for a research paper, sentence headings are probably preferable.

To think about and discuss

1 How do headings distinguish between main ideas and secondary ideas?

2 What are the advantages of organizing notes in outline form?

3 What is the difference between an informal and a formal outline?

4 Discuss the uses of topic headings and sentence headings — when preferred, advantages and disadvantages, etc.

Application

Read the following and prepare notes in outline form. Make your own choice as to whether you use topic or sentence headings.

WHY A CITIZEN VOTES

A summary of research on voter motivation indicates that the following are the primary indicators of whether or not a particular citizen is likely to vote. He will be likely to vote:

1. *If he believes his interests are strongly affected by governmental policy.* In other words, he tends to vote if he believes he has a personal economic, social, or ideological interest in the election. Farmers, for example, know that they have a stake in price-support policies. This gives them a strong motive for being interested in an election. In general, women are less interested in politics than men, and 41 percent of the women who were eligible to vote in the 1948 election failed to do so. But that was a time of peace and prosperity. Four years later the threats presented to them and to the very lives of their husbands and sons by the Korean conflict brought them out in much larger numbers, though 31 percent did not vote even then.

2. *If he understands the relationship of the election to his own interests.* A person may be profoundly affected by government policies, but if he does not recognize that his personal interest is at stake, they do not exist for him, and he may be blindly apathetic. In general, therefore, the better informed and educated a person is, the more likely he is to vote.

3. *If he is subjected to social pressure to vote.* Upper-middle-class persons are more likely to be expected to vote by peer groups than are members of the working class. A small-town dweller whose daily activities are highly visible is more likely to be subjected to social pressure to vote than an apartment dweller, who is shielded by the relative anonymity of the large city. A few religious groups are opposed on principle to voting.

4. *If he is not subjected to cross-pressures.* If the various factors listed above do not tug the citizen in opposing directions, he is more likely to vote than if they do. If one of his interests (say, his religion, which may be the same as that of a major candidate) conflicts with another (say, his business, which he believes would be most helped by a different candidate), he may not vote at all. Similarly, what he reads in his union newspaper may conflict so forcefully with what he reads in his daily newspaper that he may give up any attempt to understand and so not vote. He may have grown up in a family of Democrats, but he is now surrounded by Republican neighbors. Or he and his wife may not be able to agree, which tends to disrupt the political convictions of both. The conflicts that he feels may be so great that he cannot bring himself to vote for candidates of either major party.

PRINCIPLES OF NOTEHAND

73 **Nd.** The Notehand strokes for *n* and *d* are joined without an angle to represent the sound of *nd,* as in *lined.*

Nd

Compare: **line** **lined**

Spell: **lined,** *l-ī-end;* **land,** *l-a-end*

land	**signed**	**end**
trained	**kind**	**spend**
joined	**mind**	**friend**
band	**bind**	**wonder**

Reading and writing practice

THE LARK AND HER YOUNG ONES

(Concluded in Paragraph 74)

74 **Nt.** The stroke for *nd* also represents the sound of *nt,* as in *rent.*

Spell: **rent,** *r-e-ent;* **paint,** *p-a-ent;* **enter,** *e-ent-r*

rent	center	spent
went	paint	gentle
prevent	want	enter
sent	plenty	interest

Reading and writing practice

THE LARK AND HER YOUNG ONES ***(Concluded)***

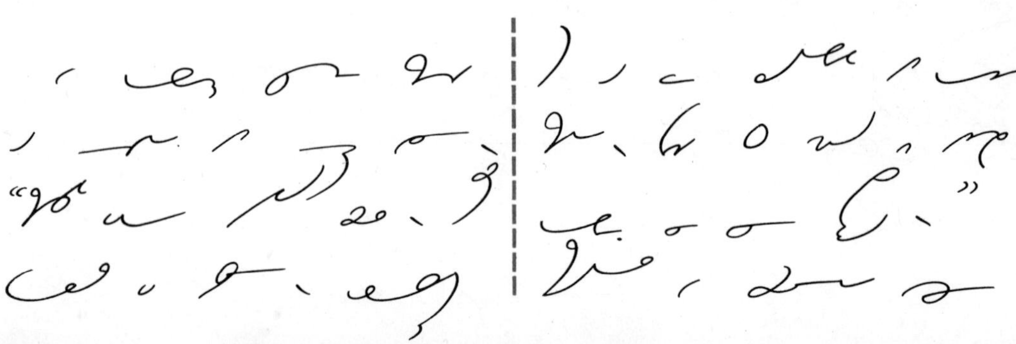

—*Adapted from Aesop's Fables*

Most-used Gregg Notehand forms

Here is another group of ten Notehand forms for common words in the English language. Add them to your card.

be, by **which** **some** **out** **now**

find **sent** **over** **how** **matter**

Unit 25

PRINCIPLES OF NOTEMAKING

Leave wide margins

A good set of notes should have wide margins all around the page, for the following very important reasons:

1 Wide margins make the notes more readable. A page crowded with notes from edge to edge and from top to bottom always appears considerably more difficult to read.

2 Wide margins leave room for corrections and for the insertion of afterthoughts. Otherwise, such additions must be squeezed illegibly into some cranny of an already crowded page.

3 Wide margins permit the notemaker to add key words that make finding and reviewing easier and faster.

Look at the example below and notice how wide margins have permitted the notemaker to add important points to his notes.

Postwar Prosperity — Europe

A. Great Britain

1. GB dependent world before.

2. Competition US, Germany, and Japan, and

USSR

3. European Common expected into GB's

exports

Application

Read the following paragraph and recite the gist of it in your own words. Develop an appropriate heading for notes.

One of the reasons why Shakespeare gave such a fresh interpretation to the English language is that he was not hampered by formal English grammar. Little boys in Elizabethan England did not have to learn formal English. All the rules and ritual and reverence were focused on Latin, with the result that Shakespeare and the other writers of his day leapt into English lighthearted and free. There was no English dictionary to hamper them. They could pick up words where they found them, put them into any combinations, or make up new ones.

PRINCIPLES OF NOTEHAND

75 **Md, Mt.** The Notehand strokes for *m* and *d* are joined without an angle to represent the sound of *md,* as in *framed.* The same stroke also represents the sound of *mt,* as in *prompt.*

Md, Mt

Compare: **clean** **cleaned**

claim **claimed**

Notice that the *md, mt* stroke is considerably longer than the *nd* stroke – at least twice as long.

Md

Spell: **framed,** *f-r-a-emd*

framed **ashamed** **blamed**

seemed **climbed** **named**

trimmed **claimed** **famed**

Mt

Spell: **prompt,** *p-r-o-emt*

prompt **promptly** **empty**

prompted **promptness** **emptied**

Reading and writing practice

STUDY

PRINCIPLES OF NOTEHAND

RECALL

In Unit 26 there are no new Notehand devices for you to learn; you will have a little time to digest the material you studied thus far.

76 Recall chart. Can you read the 84 words and phrases in this chart in 7 minutes or less? After you have read the chart from left to right, read down each column. If you can also read the entire chart in this way in 7 minutes, you are to be congratulated; you are making fine progress!

Words

1						
2						
3						
4						
5						
6						
7						
8						
9						

Brief-form derivatives and phrases

10						
11						

12						
13						
14						

77

Reading and writing practice

FARMING

cold

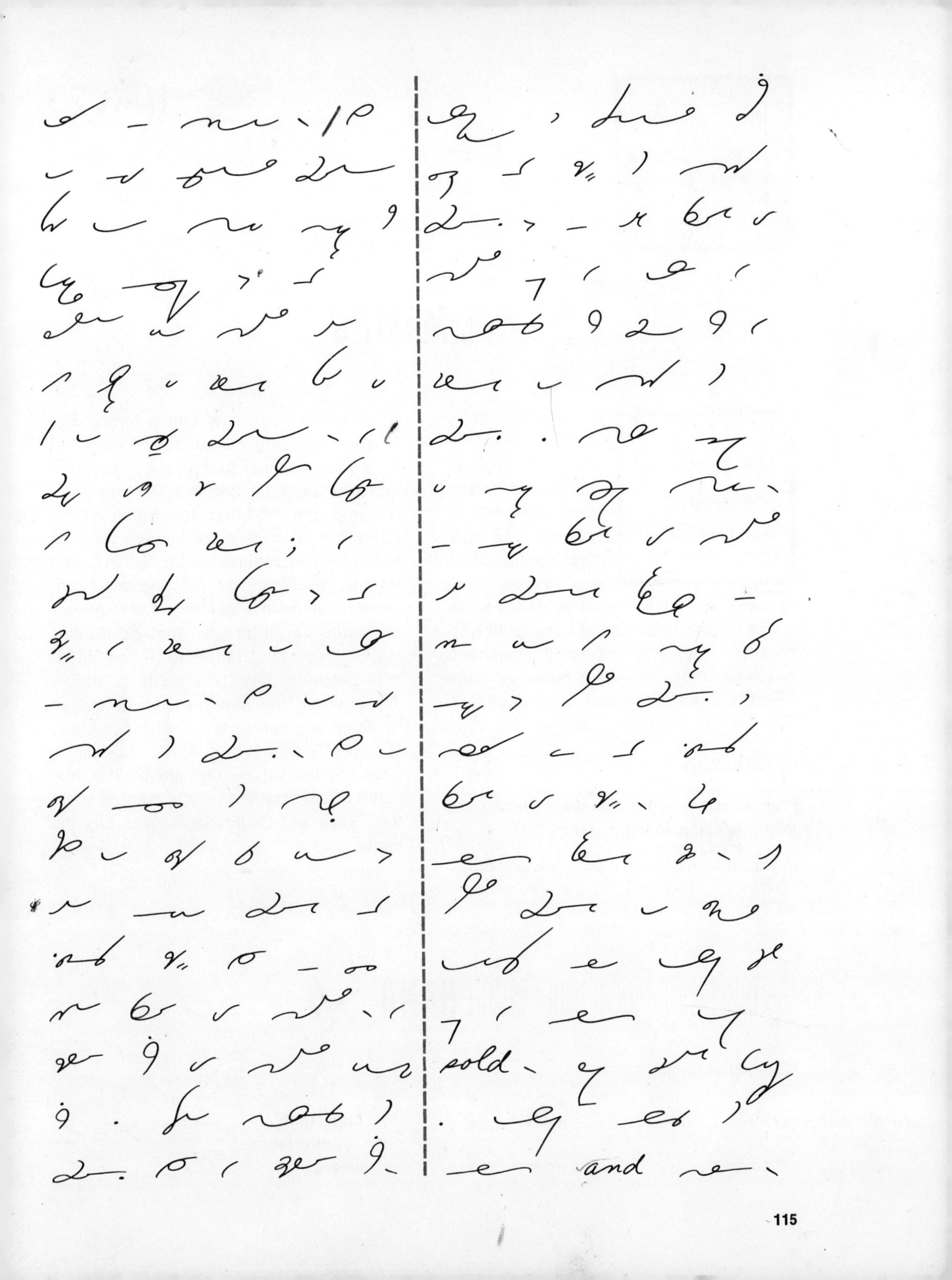

sold

and

Unit 27

PRINCIPLES OF NOTEMAKING

Use longhand headings in your notes

In all notes, it is best to write the major headings in longhand to make them stand out so that you can spot them readily when you review your notes. The longhand headings in your notes are as helpful as the use of large, bold type on a printed page. Notice how the longhand headings stand out in the notes on page 117. The key to the notes is on page 322.

Application

Prepare notes on the following, writing the major headings in longhand.

In classical economic theory, several types of utility are recognized. One is form utility, in which something is added in a chemical or physical manner to a product to make it more valuable. Lumber is made into furniture and flour into bread, thus creating form utility. Other utilities are equally valuable to the final user. Furniture located in Grand Rapids, Michigan, or High Point, North Carolina, in April is of little value to people in Austin, Texas, or Los Angeles, California, who want the furniture to give as Christmas presents; thus time utility is added. Transporting the furniture from Michigan to Texas increases its value; place utility is added. Storing it from April to December adds another value—time utility. The final value of possession utility is created when the Texas and California families buy the items.

PRINCIPLES OF NOTEHAND

78 Brief forms

and		**short**		**important, importance**	
suggest		**work**		**where**	

Woodrow Wilson

Education

1. Early edu. [illegible]
2. Entered Princeton U. [illegible] 1875.
3. [illegible] debater [illegible] scholar.
4. [illegible] prof. and [illegible] pres. [illegible]

Politics

1. Dems. elected W Gov. [illegible] N.J. [illegible] 1910.
2. Dems. elected W Pres. [illegible] 1912. [illegible] election [illegible] possible [illegible] Rep. [illegible]

Domestic Policy

1. Dem. [illegible] called [illegible] W [illegible] and Cong. [illegible] Underwood [illegible]
2. W [illegible] and Cong. [illegible] Reserve [illegible]

Foreign Policy

1. W [illegible] neutrality [illegible] War [illegible] 1914.
2. W's [illegible] elected [illegible] second [illegible] 1916 [illegible]

79 Brief-form derivatives

suggestion		shortly		worked	
suggested		shorter		working	

Reading and writing practice

THE MEASURE OF A MAN

—W. C. Brann

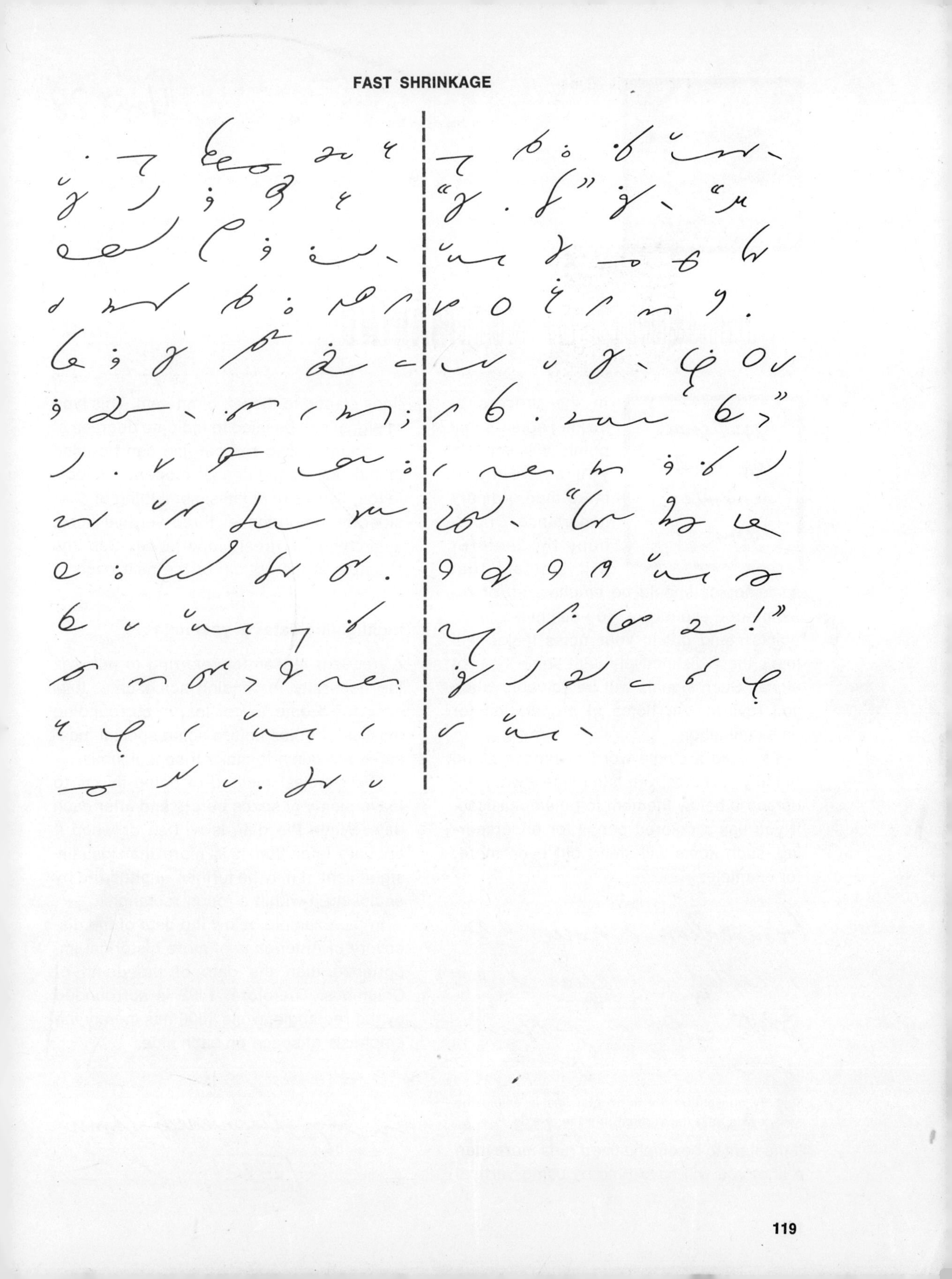

FAST SHRINKAGE

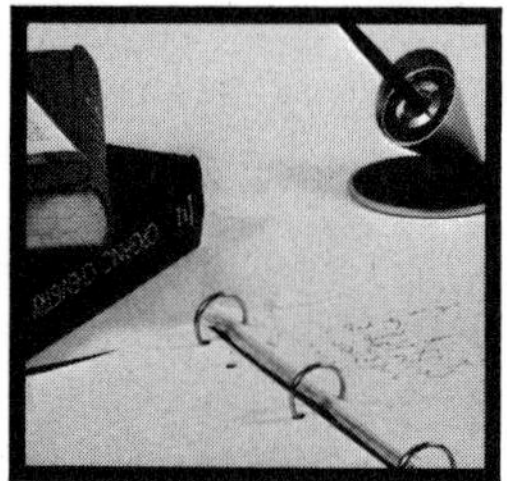

Unit 28

PRINCIPLES OF NOTEMAKING

Use signals for "must remember" items

In the process of making notes, some points will impress you as being of more than ordinary importance. Or perhaps the lecturer will indicate that some topics should be emphasized or remembered especially. You can make these points stand out in your notes if you will mark them distinctively with some type of signal. Such signals will be valuable when you review your notes in preparation for an examination.

To make a single word or phrase stand out in your notes, you can place a wavy underscore below the item to be emphasized. If you use a colored pencil for underscoring, such items will stand out even more; for example:

(convention (horiz. (called (x-axis / (vert. (y-axis.

Key: By convention the horizontal line is called the x-axis and the vertical line the y-axis.

If the item to be emphasized runs more than a line, you will save time by using vertical lines placed to the left of an item. This type of signal can be used to indicate degrees of importance. One vertical line can be used to indicate something of moderate importance; two vertical lines, something of considerable importance; three vertical lines, something of great importance. See the example at the bottom of the next page.

Highlighting dates in your notes

A frequent reason for referring to notes is the necessity for finding some date. It is easy for a date to get lost in surrounding masses of notes unless some special measures are taken to make it conspicuous.

The simplest method of doing this is to leave plenty of space before and after each date. When the date is written or when it appears later that it is more than usually significant, it may be further emphasized by enclosing it within a rough rectangle.

In the example below the date of the discovery of America is of more historical importance than the date of the death of Columbus. Therefore, 1492 is surrounded by the rectangle, while 1506 has merely the emphasis of space on each side.

discovered Amer. 1492

1506

possible

discovered. new cont.

Key: Columbus discovered America in 1492 and did not die until 1506, but it is possible that he died without realizing that he had discovered a new continent.

Application

Select a heading for the following paragraph and make notes on the material. Apply the suggestions offered in this unit.

There are several examples of contract medical service that have worked well. Among these are the following: (1) Baylor University Hospital was the first to start a medical contract plan (1929), offering it to teachers at the rate of $3 a month. This plan later became the Blue Cross, the best known of all plans. (2) The Health Insurance Plan of New York City, organized in 1946. One year later it had 15,000 members. Here each member pays a few cents a week and his employer pays an additional few cents. (3) Group Health Association, which was organized by employees of the Home Owners' Loan Corporation in Washington. The unique feature of this plan is that it operates on a prepaid basis. (4) Particularly outstanding is the Permanente Health Plan, which grew up in the Kaiser shipyards at Tacoma, Washington, and at Oakland, Richmond, and Fontana, California. The Permanente Health Plan remains very popular today.

A. Population US
WW 2 because

1. Many opportunities offered
industrial society
2. Prosperity depression
3. birth

B. US Canada

PRINCIPLES OF NOTEHAND

80 Brief forms as word beginnings. It is often possible to use the brief forms *in, be,* and *for* as prefixes in longer words.

In

Spell: income, *in-k-m*

income inside invite

Be

Spell: beneath, *b-n-e-ith*

beneath believe belong

For

Spell: forget, *for-gay-e-t*

forget form force

Reading and writing practice

SURPRISE

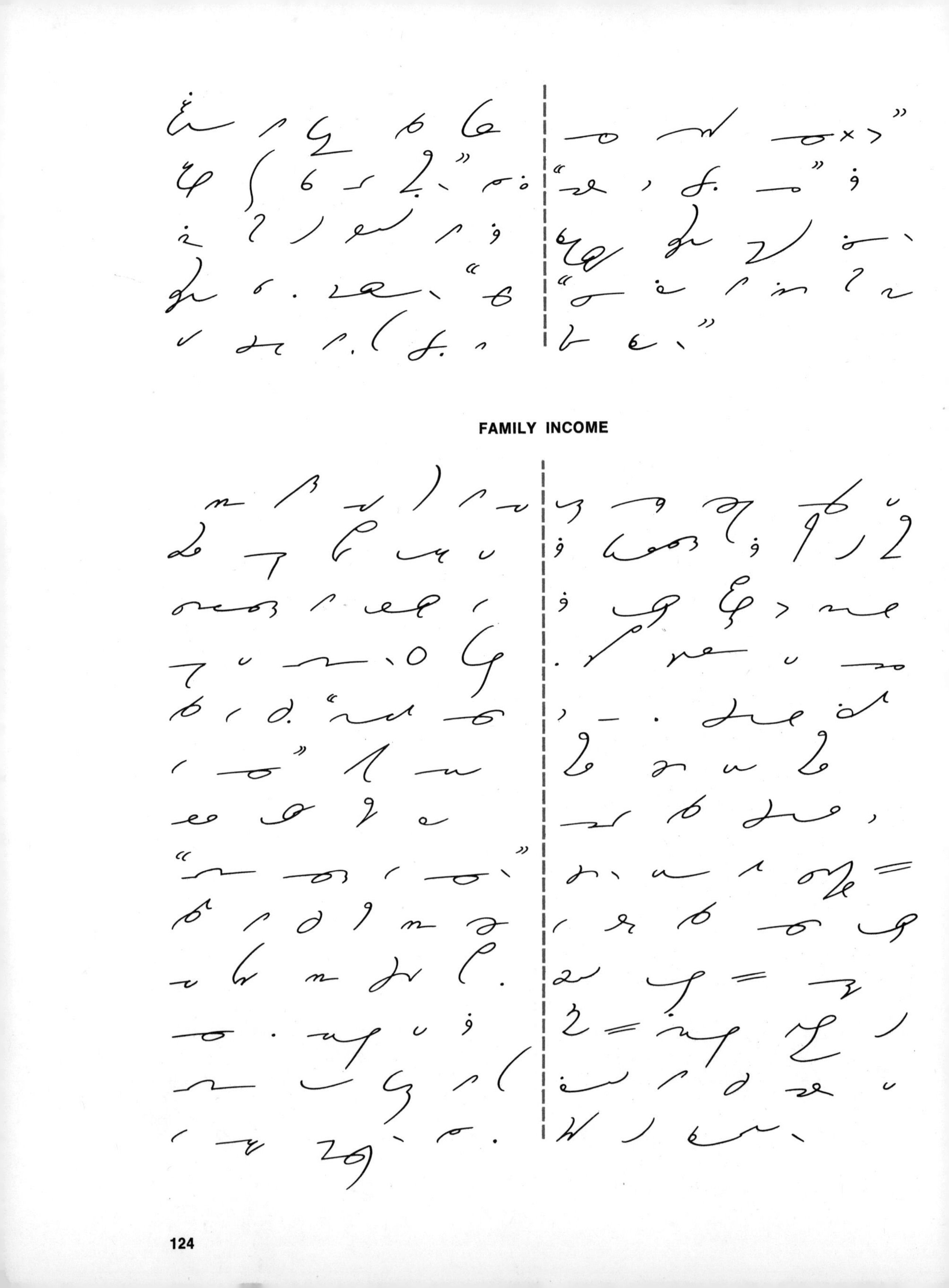

FAMILY INCOME

Most-used Gregg Notehand forms

By this time you have probably completely mastered many of the most-used Gregg Notehand forms that you wrote on your special card in the early part of your study of Gregg Notehand. Perhaps some of the more recent words added to the card may not yet be thoroughly familiar. Read through the forty Gregg Notehand forms you now have on the card as rapidly as you can. Put a circle around any forms on which you had to hesitate ever so slightly. Then transfer those words to a new card. Thus, instead of the forty words, you will now have fifteen or twenty that you need to keep for constant reference as you make notes in Gregg Notehand. Then add the ten new words given below. You could already have written any of these new Gregg Notehand forms, but they are given here for special practice and attention.

work **has** **and** **also** **advice**

when **what** **them** **us** **were**

Proportion drills

Remember to (1) read the entire list of words to be sure you know their meaning, (2) make one copy of each line, striving for accuracy of outline, (3) make a copy of the entire list.

In practicing these words, make your curves deep. Watch the size of your circles—the *a's* should be large, your *e's* very small.

Circles and curves

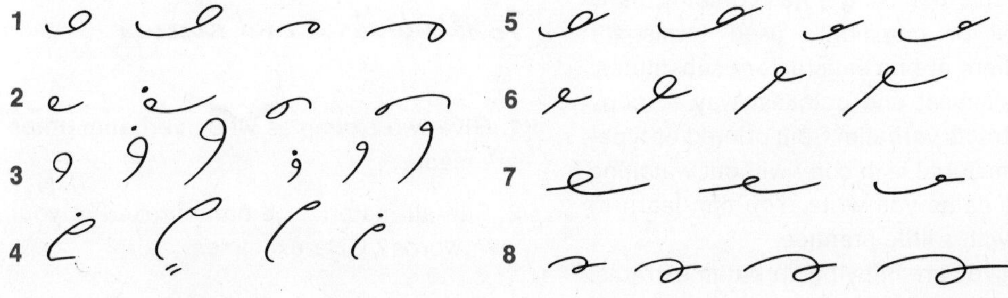

KEY

1 Ray, lay, key, gay. **2** Ear, hill, ache, egg. **3** As, half, I have, he is, if, eve. **4** Happen, Abe, ebb, hip. **5** Rate, late, writ, let. **6** Tear, tar, dear, deal. **7** Nail, mill, lean. **8** Keen, can, gain, game.

Unit 29

PRINCIPLES OF NOTEMAKING

Making verbatim notes

Sometimes you need to make notes of what you hear or read exactly as it is said or written. Examples of such occasions are (1) when you wish to make a direct quotation from what you hear or read; (2) when you wish to memorize a statement, such as a famous quotation, a poem, or a rule of law; and (3) when the material on which you are making notes contains many technical or commonly used terms for which there are no satisfactory substitutes.

The simplest and quickest way to copy long extracts verbatim from printed or typewritten material is to copy without watching your hands as you write. You can learn to do this with a little practice.

When you are copying verbatim extracts, write on every other line, glancing occasionally at the writing to be sure that your copy isn't overlapping.

Copying without watching is of no special advantage if you must write everything in longhand, because most English words require so much writing time that you have plenty of time to glance back and forth from the textbook to the notebook. The Notehand writer, however, can use the copy-without-watching rule to very good advantage. The Notehand outlines for most words, particularly for the frequently used words of the language, are so short that constant glancing back and forth slows down the speed of copying considerably. Because the Notehand outlines are so short, they need less watching than the more cumbersome longhand words.

To think about and discuss

1 Give two examples when verbatim notes are made.

2 Can all material be paraphrased in your own words? Give examples.

Application

Read the notes that appear on page 127. (You will find the key on page **323**.) Notice the application of many of the notemaking techniques you have been studying.

Personality Development

1. Dependence. com- pletely dependent weaned

2. Comfort Eating. child's comfort

3. Show-Off child attention " ", uses

4. Low Boiling Point. into

5. Gang Toward

PRINCIPLES OF NOTEHAND

81 **Ted.** The combination *ted,* as in *heated,* is formed by joining *t* and *d* together as one long stroke.

Ted

Compare: **heat** **heed** **heated**

Notice that the stroke for *ted* is about twice as long as the stroke for *d.*

Spell: **acted,** *a-k-ted;* **instead,** *in-s-ted*

acted	**visited**	**located**
waited	**quoted**	**instead**
adjusted	**noted**	**steady**

Reading and writing practice

LOYALTY

(Continued in Paragraph 82)

82 Ded. The same stroke that represents *ted* also represents the sound of *ded,* as in *needed.*

Compare: **need** **needed**

Spell: **added,** *a-ded;* **deduct,** *ded-oo-k-t*

added	**graded**	**persuaded**
provided	**headed**	**deduct**
traded	**guided**	**deduction**

Reading and writing practice

LOYALTY ***(Continued)***

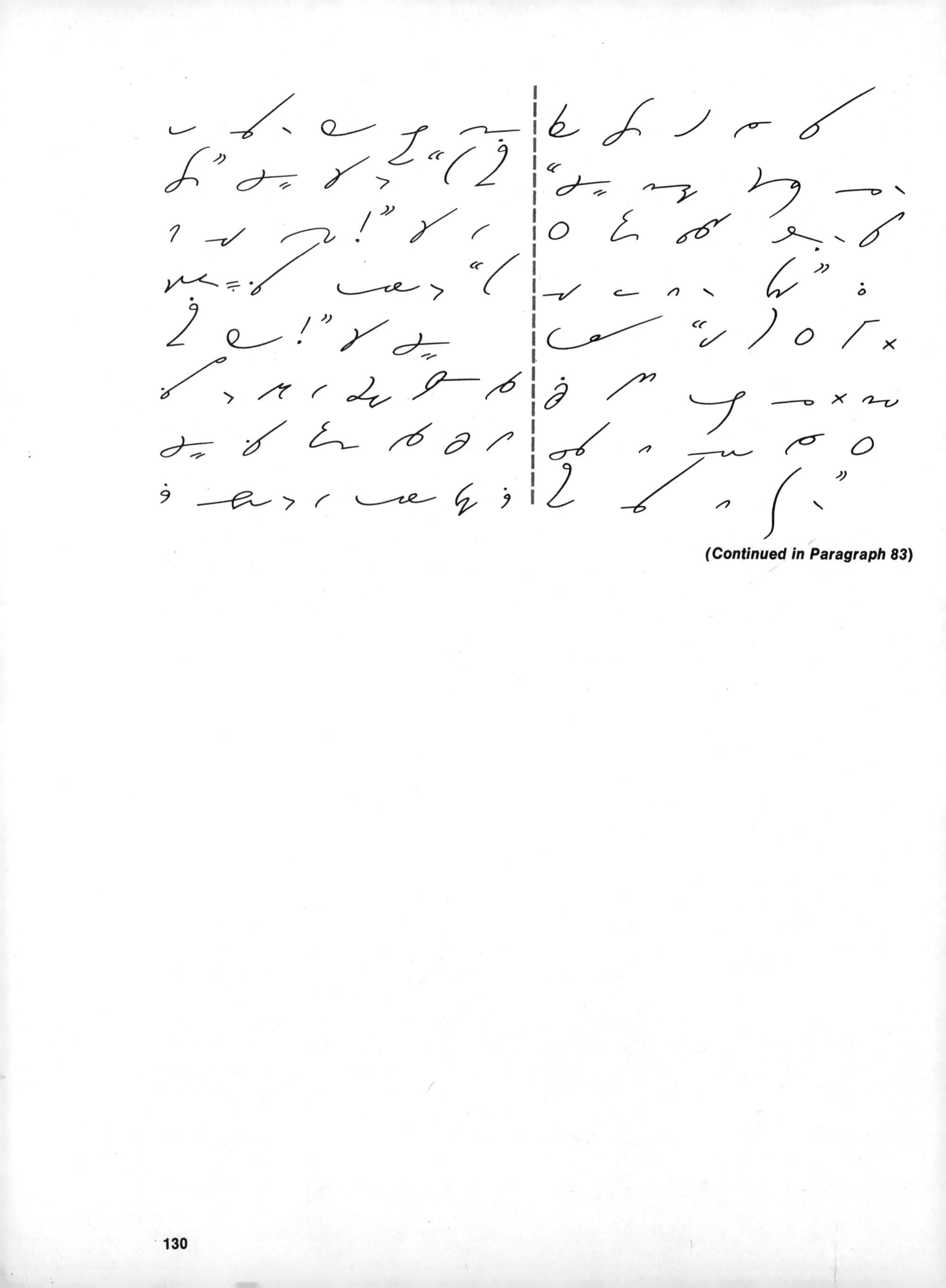

(Continued in Paragraph 83)

Unit 30

PRINCIPLES OF NOTEMAKING

The notemaker is an active listener

Do you take your listening ability for granted? Most people do. Few rank listening as equal in importance with reading, writing, and speaking. Yet most of us spend more time listening than in any of the other three communication arts. In fact, of the total time spent communicating, about 45 percent is spent in listening!

The ability to listen effectively and the ability to hear well are not the same thing. You may hear every word your Aunt Gracie said in that long telephone conversation, and yet you may not have actually *listened* to much of it. You may sit in the front row in a World Literature class, with your ears wide open and your eyes glued to the instructor, and still not be able to give even a hazy account of what he said.

Casual listening and active listening

Basically, there are two kinds of listening: casual listening and active listening. Casual listening usually results in absorbing just enough of the speaker's remarks to keep a conversation going. In a conversation with a friend, a chat on the telephone, or a group discussion at the bridge table, you can get by with casual listening. It doesn't usually matter whether what you hear really "soaks in." Because we do so much of this kind of listening, we are inclined to forget that there is any other kind!

Active listening, on the other hand, means concentrating on what you are hearing, trying to absorb and fix in your mind as much as you possibly can. It calls for actively participating mentally in what you hear and thinking about the speaker's remarks as he makes them. Active listening is vitally important in many situations — for example, when a doctor listens to a patient describe an ailment, when a lawyer hears his client's account of an accident in which he was involved, when an employee receives instructions from his supervisor on how to do a job.

Active listening vital for the student

Much of the student's exposure to learning is through listening — to lectures, explanations and remarks of the instructor, and comments and discussions among the students. The typical college student attends some two thousand lectures during his four-year college career! For such an investment of time, the student should be interested in improving his listening habits.

Classroom lectures call for the most difficult kind of listening. After all, the student goes to class for the purpose of learning. He cannot afford the ease of casual listening, but must strive to comprehend fully what he is listening to so that he can remember the essential ideas and information. Further, what he hears through lectures, explanations, and remarks of the instructor is perishable. If the student doesn't listen with understanding at the time of the lecture or discussion, the information is lost. What we read can usually be reread; what we hear can rarely be reheard.

Good notemaking and active listening go together

Studies of listening show that we forget about 50 percent of what we hear immediately after we hear it. And after about two months, we have forgotten another 25 percent. This factor of forgetting makes it imperative that the student make good notes while he is listening, because only through good notes can he retain in permanent form the important ideas he hears. Good listening and good notemaking, therefore, go hand in hand. In fact, the process of making notes during a lecture encourages active participation in listening. At the same time, active listening is essential to good notemaking.

To think about and discuss

1 The average speaker talks at a rate of about 150 words a minute. The average listener, on the other hand, can comprehend speech at a rate of more than 300 words a minute. What might be the danger to the listener in the difference between these two rates?

2 What is the difference between casual and active listening?

3 "Lectures are perishable." Explain.

4 When do we forget most of what we are going to forget?

PRINCIPLES OF NOTEHAND

83 Men. The combination *men,* as in *mend,* is written by joining *m* and *n* together in one long stroke, which is about twice as long as the stroke for *m.*

Men

Compare: **in** **am** **men**

Spell: **meant,** *men-t;* **women,** *oo-e-men*

men	mend	mention
meant	mended	immense
mental	many	women

Reading and writing practice

LOYALTY *(Continued)*

(Concluded in Paragraph 84)

84 Min. The stroke that represents *men* also represents *min,* as in *minute.*

Compare: **meet** **minute**

Notice that the stroke for *min* is at least twice as long as the stroke for *m.*

Spell: **minute,** *min-e-t*

minute	nominate	eliminate
mint	minister	minimum

Reading and writing practice

LOYALTY ***(Concluded)***

—Adapted from Elbert Hubbard's Notebook

WFIL
CBS

Unit 31

PRINCIPLES OF NOTEMAKING

Getting the most out of your listening

Effective listening habits can be acquired. But, like any other art, active listening must be worked at if it is to be mastered. There is no magic formula for learning how to listen effectively. It is something you must do for yourself. First, realize the importance of good listening; then, want to listen effectively; and finally, practice listening effectively until it becomes an established habit.

For the student, participating actively in listening has six fundamental requirements:

1 A desire to listen

2 An open mind

3 Concentration

4 Alertness in grasping essential ideas

5 Alertness in listening for related ideas

6 Notemaking

A desire to listen

Listening is a strictly voluntary activity, and the incentive has to come from you. Listening is important to your own goals. Since the basic purpose of a lecture or class discussion is learning, then you should "listen to learn."

An open mind

Bring an open mind to the listening situation. We often assess people and ideas in an introspective, personal manner, basing our assessments on our pet likes and dislikes. For example, the speaker's appearance, his pronunciation, his voice, his mannerisms—perhaps even an occasional error in grammar—may annoy the listener so much that he cannot concentrate on what is being said. Or perhaps the listener has a special prejudice or strong feeling concerning the subject. These prejudices close the listener's mind and limit his ability to listen.

To be an effective listener, try to overlook personal irritants and concentrate on what is "coming out" rather than on the person or on your prejudices.

Concentration

Do not allow the annoyances just mentioned to interfere with your receptivity to what is said. You are in a position to "tune in" or "tune out" the speaker as you wish. Your willingness to pay attention to what is being said is your "tuning device." And you may be tempted to "tune out" because many speakers speak much more slowly than you, as a listener, can comprehend. In fact, the typical listener can comprehend at a rate approximately four times faster than some speakers talk. The listener should use this "spare" time for concentration—not for woolgathering.

The typical listener frequently indulges in daydreaming or detouring into unrelated thoughts. Once the listener is tuned out, he may get hopelessly lost when he tries to reenter the discussion because he will have lost a part, perhaps a significant part, of what has been said. Concentration is practically a full-time job for the active listener—not something to "put on and take off" as the fancy pleases him. Concentration requires self-discipline and means paying attention and sustaining it throughout the lecture or discussion.

Alertness in grasping essential ideas

Be on the alert to grasp the speaker's essential ideas. Try to think along with the speaker. You may even anticipate what he is going to say next—or at least the direction of his remarks. When an essential idea, fact, or piece of information is conveyed to you, rephrase it mentally in your own words. This process of rephrasing mentally to yourself what you hear will help you understand and remember what you hear. Note the example below.

The Speaker Is Saying:	You Might Be Thinking:
Many of the Mediterranean cities were already thriving veterans of trade. They had been toughened and enriched by the Crusades. In Italy, besides Venice, there were Genoa, Lucca, Pisa, Florence, Milan, and a good many others. In Southern France there were Narbonne, Montpellier, and Marseilles, and in Spain there was Barcelona. Through most of the thirteenth and fourteenth centuries, however, Venice was the undisputed mistress of Mediterranean trade. In the 1300s she won a feud with her strongest rival, Genoa, for leadership.	**Several Mediterranean cities were old hands at trade. Crusades helped to build them. A number of cities were in Italy, France, and Spain. Venice, though, was undisputed leader through most of the thirteenth and fourteenth centuries. Surpassed her old enemy, Genoa, in 1300s.**

Alertness in grasping related ideas

Listen for related ideas and information, such as illustrations, anecdotes, and "asides" that elaborate, provide insight, and give support to the main ideas and information. For example, in the lecture on Venice just illustrated, the speaker may continue:

> **Incidentally, this rivalry between Venice and Genoa had some interesting sidelights. Captains of Venetian ships were instructed to get there and back before the Genoese ships at all costs, regardless of who else was involved, and many unscheduled races were staged in the Mediterranean. To keep ahead of her rival, Venice even had an ambassador to England to smooth the way for her merchants there. The city fathers gave specific instructions, too, to the ambassador about putting up a good front. He was instructed to wear a fine scarlet gown and he was required to maintain four servants, two pages, a cook, and a secretary. . . .**

You can see that these sidelights add both color and interest, even though they are not worth recording in your notes. If you are listening actively, however, your impressions of Venice as a leader in Mediterranean trade are much more vivid.

Notemaking

Make notes as you listen. Since what we hear is perishable, the main ideas (along with related and supporting ideas) must be captured and retained for reference, for reviewing, and for preparing for examinations. Making notes is no more than an extension of active participation in listening. It simply consists of putting on paper, in your own words, the essential ideas and information. And the very process of making notes contributes to concentration, learning, and remembering.

Gregg Notehand gives the listener more time to think about what is being said and gives him time to record more complete notes than he would be able to make by longhand. "More complete notes" does not mean verbatim notes. Even though Gregg Notehand gives the listener an efficient writing tool, he should not attempt to record lecture notes verbatim. Verbatim notes are seldom the most useful notes.

To think about and discuss

1 What are the six fundamental requirements of active listening?

2 Why is it important to rephrase mentally what you hear?

3 Why do you think verbatim notes are less useful than carefully selected notes?

Application

Assume that the following is a part of a lecture that you are hearing.

1 Condense it in your own words.

2 Find the essential idea and the related ideas.

3 Prepare a set of notes in outline form.

Every state is legally separated from every other state, and each has jurisdiction only within its own boundaries. Massachusetts cannot project her laws into Connecticut; an Illinois state judge cannot hold court in Indiana. Every state, however, must constantly have dealings with other states, and the populations of all the fifty are perpetually commingling in pursuit of the various trades and professions. It therefore becomes a practical necessity that the states accept in common certain obligations toward one another. Four specific obligations were, indeed, imposed by the national Constitution as originally adopted. One of them—the duty to deliver up fugitive slaves escaping from one state into another—became obsolete when the Thirteenth Amendment abolished slavery in 1865. The other three continue in effect and pertain to (1) recognition of legal processes and acts, (2) interstate citizenship, and (3) rendition of persons accused of crime.

PRINCIPLES OF NOTEHAND

85 Brief-form review. The following chart contains the 36 brief forms you have studied thus far. Can you read the entire chart in half a minute or less? Can you then make a copy of the brief forms in your notebook in one minute or less?

86 **Brief forms.** This is the last set of brief forms that you will have to learn.

question	send	difficult
yesterday	probable	into

87 **Phrases**

to question	send them	into this
send the	into the	into that

Reading and writing practice

TEN SIGNS OF A MATURE MAN

(Concluded in Paragraph 88)

88 **Ses.** The sound of *ses,* as in *senses,* is represented by joining the two forms of *s.*

Compare: **sense**   **senses**

face   **faces**

Spell: **addresses,** *a-d-r-e-ses*

addresses   **chances**   **closes**

leases   **cases**   **necessary**

This stroke also represents the similar sounds heard in *sis,* as in *sister;* and in *sus,* as in *versus.*

Spell: **sister,** *ses-t-r;* **versus,** *v-e-r-ses*

sister   **basis**   **census**

system   **analysis**   **versus**

Reading and writing practice

TEN SIGNS OF A MATURE MAN *(Concluded)*

Unit 32

PRINCIPLES OF NOTEMAKING

Writing names in your notes

When an expression or name recurs frequently in your notemaking, devise a special abbreviation for it, using longhand initials. For example:

L = Lincoln
Mc = McClellan
dg = de Gaulle
Py = Pythagoras
VN = Viet Nam
WW 2 = World War 2

So that there will not be any question in your mind as to the meaning of an abbreviation when you review your notes later, put a key at the top of your notes like this:

dg = de Gaulle

The examples above are merely suggestions. You will want to devise your own abbreviating methods. Just be sure you are consistent with whatever abbreviating device you choose.

Of course, if it is easier to write the name or expression in Notehand and you are sure it will stand out in your notes, by all means use Notehand either in full or abbreviated. For example:

= Lee
= Grant
= Poe
= Populist
= Brahms
= Faulkner
jq = John Quincy Adams
= Michelangelo

Don't try to remember such abbreviations from month to month. Use them the day you devise them or as long as that subject continues to be part of your work. Somewhere at the beginning or end of the notes make a record of them. Then forget about them. Perhaps the next day – perhaps even the same day – you may use the same abbreviation to represent a totally different expression. In the morning you may make notes on the rise of the Dutch Republic and use the small joined longhand initials *da* to represent the Duke of Alva. In the afternoon you may be making notes for a talk on law enforcement in your community, and *da* will represent *district attorney.*

Application

Devise your own methods of writing the expressions in the next column. In some cases you will probably want to write the name in Notehand or a Notehand abbreviation.

1 George Bernard Shaw
2 Napoleon
3 Middle Ages
4 Emancipation Proclamation
5 Queen Victoria
6 centrifugal force
7 Huckleberry Finn
8 Keats
9 law of diminishing returns
10 binomial

PRINCIPLES OF NOTEHAND

89 Ten. The combination *ten,* as in *written,* is represented by an upward curve about three times as large as the curve for the over *th.*

Ten

Compare: Th **Ten**

Spell: written, *r-e-ten;* **stand,** *s-ten-d;* **bulletin,** *b-oo-l-e-ten*

written **intend** **tonight**
threaten **tender** **stand**
attend **gotten** **bulletin**

This blend also represents *tain.*

Spell: captain, *k-a-p-ten*

captain **maintain** **retain**
certain **obtain** **attain**

Reading and writing practice

STRICTLY THE TRUTH

90 **Den.** This stroke also represents the sound of *den,* as in *sudden.*

Spell: **sudden,** *s-oo-den;* **dinner,** *den-r;* **guidance,** *gay-ī-den-s*

sudden	**deny**	**evident**
hidden	**dentist**	**guidance**
broaden	**dinner**	**incident**

Reading and writing practice

TIME TO FORGET

91 Word ending -ment. The word ending *-ment,* as in *agreement,* occurs in a great many English words. The ending is expressed by the Notehand *m.*

Spell: agreement, *a-gay-r-e-ment;* **elementary,** *e-l-e-ment-r-e*

agreement		**payment**		**moment**	
arrangement		**judgment**		**elementary**	
measurement		**appointment**		**fundamental**	

Reading and writing practice

BIG BUSINESS AND SMALL BUSINESS

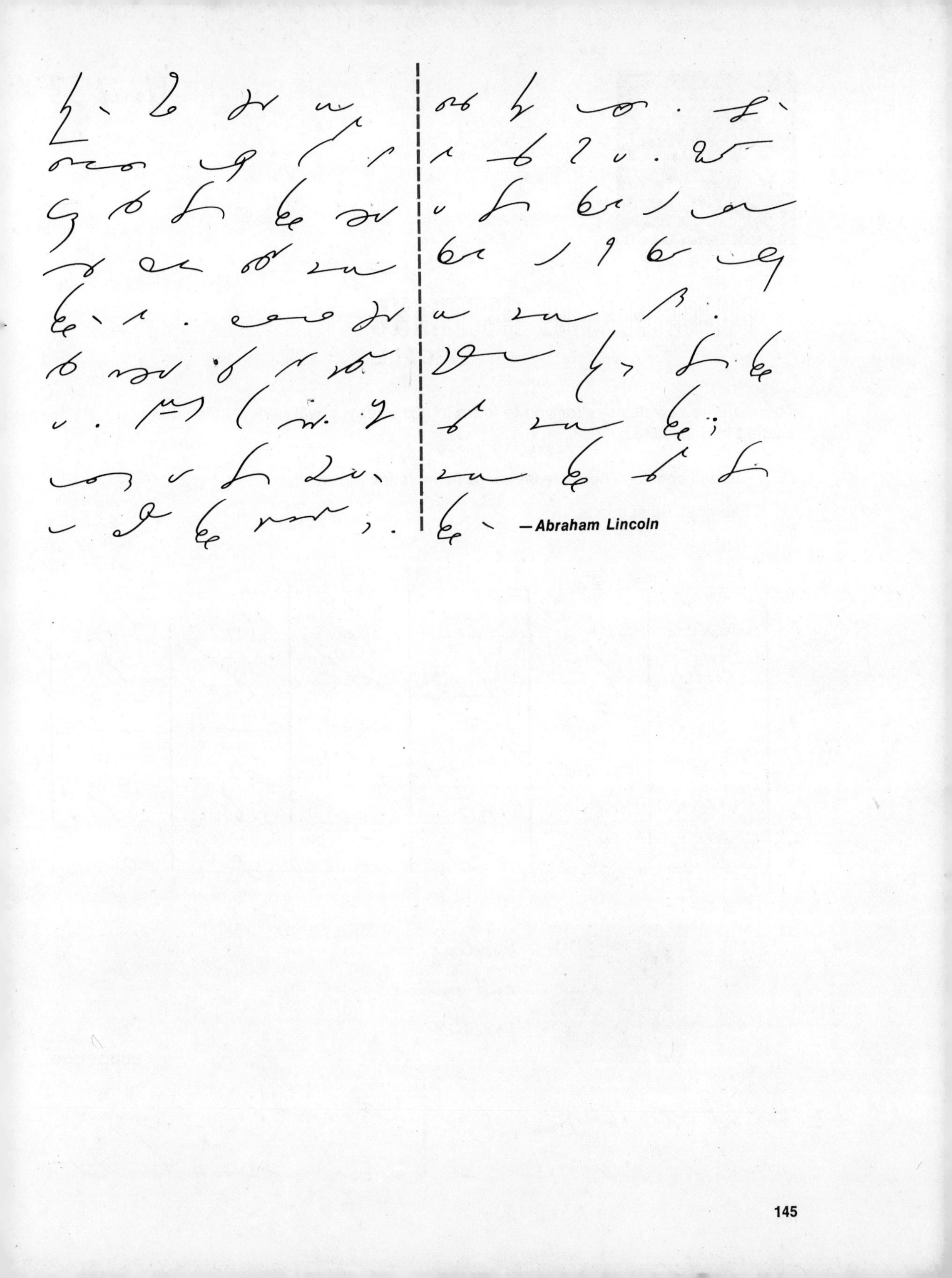

—Abraham Lincoln

Unit 33

PRINCIPLES OF NOTEHAND

RECALL

There are no new devices for you to learn in this unit; you will review those that you studied in Units 28-32.

92 **Recall chart.** There are 36 words in the following chart.

Time goal: 30 seconds.

Words

1

2

3

4

5

6

93 *Reading and writing practice*

BUDGETING

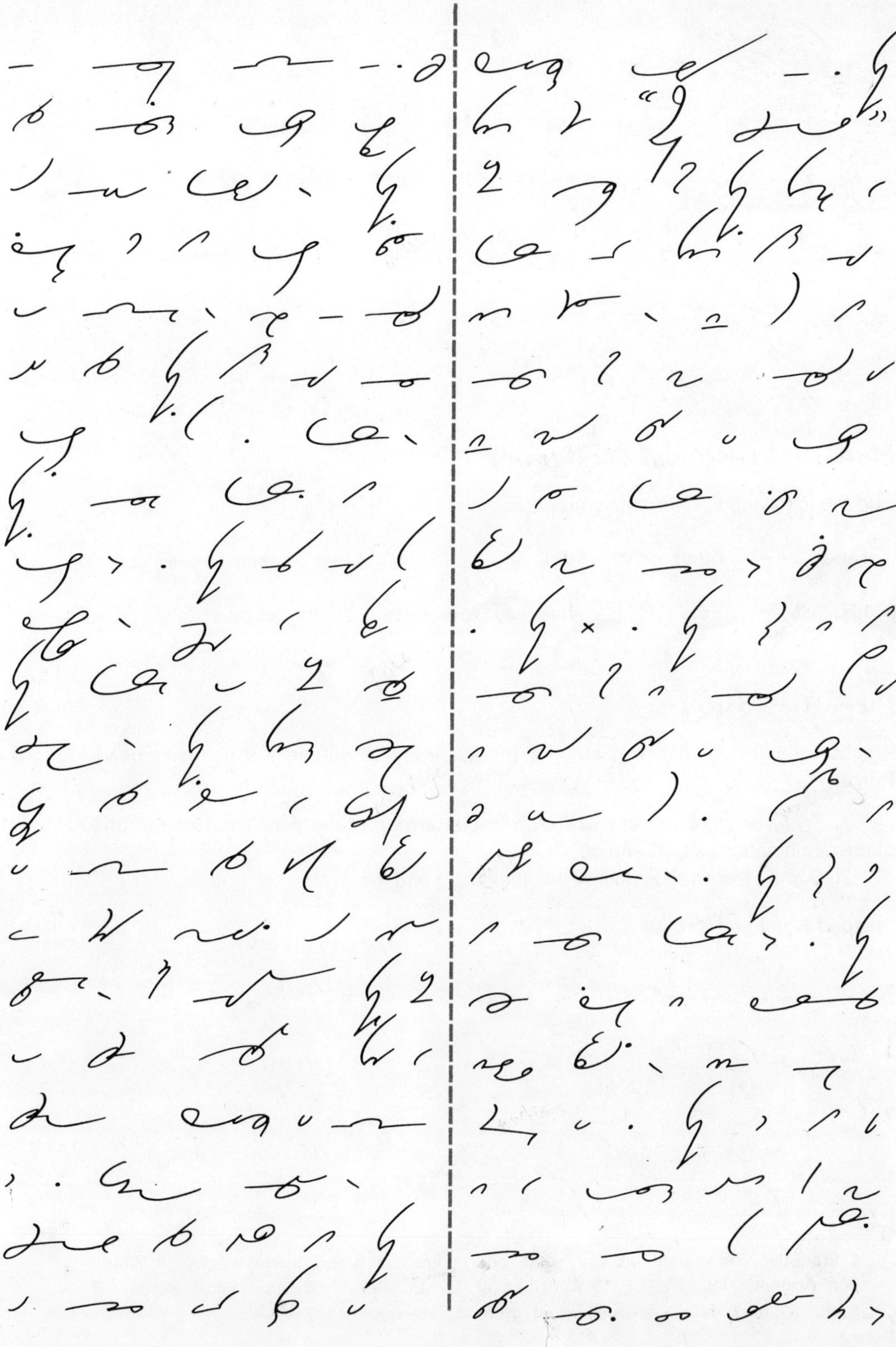

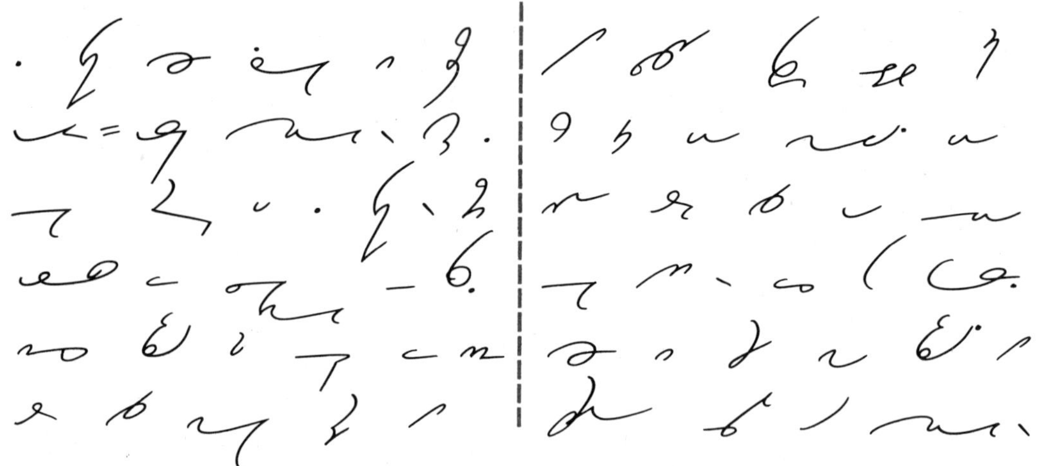

Most-used Gregg Notehand forms

Add the following ten words to your card:

same other did him take

his time had date copy

Proportion drills

Practice the following drills, striving for accuracy of outline rather than speed. Notice:

1. *Fr, fl; pr, pl; br, bl* are written with one sweep of the pen. The same is true of the combinations *kr, rk,* and *gl.*
2. *G* and *r* join with a "bump" between the *g* and the *r.*

Blended Notehand strokes

KEY

1 Free, flee, fret, freight. **2** Pray, play, prim, plane. **3** Breed, blade, blame. **4** Wrapper, neighbor, labor, label. **5** Acre, maker, baker, sticker. **6** Glow, glide, gleam. **7** Park, lark, bark, dark. **8** Green, great, greet.

Unit 34

PRINCIPLES OF NOTEMAKING

Following are practical suggestions to help you achieve active participation in listening and making good notes.

Prepare in advance

The more you know about the subject that is being discussed, the more fruitful your listening efforts will be. If possible, therefore, read in advance about the topic or subject on which you are to hear someone speak.

Choose a good location

Make sure you are seated where you can hear the speaker without strain. If the speaker uses the chalkboard or other visual aids to outline important points or to illustrate complicated explanations, try to sit where you have a clear view of the visual device.

Come equipped

Come equipped with proper and adequate supplies for making notes—plenty of note paper, a good pen, and an extra pencil or two.

Use a good writing surface

Don't try to make notes on top of a pile of books or with your lap full of books. Give yourself as much uncluttered writing surface as you can manage.

Label your notes

Identify your notes—the name of the course ("History 202" or "Hist of Western Civ"), date, and, if there is a guest speaker or if instructors alternate, the name of the lecturer.

Application

Prepare a set of notes from the following, using as much Notehand as you can.

An important part of planning window displays is determining the frequency of window changes. Change keeps customers interested and increases the opportunity to give them a picture of the various kinds of merchandise the store carries. The frequency with which windows should be changed depends on the location of the store, its character, and the kind of merchandise carried. In the small community or in the business section of a large city where the same people pass by repeatedly, display windows should be changed every week. A display of fashion goods should remain for a shorter period of time than a display of staples. Displays should also be changed frequently to prevent merchandise from soiling or fading.

PRINCIPLES OF NOTEHAND

94 **Rd.** The combination *rd,* as in *heard,* is represented by giving the *r* an upward turn at the end.

Compare: **hear** [shorthand] **heard** [shorthand]

Spell: **hired,** *h-ī-ard;* **garden,** *gay-a-ard-n*

hired	 [shorthand]	hard	 [shorthand]	card	 [shorthand]
tired	 [shorthand]	word	 [shorthand]	garden	 [shorthand]

Reading and writing practice

HARD WORK

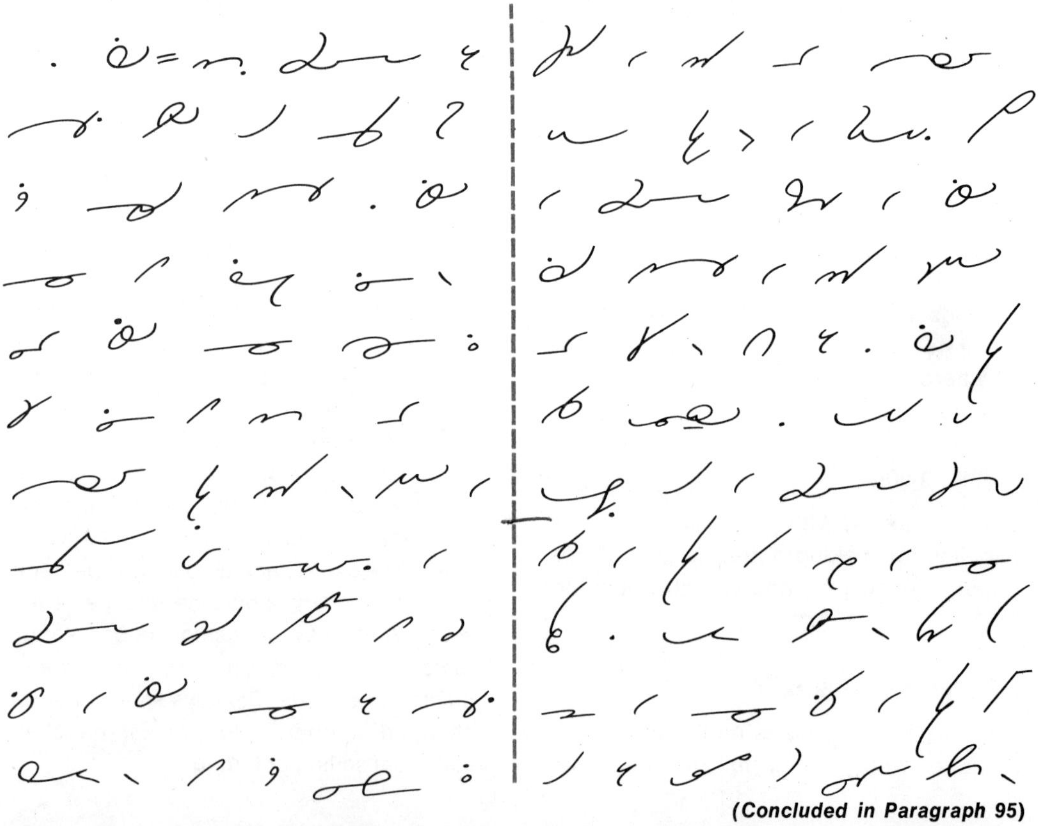

[shorthand passage]

(Concluded in Paragraph 95)

95 Ld. The combination *ld,* as in *told,* is expressed by writing the *l* with an upward turn at the end.

Compare: roll [shorthand] **rolled** [shorthand]

Spell: field, *f-e-eld;* **seldom,** *s-e-eld-m*

field	[shorthand]	settled	[shorthand]	sold	[shorthand]
cold	[shorthand]	drilled	[shorthand]	gold	[shorthand]
spoiled	[shorthand]	hold	[shorthand]	seldom	[shorthand]

Reading and writing practice

HARD WORK (*Concluded*)

[shorthand passage]

Unit 35

PRINCIPLES OF NOTEMAKING

Rules for effective listening (continued)

Listen for cues

If the speaker speaks from an outline, the framework of your listening and notemaking will be pretty well organized for you. The instructor may even have supplied you with a copy of the outline. If so, bring it to class with you each time for your notemaking "blueprint."

If there is no outline in either your or the instructor's hands, you will have to listen for cues from the speaker. The most important ideas and information will often be cued by such words and phrases as "First," "Second," "Third," "Another important consideration," and "Finally." Or they may be cued by superlatives, such as "The most significant thing that happened during this period was," or "The best explanation is," or "The most successful method was . . ." Watch for these cues; in many cases, they will provide important headings in your notes.

Contrasts and comparisons are often introduced by such cues as "On the other hand," "Besides," "On the contrary," "Moreover," "However," and "Furthermore." In your notes these become subpoints or parenthetical statements. Or, if you have followed the good practice of leaving a wide left margin on your notepaper, you may use this space to make notes of interesting contrasts and comparisons.

Questions posed by the speaker are helpful cues. For example, he may ask, "Why did Columbus return to Spain rather than to Italy after his discoveries?" or "What are some of the factors that influenced Lincoln's decision to retain Grant?" Since the lecturer is sure to proceed with the answers, the notemaker turns the questions into positive statements: "Columbus returned to Spain because . . ." and "Factors that influenced Lincoln's decision to retain Grant are . . ."

Speakers will often cue in a listener with such signals as "In summary," or "Note particularly that," or "Now, let's turn our attention to . . ." Pauses, intonations of voice, gestures, and other techniques used for emphasis are other helpful cues.

Flag important things in your notes

Flag your notes with signals of importance. These might be brackets, underscores, arrows, vertical lines, or indentions. Whatever the device, flagging notes will be helpful in using the notes later.

Listen for special instructions

Listen closely for, and note carefully, instructions and special directions—assignments, sources of other information, special preparation, examination dates and what examinations will cover, and so on.

Go over your notes promptly

After you have made your notes, go over them promptly. In this way you can review your notes, make additions and changes in them, plan further study, and so on. Using notes in reviewing is treated in detail in Units 49 and 50.

To think about and discuss

1 Give examples of cues often used by speakers.

2 Give examples of contrasts and comparisons.

3 What types of "flags" may be used to signal important things in your notes?

4 When is the best time to go over your notes, once you have made them?

Application

Study the lecture notes on page 154. Observe how the notemaking suggestions presented in the past few units are applied. (The key to these notes appears on page 326.)

PRINCIPLES OF NOTEHAND

96 **Word ending -ble.** Another frequent word ending in the English language is *-ble,* as in *available.* It is represented by the Notehand *b.*

Spell: **available,** *a-v-a-l-bul*

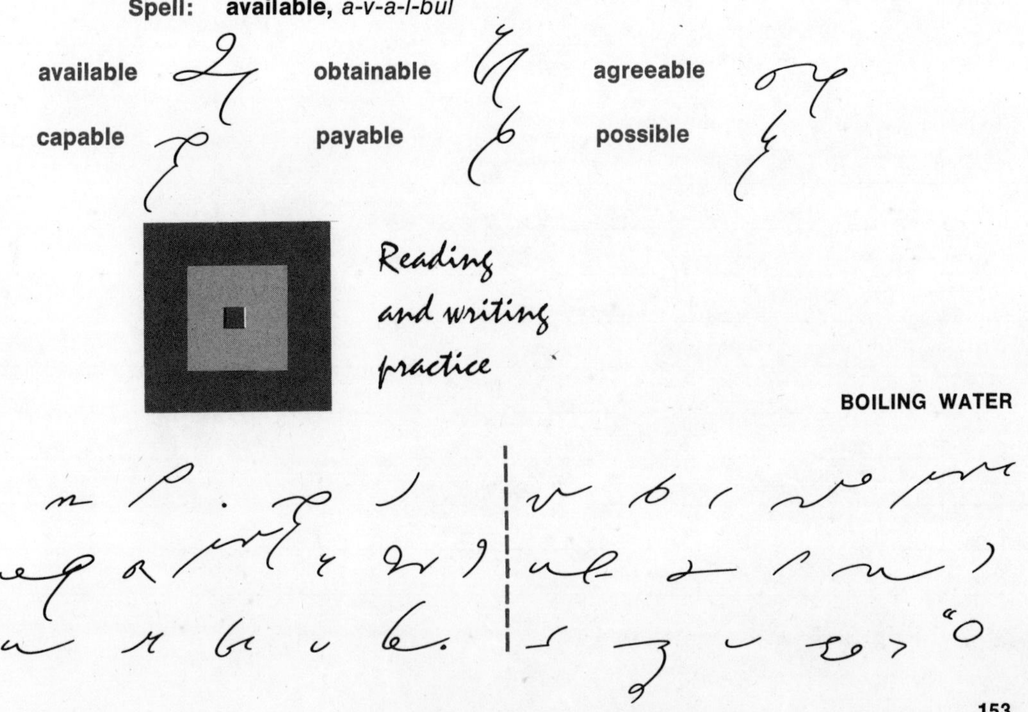

First Aid

I. Treatment Wounds

A. skin

1.

2. iodine Caution:

deep

2% tincture

B. Burns

1. carefully.

2.

3. sterile

4. Extensive

II. Fainting

A. Cause:

B.

1. forward knees.

2. unconscious

97 **Word ending -ful.** The word ending *-ful,* as in *careful,* is expressed by *f.*

Spell: **careful,** *k-a-r-ful*

careful		beautiful		thoughtful	
grateful		tactful		useful	

Reading and writing practice

WASTED TIME

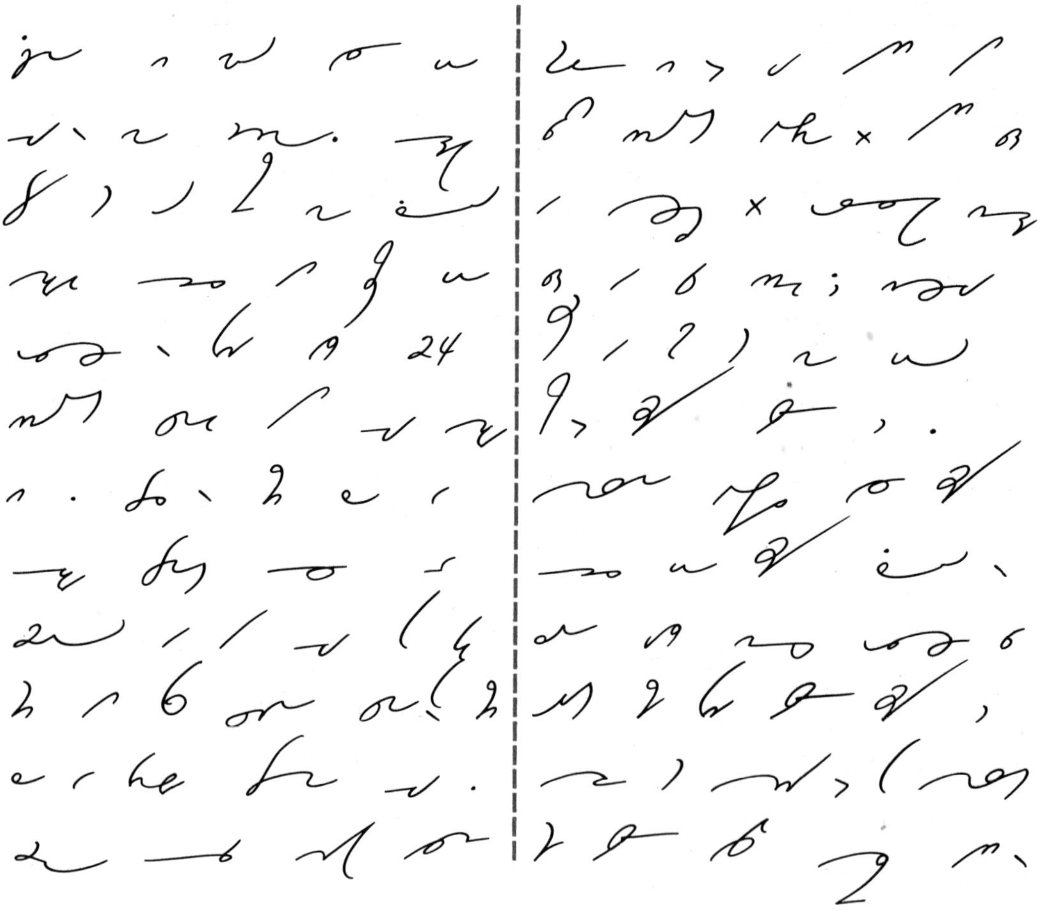

Unit 36

PRINCIPLES OF NOTEMAKING

Preserve difficult longhand spellings

When you are listening to a lecture, the lecturer will sometimes write an unusual word (or pronunciation of a word) on the chalkboard. By all means, preserve the word in longhand in your notes. The name of the great economist, Keynes, is pronounced *canes,* and you may have difficulty in recognizing it from the pronunciation. Of course, you can abbreviate the name with your own device in your notes, but make sure that you have the correct spelling somewhere in your notes.

Also, when you are making notes or copying from a book, preserve the correct spelling of unusual or troublesome words. It may be a common "spelling demon" like *mnemonics* or *syzygy.* Either word would be easy to write in Notehand, but if either word presents a spelling problem to you and if you have the correct spelling available when making your notes, by all means use longhand to keep that spelling readily available in your notes.

Application

Prepare a set of notes from the following. Be sure to write in longhand the words that may present spelling difficulties.

Thus, enzymes are destroyers as well as builders. They have the task, for example, of destroying excess hormones—otherwise, we would be like cars with accelerators but no brakes. Many of the hormones are fat-soluble and kidneys cannot dispose of them. Magical enzymes in the liver convert excess amounts of such hormones into water-soluble substances which the kidneys can then discard.

Already many enzymes are being put to work by physicians. Body cells are cemented together by a substance called hyaluronic acid.

PRINCIPLES OF NOTEHAND

98 Word beginning Con-. The word beginning *con,* as in *concern,* is expressed by the Notehand *k.*

Spell: **concern,** *con-s-e-r-n*

concern contest conclude

conduct contract constant

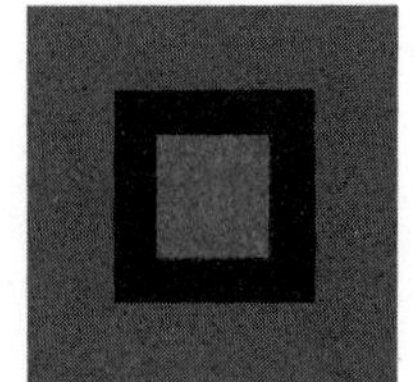

Reading and writing practice

ON THE ALERT

99 Word beginning Com-. The Notehand *k* represents the word beginning *com-*, as in *comply*, as well as the word beginning *con-*, as in *consider*.

Spell: comply, *com-p-l-ī*

comply · compliment · combine
competent · complain · comparative
compare · complete · comfortable

Reading and writing practice

HEARING AID

Unit 37

PRINCIPLES OF NOTEMAKING

Showing contrasts and comparisons in your notes

In many notemaking situations, the writer or speaker compares one quality, characteristic, or point of view with another. In these instances it is a good idea to divide the page in two or more sections and show the contrasts or comparisons side by side, so that they stand out boldly in your notes.

In the example below the author is comparing the competitive positions of large-scale and small-scale retailers. Notice in the illustration on page 161 how the notemaker shows these comparisons in his notes.

The relative competitive positions of large-scale and small-scale retailers may be evaluated in the light of several factors.

Division of Labor. The opportunity to enjoy the advantages of division of labor both at the executive level and in the manpower ranks is one of the strongest factors favoring large-scale retailers. Large retailers can afford to hire managerial specialists for each major function, such as buying, promotion, and accounting. The small store usually cannot pay enough money or offer enough future opportunity to attract a high-caliber full-time person to perform these functions. The owner-manager may be a good executive, but he has to divide his time among too many activities to be effective in all of them.

Flexibility of Operation. Small stores generally are more flexible in their management practices than are large units. Small retailers can stock merchandise to suit specific local needs, and they can adopt a flexible policy regarding services. In short, they do not have to check with headquarters or follow a company manual as large-scale retailers do.

Buying Power. Large-scale institutions have a buying-power advantage. They can buy in bigger quantities than small stores and secure higher discounts. They can achieve additional economies by purchasing from manufacturers. Sometimes this buying power is instrumental in acquiring other benefits, such as allowances for advertising, preferential treatment in case of shortages, and sole dealership rights in a given market.

Store Image. A small store usually projects a warm or friendly image to the public. Salesclerks often know the customers by name. The pace is slower than in a large establishment, and management often seems genuinely glad to see regular customers and give them personal attention. On the other hand, a large store often has high prestige and a broad reputation. The label in a coat from Saks Fifth Avenue, I. Magnin and Company, or Marshall Field means far more to a fashion-conscious customer than does a label from a small dress shop.

Application

Prepare a set of notes from the article on page 162 showing contrasts and comparisons according to the example in this unit. Use as subheadings the following: "In-

LARGE-SCALE RETAILERS	SMALL-SCALE RETAILERS
Division of Labor	
1. Ability to exercise division of labor at all levels is one of the strongest factors.	1. Can't pay enough or offer sufficient opportunity to attract high-level specialists.
2. Can afford to hire managerial specialists--buying, promotion, etc.	2. Owner-manager can't be effective in all the store activities.
Flexibility of Operation	
Not so flexible; inclined to check with headquarters or follow a company manual.	1. More flexible than large retailers. 2. Can buy for specific local needs and offer special services.
Buying Power	
1. Big advantage in buying power. Can buy in larger quantities and get higher discounts.	No advantages.
2. Can purchase direct from manufacturers.	
3. May have other advantages--allowances for advertising, preferential treatment, dealership rights.	
Store Image	
1. Often has high prestige and a broad reputation.	1. Projects a warm, friendly image.
2. Fashion-conscious usually prefer a large exclusive store (Saks Fifth Avenue).	2. Slower pace, more personal attention.

come," "Fringe Benefits," "Working Hours," "Opportunities for Advancement," and "~~Responsibility.~~"

SELF-EMPLOYMENT VS. WORKING FOR OTHERS

Perhaps the greatest advantage of being an employee with a good job in a good firm is that of regular income. The salaried employee gets his paycheck every week or month, knows exactly what the amount will be, and can thus plan his standard of living accordingly. With the application of the guaranteed annual wage plans and governmental unemployment insurance, even the fear of layoffs is no longer a major worry for many production workers.

The income of the owner of a small business, on the other hand, is dependent on the fluctuating sales and expenses of his business. It is the fortunate small-business enterpriser indeed who can accurately forecast what his income from period to period will be. In fact, the income of a small enterpriser may be lower than the salary he could be making as an employee doing similar work.

Perhaps the greatest advantage of being self-employed, however, is the possibility of earning a great deal of money. If the business is successful, the profits all go to the owner; his income is not limited to a specific salary—it might be considerably greater.

Another advantage of regular employment with a good firm is fringe benefits. Vacations with pay, sick leave, pensions, medical care, and other special services are examples. The small-business owner enjoys no such benefits. To him, sickness is a calamity; vacations mean either closing the shop and having no business during that period or no vacation. Instead of receiving a pension, the aging enterpriser often finds his income from the business dropping off as his old age makes him less active.

The employee has the advantage of regular working hours with overtime pay. The owner of a small business works long hours—sometimes seven days a week—because he cannot afford help and needs to keep the store open as long as possible so as not to lose any business. There is no overtime pay for him.

An employee of a large firm has tremendous opportunity for advancement to a better position in the company or even to a bigger job in another firm. The expansion of even a mildly successful business is often limited, however, by the owner's inability to raise sufficient capital or to delegate some of his supervisory work to others.

PRINCIPLES OF NOTEHAND

100 Word beginning Trans-. The word beginning *trans-,* as in *transmit,* is expressed by a disjoined *t* placed above the following character.

Spell: transact, *trans-a-k-t*

transact	**translation**	**transfer**
transmit	**transformed**	**transcript**
transport	**transcribe**	**transparent**

Reading and writing practice

A LITTLE LATE

101 Word beginning Ex-. The word beginning *ex-*, as in *express*, is represented by the Notehand characters for *es*.

Spell: **express,** *ex-p-r-e-s*

express	explain	extent
excellent	experiment	extra
except	expense	extreme
export	exclude	excessive

Reading and writing practice

A TOOTH FOR A TOOTH

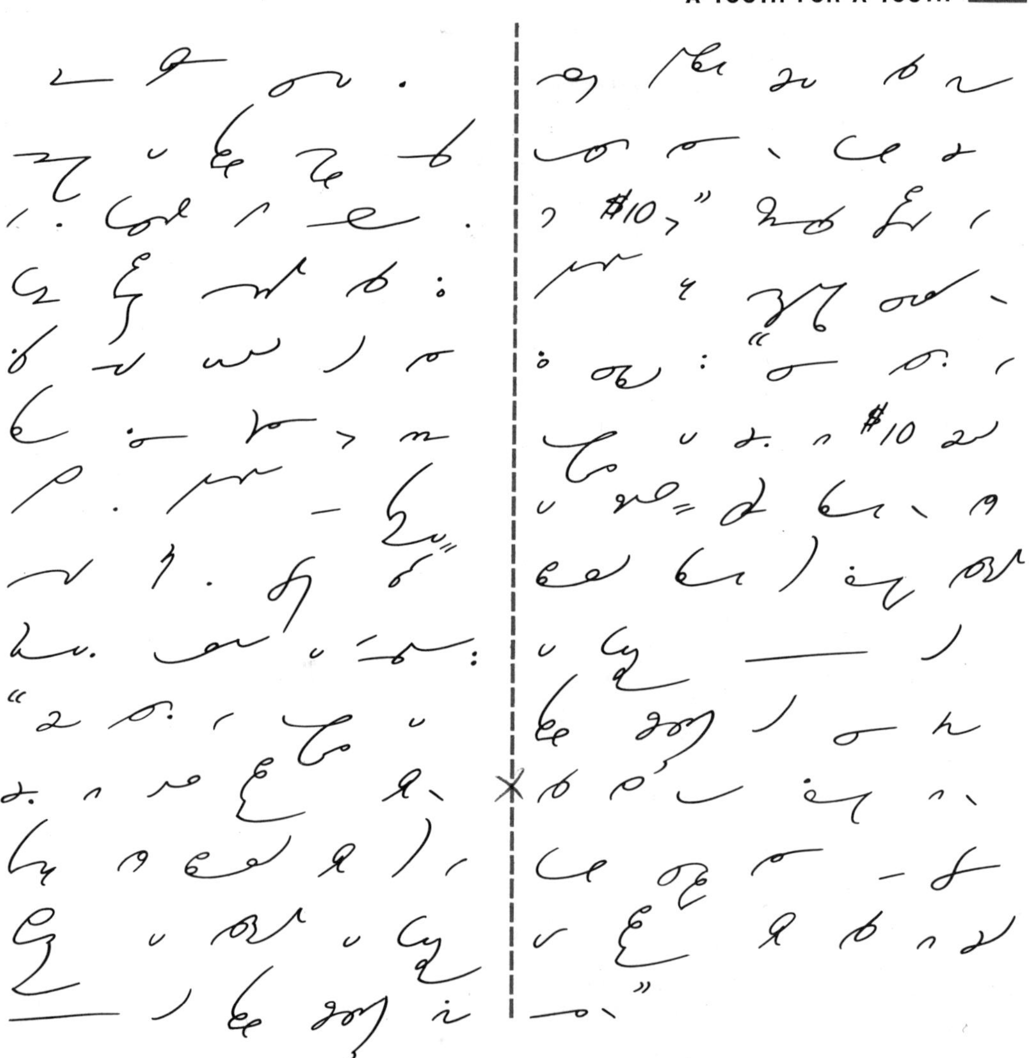

102 Word beginnings De-, Di-. The word beginnings *de-*, as in *delay*, and *di-*, as in *divide*, are expressed by the Notehand character for *d*.

Spell: delay, *d-l-a;* **direct,** *d-r-e-k-t*

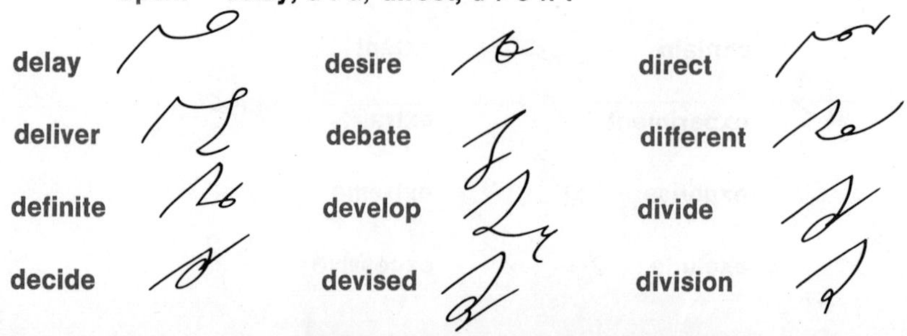

delay	**desire**	**direct**
deliver	**debate**	**different**
definite	**develop**	**divide**
decide	**devised**	**division**

Reading and writing practice

SHOCK

Unit 38

PRINCIPLES OF NOTEMAKING

Definitions, background information, and examples

In making notes from reading and listening, the notemaker often finds that the speaker or author has supplied certain background information, definitions, and examples of the main subject before getting to the "meat" of his discussion. This information is often extremely important and, generally speaking, should appear in the notes. However, when it merely leads up to the main theme of the discussion, it should be separated in the notes. Let's take an example.

> A tax is money raised to run government, and the major problem of any tax system is to make taxes fair to all. In our present tax system, we still adhere to the principles of a just tax system laid down by Adam Smith. Adam Smith was a Scotch professor at the University of Edinburgh in the eighteenth century and is the father of political economy. His principles were:
>
> 1. Ability. The subject of every state should contribute to the support of his government, as nearly as possible, in proportion to his respective ability.
> 2. Certainty. The tax which each individual is bound to pay ought to be certain, and not arbitrary. The time and manner of payment and the quantity to be paid should be certain.
> 3. Convenience. Every tax ought to be levied at the time or in the manner which is most likely to be convenient for the contributor to pay for it.
> 4. Economy. Every tax ought to be so continued as both to take out and to keep out of the pockets of the people as little as possible over and above what it brings into the public treasury.

In making notes from this material, you will probably choose as the central idea—and your major heading—"Principles of Taxation." The definition of a tax and the origin of the principles of taxation represent "kick-off" information; however, this information should be included in your notes. Thus, your notes might appear as follows.

```
PRINCIPLES OF TAXATION

  Definition: A tax is money raised to
              run government.

  Background

     1. Major problem of a tax system is
        to make taxes fair to all.
     2. Present tax system based on
        principles laid down by Adam
        Smith, Scotch professor and
        father of political economy
        (eighteenth century).

  Principles

     1. Ability. Each person should
        pay in proportion to his ability.
     2. Certainty. Time, manner, and
        amount should be certain--not
        arbitrary.
     3. Convenience. Taxes levied when
        payment is most convenient.
     4. Economy. Should cover expenses
        of government and no more.
```

Here is another example.

> Water in a lake or in the ocean is a free good. But water piped into a house is no longer a free good. Similarly, the cool breeze of a mountain retreat is a free good, but not the cool air of an air-conditioned office building. The difference in these cases is that human effort was applied to give an added utility to the good. Any good to which human effort has added utility, or usefulness, is an economic good.
>
> Human effort adds several kinds of utility to economic goods. Here we will consider only three—form utility, place utility, and time utility.
>
> Form Utility. Crude petroleum as it comes out of an oil well is limited in its uses. Only after it is separated and refined into its several products—such as gasoline, kerosene, fuel oil, and lubricating oil—is it fully useful. By changing crude petroleum into its useful products, man gives it "form utility." A good has form utility when its form or shape is such that it is useful. All manufactured goods have form utility. . . .

And so on. The other forms of utility added to economic goods would be continued.

What will you choose as your major heading for the foregoing material? Probably you will select "Economic Goods," even though the "meat" of the material is concerned with kinds of utility. Let's see how the background information leading up to "kinds of utility" might be handled in your notes.

```
ECONOMIC GOODS

  Definition: Any good to which human
              effort has added utility
              or usefulness.
  Example:    Water in the ocean is
              a free good; piped-in
              water, an economic good.

  Kinds of Utility Added by
  Human Effort

   Form Utility--changing a good in
                 form or shape to make
                 it useful. (Example:
                 Crude petroleum into
                 gasoline. All manu-
                 factured goods have
                 it.)
```

And a last example.

> After much discussion and opposition, the Pendleton Act, which provided for a real civil service, was signed in January, 1883, and became the keystone of civil service reform. It has grown rapidly, and its principle has been extended to both states and cities. The law made these provisions: (1) The President was given the power to appoint a bipartisan commission of three members to supervise the civil service. (2) This commission was given power to draw up rules acceptable to the President to be applied to the "classified list." (3) Appointments were to be made according to the highest grade received in open competitive examinations. . . .

And so on. There are ten provisions of the law, and all would be included in the notemaker's notes.

Let's assume that you have chosen the heading "The Pendleton Act" for your notes. The "meat" of the paragraph consists of the ten provisions of the act; the first two sentences are background material. Here is how your notes might appear.

```
THE PENDLETON ACT

  Background

     1. Passed in January, 1883 (much
        opposition).
     2. Provided for a real civil
        service and became keystone of
        civil service reform.
     3. Has grown rapidly; principle
        adopted by states and cities.

  Provisions

     1. President given power to
        appoint bipartisan commission
        (3) to supervise the civil
        service.
     2. Commission has power (with
        President's approval) to draw
        up rules for "classified list."
     3. Appointments made according to
        highest grade in open compet-
        itive exams.
     4. Etc.
```

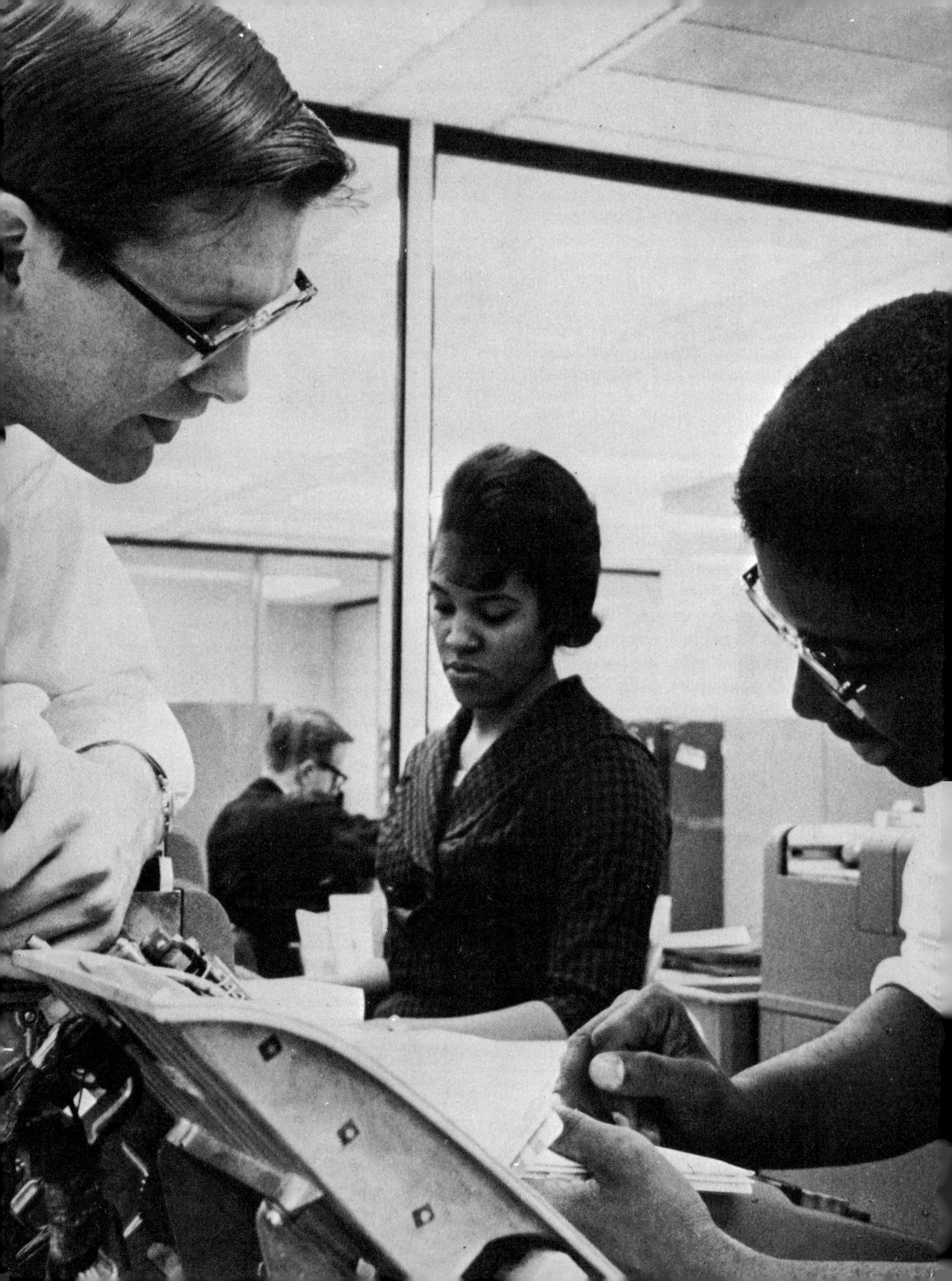

Application *Thurs.*

Prepare a brief set of notes on the following exercise, using the suggestions for definitions, background information, and examples given in this unit.

The Uniform Partnership Act defines a partnership as follows: "A partnership is an association of two or more persons to carry on as co-owners a business for profit." Partnerships may be divided into two classes: the general partnership and the special partnership. A general partnership is one that is created for the general conduct of a particular kind of business; for example, clothing store merchants, lawyers, architects, certified public accountants, and consulting engineers. The general partnership is much more common in the United States than the special partnership. It is organized to continue for an indefinite period.

A special partnership is one that is formed to carry out a special or single transaction. When the transaction is completed, the partnership is dissolved. For example, a special partnership may be formed to purchase land and then sell it as housing lots.

PRINCIPLES OF NOTEHAND

103 Word beginning Re-. The word beginning *re-*, as in *repeat,* is expressed by the Notehand character for *r.*

Spell: repeat, *re-p-e-t*

repeat	**replace**	**refuse**
report	**revise**	**reform**
residence	**reverse**	**react**

Reading and writing practice

NO SMOKING!

$3,800

$127.50 12 35

(Concluded in Paragraph 104)

104 Word beginnings Dis-, Des-. The word beginnings *dis-*, as in *display*, and *des-*, as in *describe*, are expressed by the Notehand characters *ds.*

Spell: **display,** *dis-p-l-a;* **describe,** *dis-k-r-ī-b*

display	dissolve	describe
discover	distance	description
dispose	dismissed	despite

Reading and writing practice

NO SMOKING! (Concluded)

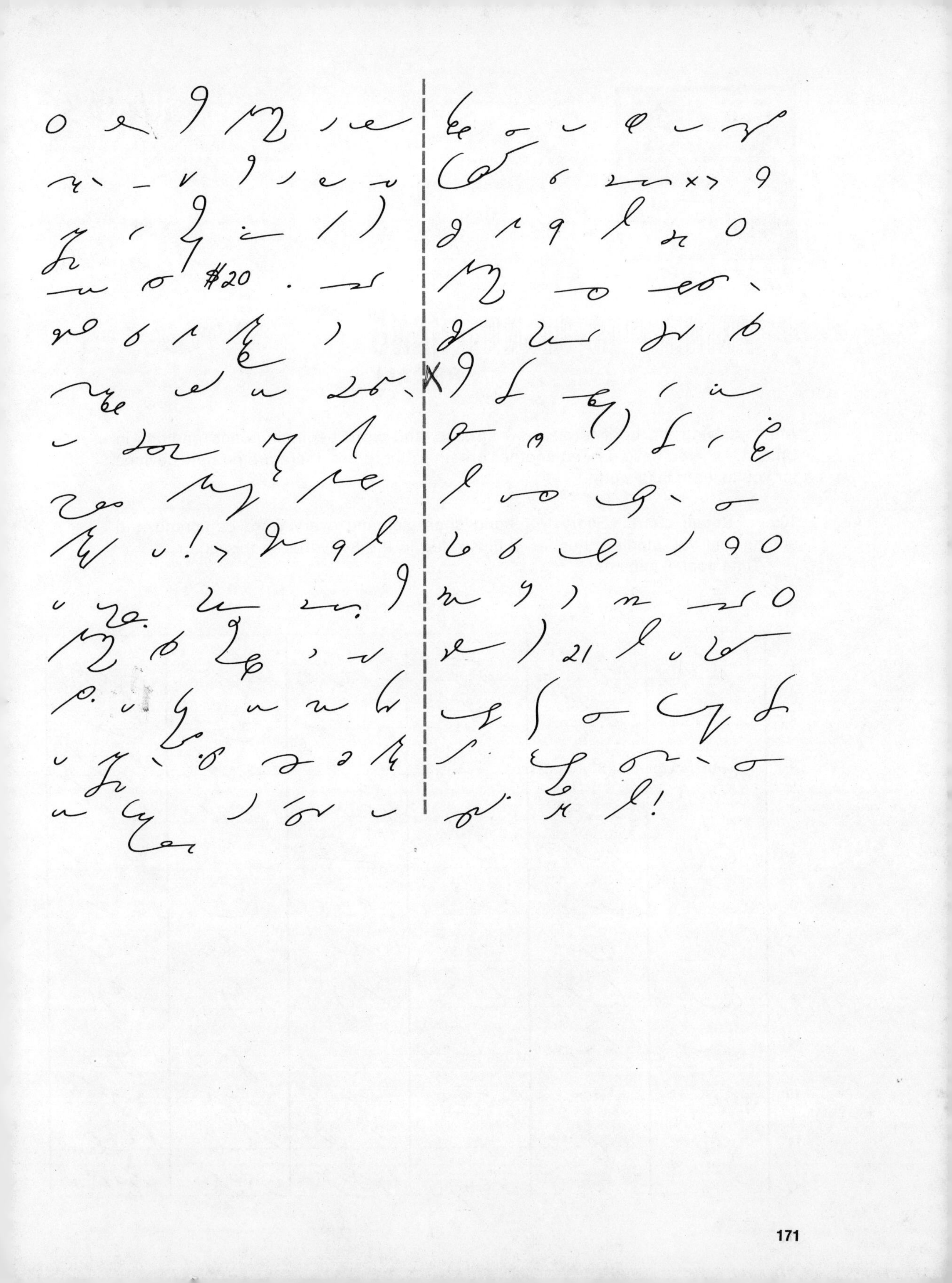

$20

21

Unit 39

PRINCIPLES OF NOTEHAND

RECALL

After studying the brief forms, new strokes, and word beginnings and endings in Units 34-38, you have earned another breather; therefore, there are no new devices for you to learn in this unit.

105 Recall chart. Every Notehand character and every word beginning and ending that you studied thus far is illustrated in the 84 words in this chart.

Time goal: 6 minutes!

Words

1

2

3

4

5

6

7

8

9

10

11

12

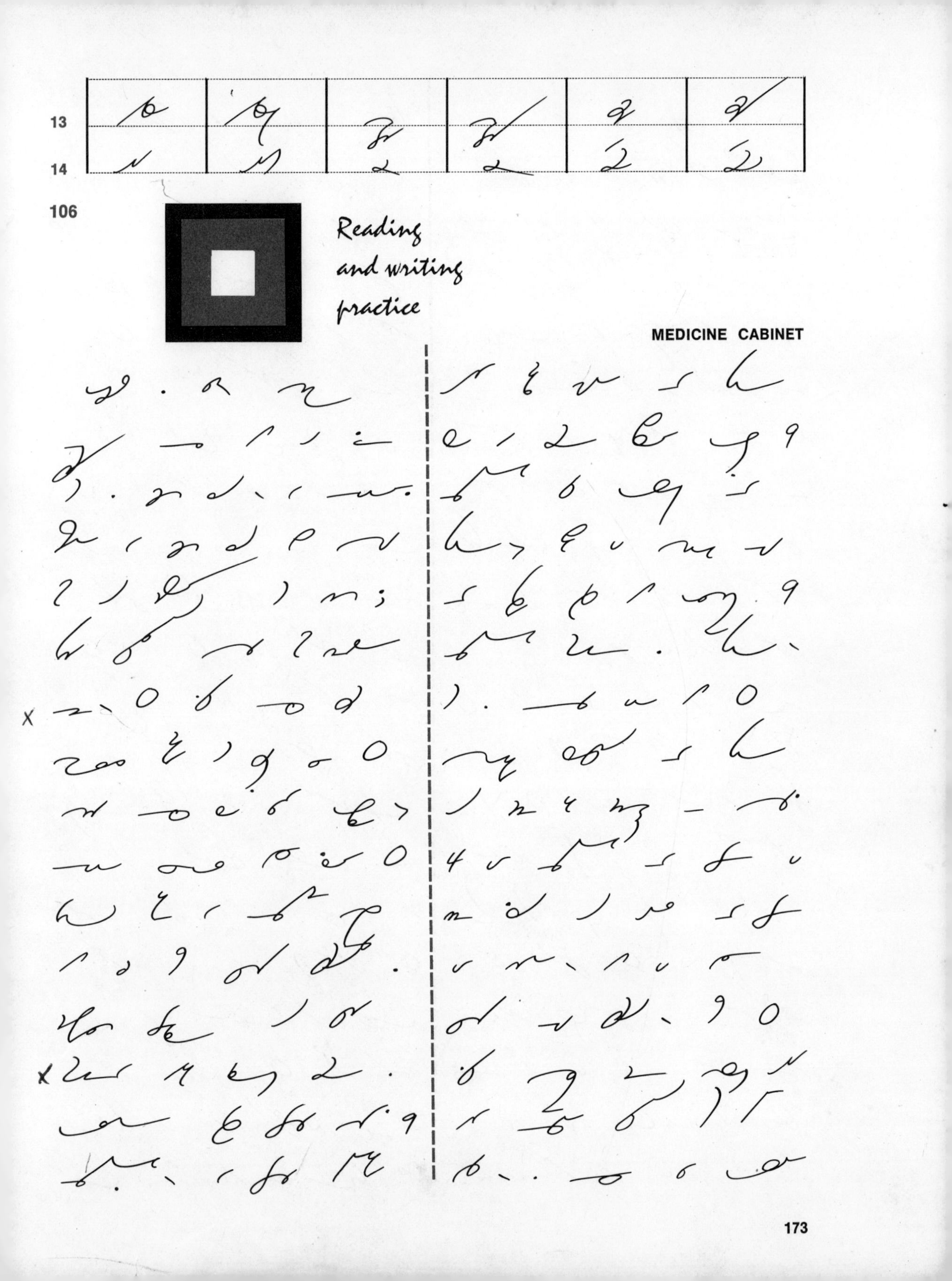

13

14

106

Reading and writing practice

MEDICINE CABINET

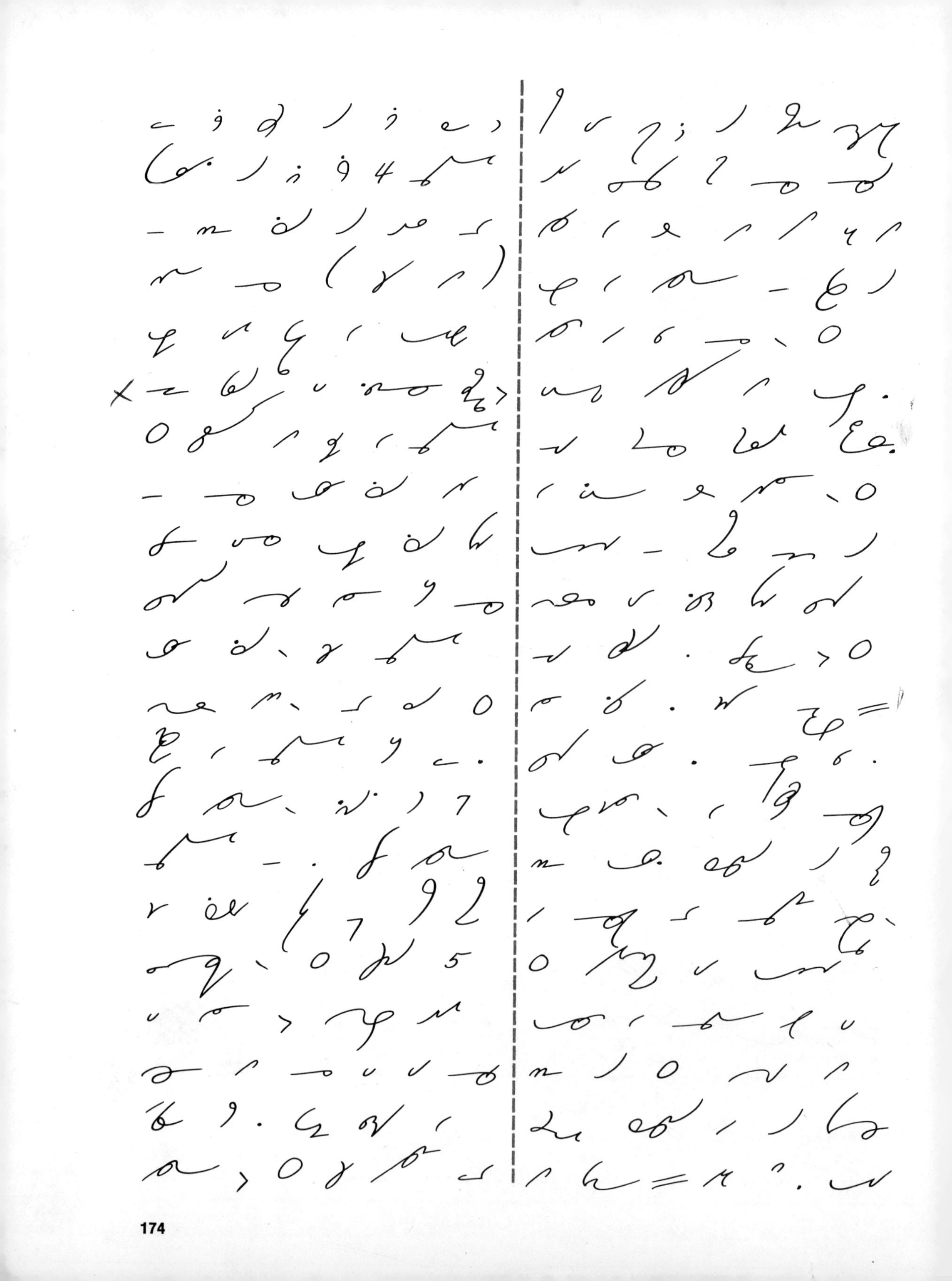

—*James Thurber*

Most-used Gregg Notehand forms

Here are ten more Notehand forms of the commonest words in the English language to be added to the card that you keep with you whenever you are making notes. Every day read over once or twice all the words that you now have left on the card. The more often you read them, the more rapidly you will be able to write them.

possible **note** **made** **make** **their, there**

just **come** **send** **they** **much**

Unit 40

PRINCIPLES OF NOTEMAKING

Using notehand in original writing

Hardly a day goes by that you as a student are not called upon to do some original writing, for example, summarizing a chapter from a history book, writing a theme or an essay for an English class, describing an experiment for a chemistry class, or preparing a research paper. Original writing plays an important part in your formal education; in fact, the success you ultimately achieve scholastically depends in large measure on the quality of your original writing.

Your ability in original writing may also play a significant part in your success in later life. It may, for example, help you get that first job through a well-written letter of application and personal data sheet.

Should you enter the field of business, you will have letters, memorandums, reports, and talks to prepare. If your choice lies in the professions, you will have articles for professional journals and papers—even books — to write. Your ability to prepare written material will stand you in good stead even though you do not enter the field of business or one of the professions. The modern housewife finds time for the Cub Scouts or the PTA, the man of the family may help with the Red Cross or the community chest, and all these activities require some writing in the form of social letters, announcements of meetings, committee reports, and even the preparation of informal talks.

In short, ability in original writing is a valuable asset for just about everyone.

Gregg Notehand is an aid to original writing

Three forms in which you can do original writing are (1) in longhand, (2) on the typewriter, (3) in Gregg Notehand.

In Longhand. Longhand is least efficient because of the time required to write down your thoughts. Longhand is slow and cumbersome. Each time you make a false start or change a word or a phrase all the time and effort expended in the original writing is wasted. In addition, you may lose your train of thought simply because your longhand writing cannot keep up with your thinking.

On the Typewriter. Typewriting is more efficient than longhand, assuming that you have a fair degree of typing skill. Much time can be lost, however, when you make additions or corrections or deletions in the process of x-ing out and moving the carriage back and forth. Then, too, a typewriter may not be available to you when you wish to compose—while you are working in the library, for example.

In Gregg Notehand. Gregg Notehand is a very efficient medium for original writing. Why?

FAC SIMILE OF AN EXTRACT FROM THE SHORT-HAND M.S. DIARY.

(Vide Page 1. 3rd sentence)

The condition of the State was thus - viz. The Rump after being disturbed by my Lord Lambert, was lately returned to sit again. The Officers of the Army all forced to yield — Lanson, lies still in the River, & Monk is with his Army in Scotland.

Courtesy of Culver Pictures, Inc.

An extract from the diary of Samuel Pepys written about 1700.

1 You can record your thoughts rapidly as they come to you.

2 You are not likely to lose an idea or interrupt your train of thought because your thinking outruns your writing speed.

3 When you make changes or corrections and must scratch out, you waste only a fraction of the time it would take if you had written in longhand or on the typewriter. Insertions and additions can often be made in Notehand with a stroke or two of the pen.

4 Since corrections and additions are so easy to make with Notehand, you are likely to revise and correct more freely than you would in longhand or on the typewriter. As a result, you will produce a better composition.

5 With Notehand you can write anywhere —in the streetcar, bus, plane, study hall, library—places where it would be either impossible or impractical to use a typewriter.

Many famous people have used some form of shorthand for original writing.

Sir G. Kneller. Pinx.t J.W. Steel. Sculp.t

Among them were Samuel Pepys, who wrote his diary in shorthand; Woodrow Wilson, who drafted all his state papers in shorthand; and George Bernard Shaw, who wrote his plays in shorthand for his secretary to transcribe.

The briefest study of the following rough draft of a paragraph of a paper, "Differences of Opinion," written in longhand, on the typewriter, and in Notehand will convince you of the timesaving advantages of using Notehand for original writing.

LONGHAND COMPOSITION

Differences of Opinion

~~When you find yourself in disagreement~~ What usually ~~transpires~~ happens when you ~~do not agree~~ disagree with another's opinion? ~~Doesn't~~ Do you ~~invariably~~ always find it easy to ~~reconcile~~ settle your differences? Or ~~do you~~ does a ~~difference of opinion~~ disagreement frequently lead to harsh words or strained feelings? One of ~~T~~the most important ~~principles~~ things to remember is that ~~you can't always be right~~ your opinion cannot always prevail.

TYPEWRITTEN COMPOSITION

Differences of Opinion

~~Whenxyouxfindxyourselfxinxdisagreement~~ What usually ~~transpires~~ happens when you ~~doxnotxagree~~ disagree with another's opinion? ~~Doesxit~~ Do you ~~invariably~~ always find it easy to ~~reconcile~~ settle your differences? Or ~~doxyou~~ does a ~~differencexofxopinion~~ disagreement frequently lead to harsh words or strained feelings? One of ~~T~~the most important ~~principles~~ things to remember is that ~~youxcan'txalwaysxbexright~~ your opinion cannot always prevail.

To think about and discuss

1 Why is longhand least efficient for original writing?

2 What are two disadvantages of the typewriter as an instrument for original writing?

3 List and discuss the advantages of Notehand as a medium for original writing.

PRINCIPLES OF NOTEHAND

107 **Abbreviation.** As you make notes in Notehand, you should always feel free to use any longhand abbreviations that are familiar to you. You may also abbreviate long words in Notehand simply writing enough so that your outline suggests the word to you; for example, *s-a-t-e-s* for *satisfactory.* However, before you abbreviate a word in Notehand, be sure that it occurs frequently in your work. A word that does not occur frequently is better written in full.

Here are some examples of the abbreviating principle:

Mr.

Mrs.

satisfy, satisfactory

particular

anniversary

convenient, convenience

consequent, consequence

arithmetic

privilege

mathematics

reluctant, reluctance

memorandum

Reading and writing practice

TABLE CONVERSATION

(Continued in Paragraph 108)

108 Word ending -ingly. The word ending *-ingly,* as in *accordingly,* is represented by a disjoined *e* circle.

Spell: accordingly, *a-k-o-ard-ingly*

accordingly **knowingly** **seemingly**

increasingly **willingly** **convincingly**

Reading and writing practice

TABLE CONVERSATION (*Continued*)

(*Concluded in Paragraph 109*)

109 Word ending -ings. The word ending *-ings,* as in *feelings,* is represented by a disjoined left *s.*

Spell: feelings, *f-e-l-ings*

feelings		earnings		drawings	
savings		awnings		ratings	

Reading and writing practice

TABLE CONVERSATION (*Concluded*)

—Robert Benchley

Proportion drills

The following drills concentrate on the joining of the Notehand *o.* As you write each *o* hook, keep it small and narrow. Be careful of the proportions of the strokes you join to the *o* hook.

Joinings of Notehand O

1

2

3

4

5

6

7

8

KEY

1 Owe, was, hope, obey, offer, office. **2** Toe, dough, know, row, low. **3** Own, stone, dome, known, moan. **4** Note, wrote, float, flowed. **5** Course, calls, nor, more. **6** Pore, bore, pole, ball. **7** Rock, lock, knock, rogue. **8** So, zone, foam, fought, vote.

Unit 41

PRINCIPLES OF NOTEMAKING

Making rough drafts

An experienced writer would tell you not to attempt to make the final copy of an important paper on the first writing. It is the rare person indeed who can write a finished paper on his first effort. Most people—even the most talented writers — make many false starts. They scratch out. They insert. They transpose. They change a word here and there. Occasionally they tear up everything and start all over again. Their completed first draft often contains more corrections than it does original writing!

"Good writing comes about only through rewriting" is an axiom that applies to most writers, and it should guide you in your own work. You can improve your own writing only after you have put something down on paper.

Organize your materials

Before you begin your rough draft, organize your materials so that, once you sit down to write, you can complete the task without interruption. Assemble all the supplies* and reference books you will need within easy reach so that you will not have to leave your desk or table. By freeing yourself from all possible distractions, you will be able to concentrate uninterruptedly on recording your thoughts and to complete your writing with the greatest economy of time.

***A convenient place in which to do your rough drafting is the stenographic notebook that you use for your Notehand practice. However, almost any type of paper is satisfactory for the purpose.**

Concentrate on recording your thoughts

As you write your rough draft, concentrate on getting your ideas down on paper. In this creative stage don't worry about spelling, punctuation, grammar, etc. Your final paper must, of course, be correct in every grammatical detail, but the time to attend to grammar is when you reread your completed rough draft—after you have organized and recorded your ideas and thoughts.

Start writing

Perhaps the hardest job for any writer is to get that first sentence down on paper. Get *a* first sentence down even though you are quite sure it will not be *the* first sentence you will ultimately use. Somehow, writing becomes easier and more fluent when that first sentence is on paper. As you continue writing, a more suitable first sentence may suggest itself to you.

Use Gregg Notehand

Write in Gregg Notehand all the words for which the outline comes to you readily. Write in longhand any words for which the Gregg Notehand outline does not immediately come to your mind. Do not take time to devise outlines for such words. As you progress with your study of Gregg Notehand and your skill develops, you will find yourself writing more and more Gregg Notehand and less and less longhand.

Make a special effort to write the commonest words in Gregg Notehand, especially those that you have recorded on your card.

Make changes freely

Do not hesitate to cross out and rewrite and make corrections and insertions; you can do it easily and quickly in Gregg Notehand.

If you discover that you are making a great many changes and additions in your notes, it is a good idea to write only on every second line in your notebook. And leave very generous right and left margins for changes and insertions.

Reread and edit

After you have completed your rough draft, reread it before you begin to make your final copy. While you are rereading, you may want to revise that first sentence that you put down just to "get started." While you are rereading, you should also take care of the following:

1 Insert all punctuation. Be sure each sentence ends with a period, each question with a question mark. Put in necessary commas.

2 Check the grammar. Does each sentence have a subject and a predicate? Does each noun agree with its verb? Do any participles dangle?

3 Indicate paragraphs.

4 Look up the spelling of words about which you are in doubt and write them in longhand — in the proper place in your draft. Don't take a chance on misspelling a word.

5 Make any other refinements in wording or construction that occur to you. If you follow these steps in making your rough draft, your hardest work is done; all that remains is the preparation of your final copy.

To think about and discuss

1 Do experienced writers usually make a final copy of their work on the first try?

2 Why is it important to organize your materials before you start to write?

3 True or false? "The hardest job for any writer is to edit his material after he has put it in rough draft form."

Application

Study the rough draft on page 185. Notice how the writer has applied the suggestions for preparing a rough draft that you have just read. (The key is on page 330.)

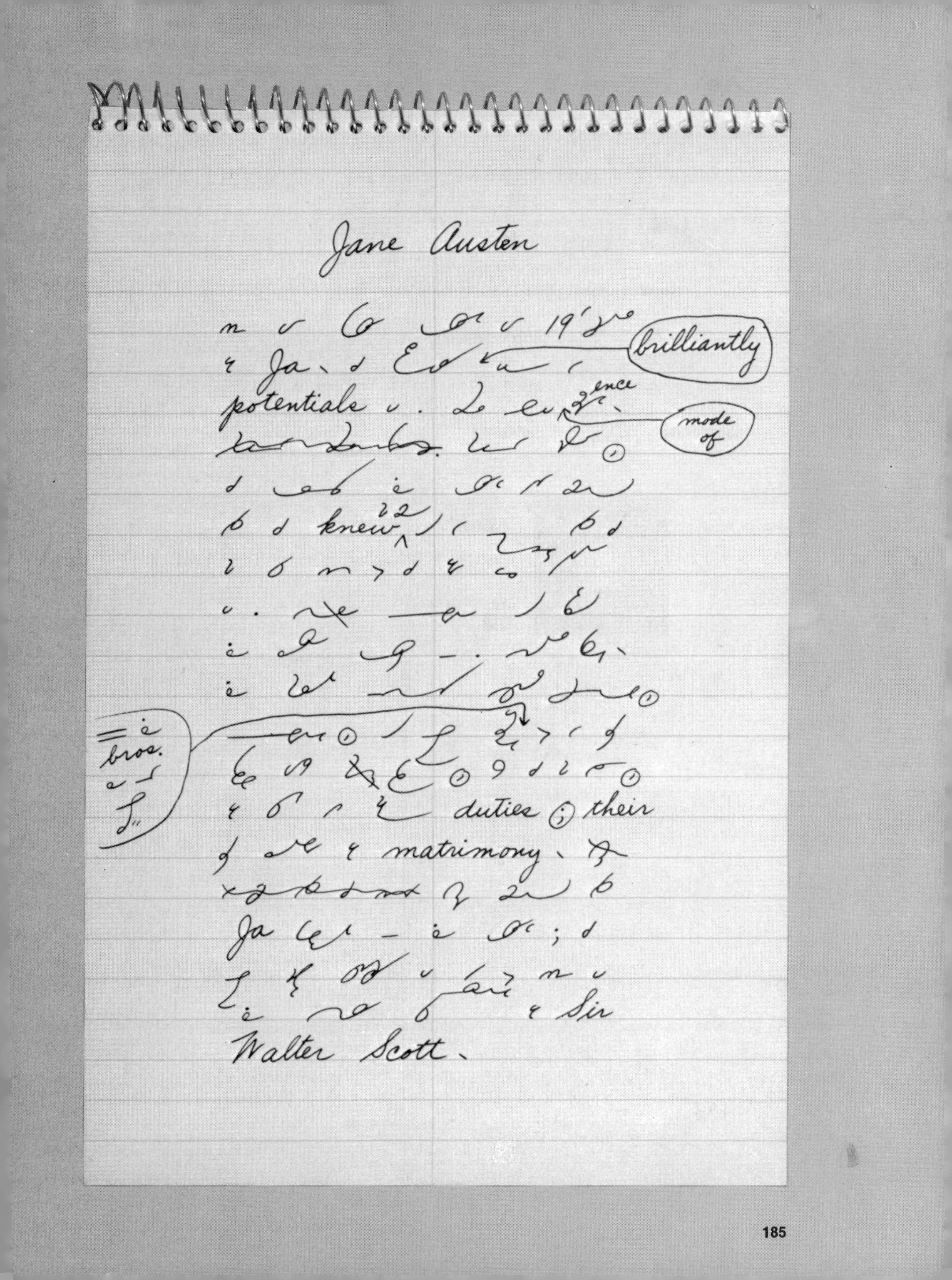

Jane Austen

brilliantly

potentials ence

mode of

knew

bros.

duties their

matrimony

Ja

Sir

Walter Scott.

PRINCIPLES OF NOTEHAND

110 Ĭa, Ēa. The sound of *ĭa* or *ēa,* heard in *piano* and *create,* is represented by placing a dot within the *a* circle.

Compare: **crate** **create**

Spell: **create,** *k-r-ĭa-t*

piano	**appropriate**	**mania**
area	**initiate**	**recreation**
appreciate	**brilliant**	**created**

Reading and writing practice

THE VALUE OF READING

(Continued in Paragraph 111)

111 Long I and a following vowel. The sound of long *ī* followed by any other vowel, as in *diary, diet,* is expressed by a double circle.

Compare: **signs** **science**

Spell: **science,** *s-īa-n-s*

diary	quiet	diagnosis
diet	dial	appliance
prior	trial	reliance

Reading and writing practice

THE VALUE OF READING ***(Continued)***

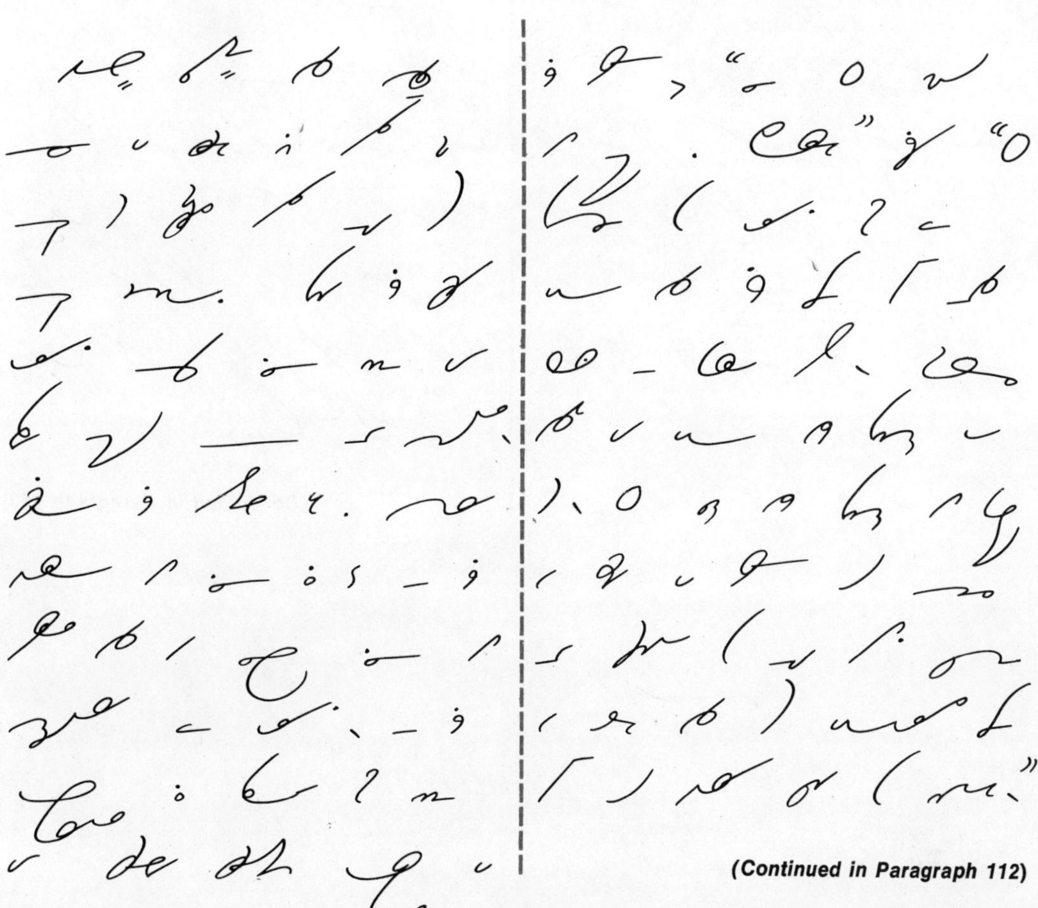

(Continued in Paragraph 112)

112 **Aw, Ah.** When *aw* or *ah,* as in *away* and *ahead,* occur before a vowel, the initial *a* is expressed by a dot.

Spell: **away,** *a-oo-a;* **ahead,** *a-h-e-d*

away		award		await	
awake		aware		ahead	

Reading and writing practice

THE VALUE OF READING *(Continued)*

Ford

(Concluded in Paragraph 113)

Unit 42

PRINCIPLES OF NOTEMAKING

Footnotes

In copying from books or composing a rough draft for a research paper, it is often necessary to provide for a footnote. The inexperienced notemaker usually puts the footnote at the bottom of the page of notes on which the reference appears, which seems reasonable. Actually, it is much better to follow the same practice in writing footnotes that is used in preparing manuscripts for the printer.

Instead of writing the footnote at the bottom of the page of notes, place it immediately below the line to which it applies. First, leave a blank line. Then draw a single line clear across the page, write the footnote, draw another line across the page and proceed with your notes on your draft. In your notes simply indicate the word to which the footnote belongs by placing an asterisk or a small cross after the word. Later, when you prepare your final copy, you can substitute raised numbers for the asterisks or crosses. See the example below.

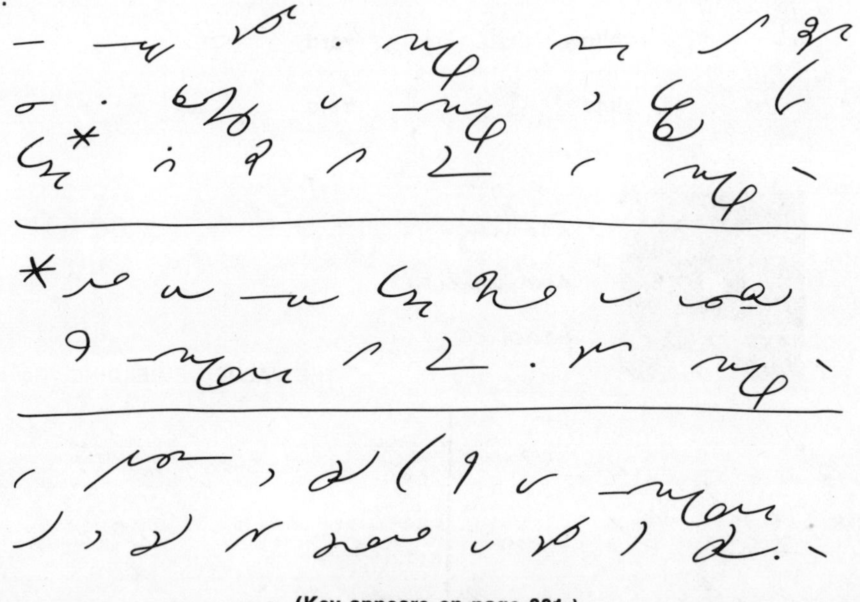

(Key appears on page 331.)

Placing the footnote immediately following the reference is desirable for two reasons:

1 In your original draft it is sometimes difficult to know how much room to allow for footnotes; some footnotes are quite long.
2 As you prepare your final copy, you may find that the word on which the footnote hangs may be at the very bottom of the page, leaving no room for the footnote which was inconspicuously placed at the foot of the page. When the footnote follows on the line after the word on which it depends, it is considerably easier to plan for the placement of the footnote on the proper page.

Application

Read the rough draft on page 191. As you do, notice how the footnote is indicated and how words are written out that might present spelling difficulties to the notemaker. (The key to this exercise is on page 331.)

PRINCIPLES OF NOTEHAND

113 **Ye, Ya.** The sound of *ye,* as in *yet,* is expressed by a small loop; the sound of *ya,* as in *yard,* is expressed by a large loop.

Spell: **yet,** *ye-t;* **yard,** *ya-ard*

yet	**yell**	**yes**
year	**yellow**	**yard**
yearly	**yield**	**Yale**

Reading and writing practice

THE VALUE OF READING (Concluded)

Stoppage – Transit

carrier

occurs

liability

10,000

US

150

114 Omission of vowel preceding -tion. When *t, d, n,* or *m* is followed by *-ition, -ation,* the circle is omitted.

Spell: station, *s-t-shun*

station	transmission	foundation
quotation	permission	explanation
combination	termination	reputation
examination	hesitation	addition

Reading and writing practice

THE TRAITS OF SUCCESSFUL PEOPLE

100

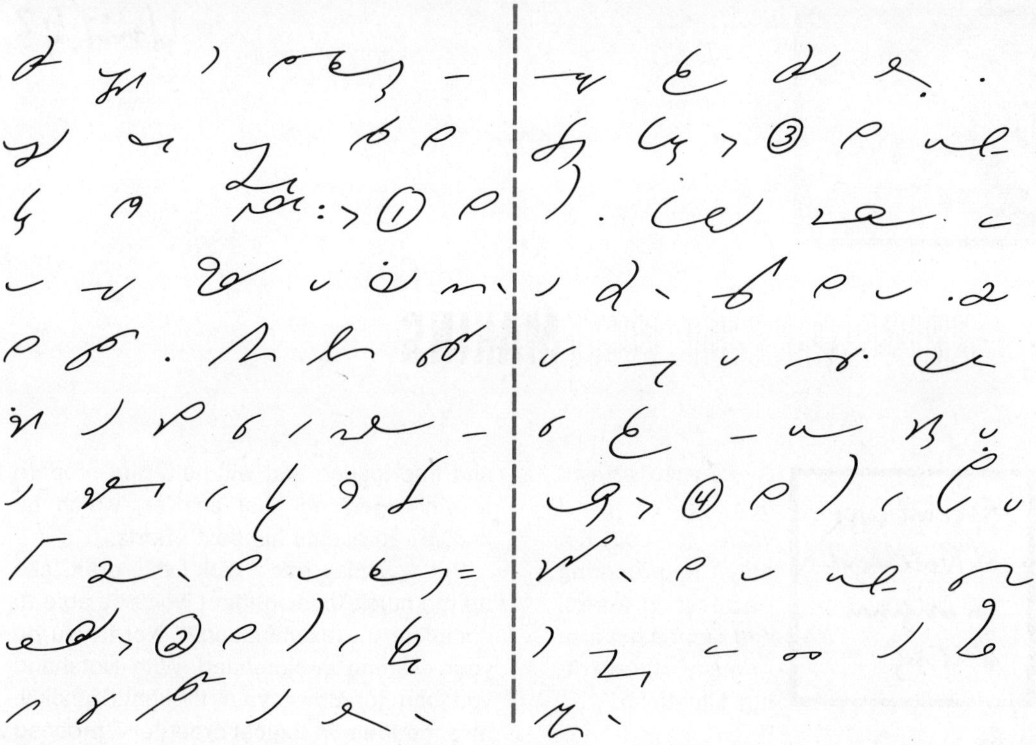

Unit 43

PRINCIPLES OF NOTEMAKING

Special uses of Notehand in original writing

Gregg Notehand can be of great value to you not only in preparing papers, themes, and reports but also in many other writing situations.

In taking examinations

Many examinations consist of questions that require an essay-type answer of several paragraphs or even pages. If you read the question and immediately start writing down your thoughts, the result is usually a disorganized answer that doesn't do justice to your ability to answer the question. A thought may occur to you while you are writing the second paragraph that should be included in the first. When you reread your answer, you find many opportunities for improvement, some of which you can make; others you cannot make because that would mean rewriting the whole answer, and there just isn't time for that. As a result, you must turn in an answer that doesn't represent your best work.

The wise student will not start writing his final answer immediately but will take a little time to plan his answer in the form of a rough draft on a piece of scratch paper. This very act of drafting will suggest facts and information that will help him prepare a well-organized final answer, which he knows represents his best efforts.

But you may ask, "Won't this draft take up too much time so that I won't be able to complete the examination?" Not if you do your drafting in Notehand. With Notehand you can jot down your thoughts quickly, arrange them in logical order, and proceed with the writing of the final answer, which will be rapid and easy because you have already done your thinking while preparing your draft.

In filling out forms

Perhaps you have already had some experience in filling out application forms of various kinds—applications for jobs, for admission to college, for membership in a club. If you haven't, you soon will.

Many of the questions on these forms are routine and simple, for example, your name, your address, your age, etc. Some, however, call for an essay-type answer, such as "Describe your duties on your last job," or "Why did you choose Midwestern University?" Usually only a few lines are provided on the form for the answer.

Again, the average person will start writing the answers immediately on the final form only to find that he must make changes and insertions or that he has run out of space—with the result that the filled-out form does not present a pleasing picture to the person who must read it and perhaps act on it.

Doesn't it make good sense, therefore, to draft answers to such questions on a piece of scratch paper before you fill out your application form? It's easy and quick with Notehand.

To think about and discuss

1 What is the advantage of drafting answers on examinations before putting them in final form?

2 How can Gregg Notehand be useful in getting ready to fill out forms?

Application

Study the lecture notes on page 196. Notice that some of the words are written in longhand, but the common words are always written in Notehand. (The key to these lecture notes appears on page 332.)

PRINCIPLES OF NOTEHAND

115 Word beginning Sub-. The word beginning *sub-*, as in *submit*, is expressed by either form of the Notehand *s*.

Spell: **submit,** *sub-m-e-t*

submit	substantial	suburb
subscribe	subway	sublease
subject	subdivide	sublet

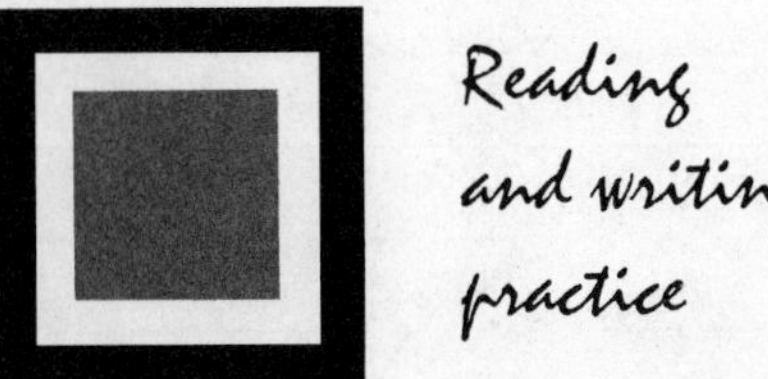

THE ART OF SAYING "NO"

Making a Speech

Appearance

"right."
well
confidence.

Posture

weight on
forward.
loosely shoulders.
pocket.

Platform Manners

attention
exceed allotted
audience.

Delivery

everyone
audience.

(Continued in Paragraph 116)

116 Word endings -cal, -cle. The word endings *-cal* and *-cle,* as in *chemical* and *article,* are expressed by a disjoined *k.*

Spell: chemical, *k-e-m-ical;* **article,** *a-r-t-ical*

chemical	**typical**	**physical**
surgical	**medical**	**mechanically**
logical	**clerical**	**articles**

Reading and writing practice

THE ART OF SAYING "NO" ***(Continued)***

(Continued in Paragraph 117)

Proportion drills

The following drills concentrate on the various joinings of the Notehand *oo.* Be sure to keep the *oo* hook small and deep. Watch carefully the proportions of the strokes joined to the *oo* hook.

Joinings of Notehand OO

1
2
3
4
5
6
7
8

KEY

1 You, hut, hood, other, hook. **2** To, do, to you, do you, wood. **3** Noon, numb, moon, enough. **4** Us, just, adjust, bus, campus. **5** Look, plug, rug. **6** Up, hub, cup, cub, couple. **7** Chorus, plus, rust, trust. **8** We, way, wash, watch, wise, wife.

Unit 44

PRINCIPLES OF NOTEMAKING

How to make notes for research papers

Many people—especially students and those in the professions—often need to make notes from reading for such purposes as writing an article, a report, a speech, a term paper, or any project that calls for research. Although the final product of each of these projects may vary in purpose and form, the procedures for all of them are quite similar. For our purposes, therefore, we shall consider the research paper.

The research paper

The research paper is sometime called a term paper. Generally, however, a term paper is not so extensive as a research paper. A single reference may provide sufficient source material for a term paper, although several sources are often required. The term paper ordinarily presents no recommendations or conclusions, but a summary statement at the end is usually desirable.

The research paper, on the other hand, is often much longer and more scholarly than a so-called term paper in that it requires the student to investigate some perplexing problem or controversial question. A topic for a research paper might be "The Defeat of Alfred E. Smith—Religion or Tammany," For such a controversial topic, the researcher must read widely, seeking various points of view. A single source or two would not provide the depth he needs for a comprehensive treatment. For a research paper, the student must weigh the evidence collected and present conclusions and, in some cases, recommendations. Any conclusions must, of course, be supported by the content of the paper.

Choosing a subject

The first step in getting ready to prepare a research paper is the selection of a subject. Avoid the pitfall of choosing a subject that is too broad. For example, unless you're writing a book, you will stay away from such a broad subject as "Ulysses S. Grant" or "City Government." It is much wiser to limit your topic so that it is manageable. For example, instead of the two broad subjects just mentioned, you might select such manageable topics as "Ulysses S. Grant as President" and "An Appraisal of the Mayor-Council Plan of City Government."

You will do a better paper if you choose a subject in which you are personally interested. If it is one that will help you along toward your career goals at the same time, so much the better.

Locating your sources

In gathering material for a short paper, you may have to consult only two or three sources. For more scholarly papers, however, you will probably have to consult many sources.

Most experts agree that the first step in locating your sources is to consult a good encyclopedia. There you will probably find an authoritative, albeit condensed, discussion of your topic or some important phase of it. At the end of the discussion may be a list of books that deal with the subject in detail. This list is a good starting point in locating sources. Write down the names of the authors and titles of these books, and then see whether these books are available in the library. The best way to find out is to use the card catalog. Consulting the card catalog will also help you locate additional sources to investigate. Make up a bibliography card for each of the books that you wish to consult. This bibliography card should contain all the following information:

1 The author's name (last name first)
2 The title (and edition if there is more than one)
3 The location and name of the publisher
4 The date of publication (latest copyright date)
5 The call number

For example, see the card below.

Some of the books you come across will probably suggest other sources to you. Before long, you'll doubtless find your problem to be one of selecting the most promising sources for your purposes. If you have no luck, however, ask the librarian to help you.

Don't overlook magazines and newspapers in your search. The best place to look for lists of magazine articles, according to subject, is the *Reader's Guide to Periodi-*

Satin, Joseph

Ideas _ Context. Boston:

Houghton Mifflin Company,
1958

808.8S

Bibliography card for a book

Perron, Alex T.

"Bacon's Interpretation of Nature," Classics Monthly

44:316-330 (— 1933)

Bibliography card for a magazine

cal Literature; for newspaper articles, the *New York Times Index.* A bibliography card for each article should also be prepared. A card for a magazine article is shown above.

The number 44 at the bottom of the card indicates the volume number of the magazine; 316-330 indicates the page numbers where the article may be found. For newspaper articles, you need the title of the article, the title and location of the newspaper, and the month, day, and year of publication.

Be sure to make up a bibliography card for every book or article that you use. These cards will come in handy later.

To think about and discuss

1 What might be the main differences between a term paper and a research paper?

2 True or False? The following title for a research paper is a good one: "Russian Literature."

3 What should a bibliography card contain?

4 Is a bibliography card desirable for a newspaper article?

Application

Assume that you are gathering material for a paper on "The Development of Office Automation." One of your sources is a book; another is a magazine. They are as follows:

Source No. 1. A book entitled *Office Work and Automation,* written by Howard S. Levin. The publisher is John Wiley and Sons, Inc., New York. The publication date is 1966. The extract you will use appears on page 54.

Source No. 2. An article entitled "Automation in the Sixties," by Robert M. Smith, in *Office Management Magazine,* January, 1967, Volume 16. The article begins on page 16 and ends on page 20.

Prepare a bibliography card for each source.

PRINCIPLES OF NOTEHAND

117 Word ending -ward. The word ending *-ward,* as in *backward,* is expressed by a disjoined *d.*

Spell: backward, *b-a-k-ward*

backward		**upward**		**afterwards**	
forward		**downward**		**inwardly**	
onward		**awkward**		**rewarded**	

Reading and writing practice

THE ART OF SAYING "NO" ***(Continued)***

(Continued in Paragraph 118)

118 Word endings -lity, -lty. The word ending *-lity,* as in *locality,* is expressed by a disjoined *l.*

Spell: locality, *l-o-k-ality*

locality		**reality**		**reliability**	

utility ability personality

mentality possibility quality

The word ending *-lty,* as in *faculty,* is also expressed by a disjoined *l.*

Spell: **faculty,** *f-a-k-ulty*

faculty loyalty penalty

Reading and writing practice

THE ART OF SAYING "NO" (*Continued*)

(Concluded in Paragraph 119)

119 Word ending -rity. The word ending *-rity,* as in *majority,* is expressed by a disjoined *r.*

Spell: **majority,** *m-a-j-rity*

majority authority charity

sincerity prosperity clarity

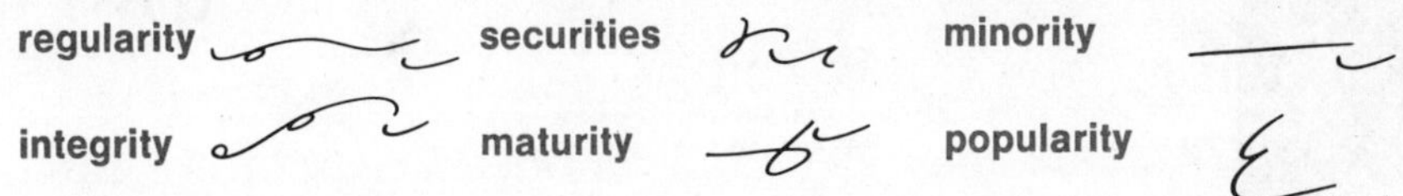

regularity securities minority

integrity maturity popularity

Reading and writing practice

THE ART OF SAYING "NO" ***(Concluded)***

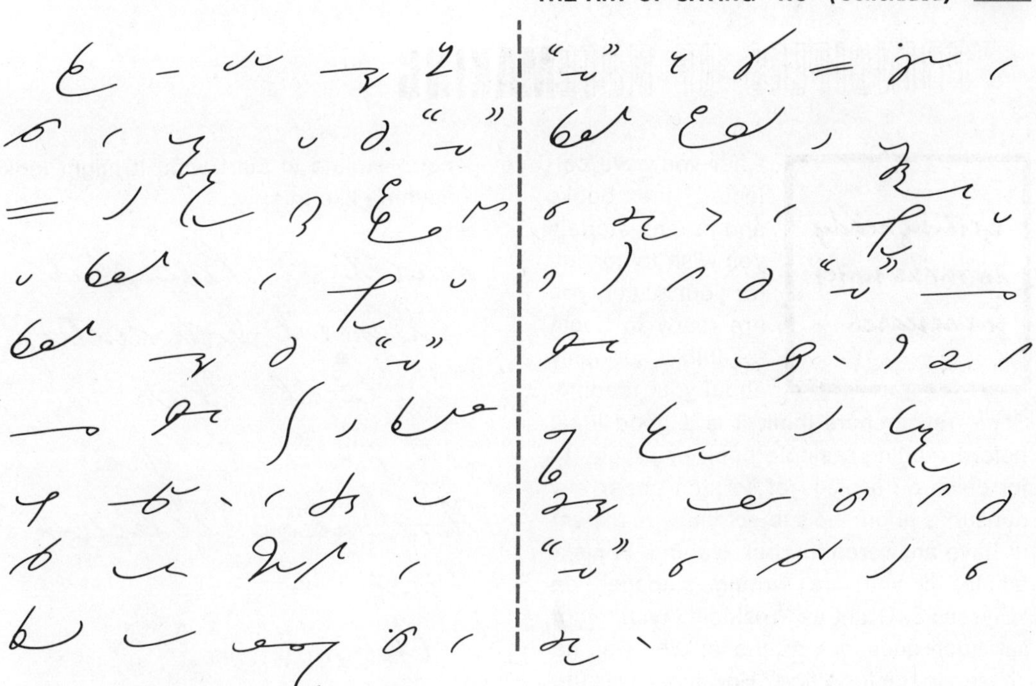

Most-used Gregg Notehand forms

Here is another group of ten most frequently used words to be added to your card. At this stage in your study of Gregg Notehand, no doubt most of them are already old friends.

my **number** **so** **she** **please**

me **get** **do** **been** **would**

Unit 45

PRINCIPLES OF NOTEMAKING

Getting ready to make notes for research

After you have collected the books and other materials you wish to consult for your paper, you are ready to begin to think seriously about your reading. Some researchers think it is a good idea, before reading a single book or article, to jot down on a piece of scratch paper any questions about the subject that you expect to have answered in your reading. For example, if you are writing a paper on "Ulysses S. Grant as President," you might ask such questions as these: Why was he chosen to run for office? How close was the race? What qualifications did he have? How did he fare during his first term? Second term? What was he like as a person? Whether you do this or not is up to you, but you should at least give a good deal of thought to your subject before you begin to dig into the materials you have gathered.

The next step in getting ready to make notes is to prepare a broad outline. Look at the table of contents of some of the books and perhaps read a chapter or two in a couple of them. This quick examination should give you a framework around which to build a tentative outline. You will need some directional signals, for you can't do a very intelligent job if you just start making notes without a purpose. You need a broad general outline to start with. It might look something like this:

Grant 9 President
  General Introduction
    Civil War
    Postwar Yrs
Nomination / Election
First e—
  Cabinet
  Domestic Policy
  Foreign Affairs
Second e—
  Scandals
  "Whiskey Ring"
  Indian Service Graft
Grant (Man
  Soldier
  Father

To think about and discuss

1 What is the purpose of jotting down on scratch paper any questions about the subject you are researching before you begin to read?

2 After you have listed the questions you want answered, what is the next step in getting ready to make notes from research?

3 Should you ever begin making notes without a purpose?

Application

Study the outline on page 208. Notice how the wide margins and plenty of white space make the notes easy to review. Notice also the use of signals that make important facts stand out. (The key to this outline is on page 333.)

PRINCIPLES OF NOTEHAND

120 Omission of vowel in -ious, -eous. The endings *-ious* and *-eous,* as in *various* and *courteous,* are expressed by *oo-s.*

Spell: **serious,** *s-e-r-oo-s*

serious	**tedious**	**envious**
curious	**obvious**	**erroneous**
previous	**industrious**	**courteously**

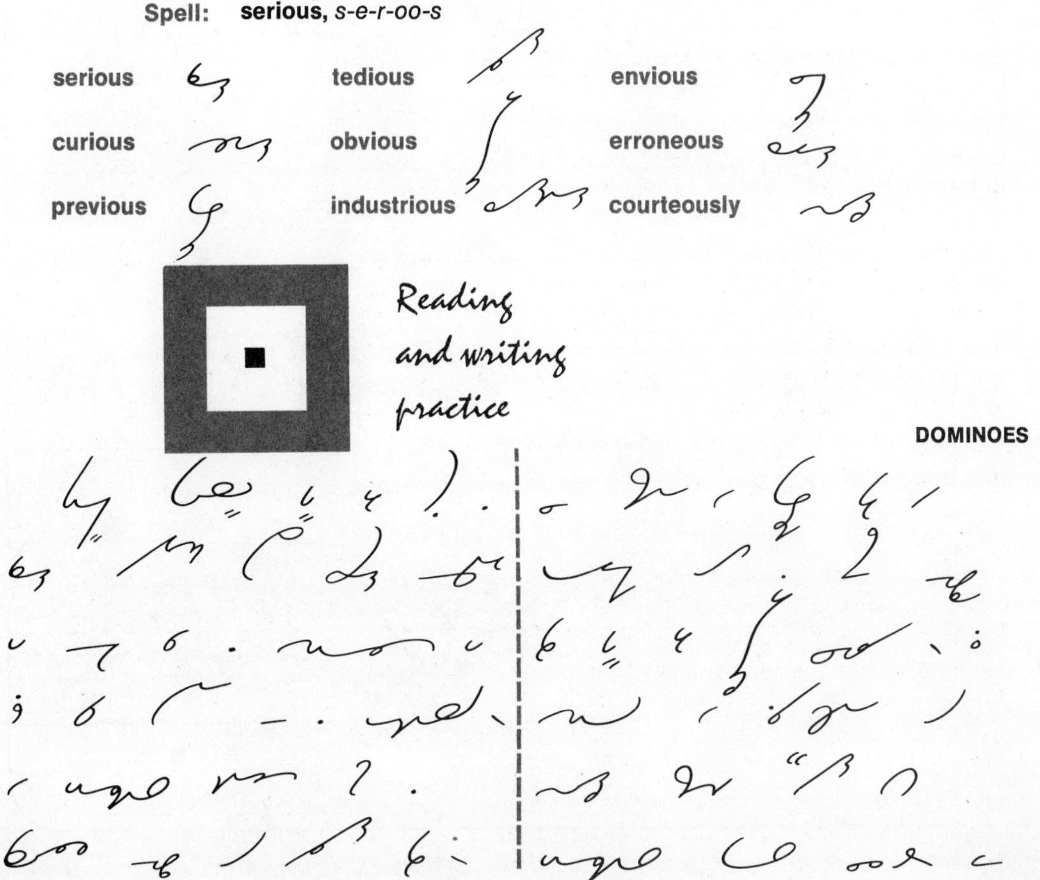

Essentials [shorthand] Good Savings Program

I. [shorthand] plan

A. [shorthand]

B. [shorthand]

II. [shorthand] safe

A. [shorthand]

B. [shorthand]:

1. [shorthand]

a. [shorthand]

b. [shorthand]

c. [shorthand]

2. [shorthand] E

III. [shorthand] earn interest

A. [shorthand] convenience [shorthand]

B. [shorthand]:

1. [shorthand]

2. [shorthand]

a. [shorthand]

b. [shorthand]

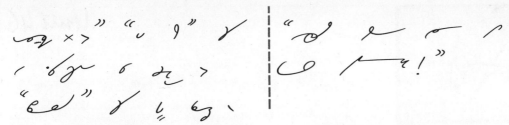

121 **Omission of E in U.** The small *e* circle may often be omitted from the diphthong *ū*, as in *new*.

Spell: new, *n-oo*

new	**reduce**	**issue**
numerous	**produce**	**avenue**
tune	**induce**	**duty**
renew	**music**	**suit**

Reading and writing practice

PRESS THE BUTTON

Unit 46

PRINCIPLES OF NOTEMAKING

Making notes from research

With your broad general outline before you, you are ready to make notes. Making notes is perhaps the most important activity in the research process. The ease with which you can organize your material and write the paper will depend largely on how well you have made notes from your reading.

Make more notes than you need

Don't skimp on quantity; make more notes than you will probably use. A good news reporter, in conducting an interview with a famous person or in preparing a report on local crime, gathers three or four times as much material as he can actually use in his final article. It is through the process of sifting this mass of material that he arrives at his best story.

The same is true of making notes for use in a research paper. The more notes you make, the more material you will have on which to draw as you write your paper. You can discover what is really important only when you have made a great many notes and begin to "shake them down" to write your paper. You also get many points of view, by gathering a great deal of material from several sources, which helps give balance to the finished paper.

Use cards for making research notes

You won't know until you are all through how much of your notes you can actually use. You must, therefore, make these notes in such a way that (1) you can easily add new material and throw out useless material, and (2) you can reorganize in different ways the material you have collected. For these purposes, cards are better than ordinary sheets of paper. Cards are sturdy and can be sorted and re-sorted without damage. And they are handy; you can spread a lot of them out in front of you as you work.

There are three common sizes of cards for this type of notemaking: 3 by 5 inches, 4 by 6 inches, and 6 by 9 inches. No one size is absolutely best, but of course you should use the same size throughout your project. The cards should be small enough to be convenient but large enough to enable you to write a fair amount on each card. You can buy cards in a variety of sizes at nearly all stationery stores, school bookstores, and other local stores. Most people prefer cards that are not ruled.

Identify your sources

As you make notes from reading, be careful to identify accurately the sources of your material. Of course, your bibliography cards contain complete information about your sources. But you should also indicate the sources on your note cards. These do not have to be so complete as the bibliography cards, but there should be no question in your mind about the source. For example, your note card on Satin, Joseph, *Ideas in Context* (see bibliography card illustrated on page 201) might be merely: Satin, *Ideas,* p. 46.

Write summary statements

For most notemaking for research papers, your notes will appear in the form of summary statements. Since there is little continuity when you read several different authors with several different approaches to a subject, you will find it almost impossible to outline as you make notes. Study carefully the examples of note cards shown below and on pages 212 and 213.

Note in the illustrations that each card carries a brief identification of the source, including the page number. If more than one card is used from one source, number the cards and group them together.

Here are two important rules for making notes on cards:

1 Write on one side of the card only.

2 Limit each card to one subject.

When you rearrange your cards later, you will be glad you followed these rules.

Did you notice in the illustrations of note cards the liberal use of Notehand? Notehand not only enables you to write the material down more rapidly than you could in longhand, but it also makes it possible for you to get more material on a card.

Use a slug line

Notice in the illustrations that follow the "slug" lines, or catch lines: "GRANT – FIRST TERM" and "GRANT – SECOND TERM." These slug lines are picked up from the general outline that you made before you began to make notes. You can see now the value of making a tentative outline of your main topics – its major headings are your directional signals for notemaking to keep you on the right road. Later on, you will find these slug lines a help in putting related topics together. Some notemakers prefer to put the slug in a different color of ink, or at least in all capital letters.

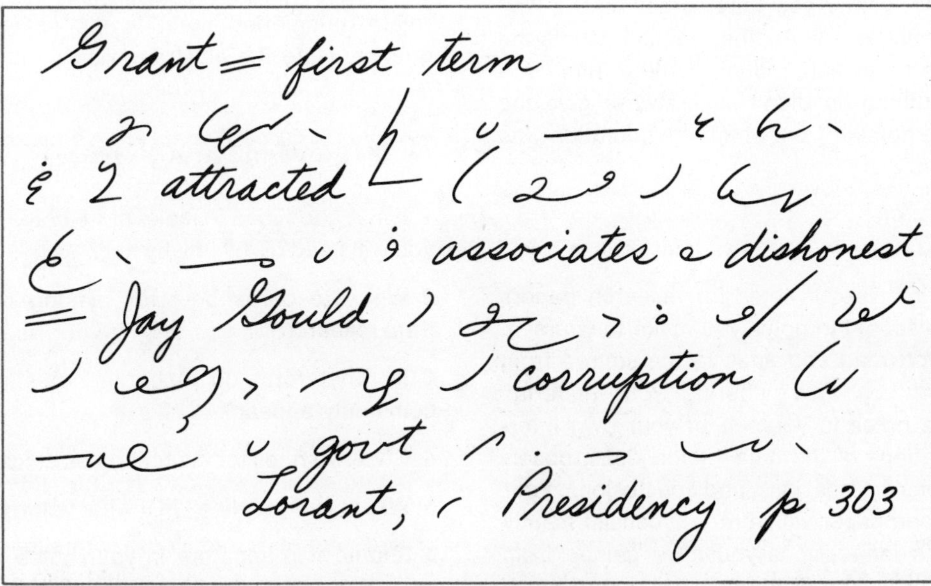

(Key appears on page 334.)

Grant = second term
"Whiskey Ring"
(persecuted)
investigators
investigations
corruption
admin
propaganda.
Faulkner, Am Pol + Soc Hist p 421

(Key appears on page 334.)

Be accurate in quotations

When you take a statement verbatim from a book, be sure to enclose the statement in quotation marks. You would not want to take credit for someone else's writing (that's plagiarism), and unless you use quotation marks, you may forget that it isn't your statement. Another caution: Quote the author correctly; don't saddle him with something he didn't say! Always give the page number from which the quotation was taken.

Make notes of your own impressions

A third type of notes for research papers consists of the notes you make to yourself. As you read and analyze the source from which you are gathering your material, make notes to yourself of your own interpretations of the data—your ideas, observations, impressions, and conclusions. Your finished paper will, after all, consist mainly of the impressions you have gained from your reading. Getting these impressions down while they are fresh in your mind will save you much time later. Prepare these cards in the usual manner, but flag them in some way so that you know the source. A large asterisk (*) in the upper left corner will do. Or just the word *me* with a circle around it is sufficient identification. Keep these cards with the material to which they relate, numbering them in the same sequence. Note the illustration on page 213.

To think about and discuss

1 Is it a good idea to make more notes than you will need? Why or why not?

2 Why are cards best for making notes from research?

3 In what form do research notes most commonly appear?

4 Give two rules for making notes on cards.

5 What is a "slug line"? Of what value is it?

6 Should you separate in your notes your own interpretations from the author's material?

Grant = the man

extrovert

entertain

30 =

dynamically

Me

(Key appears on page 334.)

Application

Refer to the exercise on page 202. From **Source No. 1** (Levin: *Office Work and Automation)* you take the following extract.

The technology of our times provides much that can contribute to more effective information handling. There is promise that clerical costs can be reduced as more accurate, comprehensive, and timely information is made available.

But these are not the only, or even the most, important reasons for improving business information systems. The more significant advantages will result from new ways of using business information to form business decisions. These improved systems will place at our command new means for initially handling information, new methods for processing information, and new techniques for utilizing information in solving business problems.

From **Source No. 2** ("Automation in the Sixties," by Smith) you take the following extract:

Business had also fallen behind generally in assessing and planning for the psychological effects of automation, either on the production line or in the office. While most instances of clerical automation have included provisions for transfer of displaced workers to other parts of the company and some planned information program in advance of the change, all the ramifications of intelligent transfer have not by any means been fully worked out. For example, how many companies have really faced the problem of what to do with senior workers suddenly moved into a new area where, in spite of their years of service, they have less experience than their juniors? How many have considered the psychological problems involved in moving a worker with a responsible job into a less demanding one?

1 Write a slug line for each note card.

2 Make appropriate notes from the extracts, identifying each note card according to the suggestions in this unit.

PRINCIPLES OF NOTEHAND

122 **Word ending -ology.** The word ending *-ology* is expressed by joined *ol;* joined *est* are added to form the ending *-ologist;* disjoined *k,* to form the ending *-ological.*

psychology		psychologist		psychological	
biology		biologist		biological	
sociology		sociologist		sociological	

Reading and writing practice

123 **Months and days**

Months

January		May		September	

February		June		October	
March		July		November	
April		August		December	

Days

Sunday		Wednesday		Friday	
Monday		Thursday		Saturday	
Tuesday					

Reading and writing practice

REVENGE

500

PRINCIPLES OF NOTEMAKING

Writing the research paper

Making an outline of your paper

The final step before beginning to write your paper is the preparation of a complete outline from your notes. When you have assembled all your notes (and you should have a good-sized stack of cards), read them all carefully. Undoubtedly you will find a few cards that contain information that is irrelevant or unimportant. Remove these from the cards you expect to use. Then arrange the remaining cards roughly in the order you are going to follow in writing the paper. Decide where each point can be most effectively presented. Don't be afraid to change your mind. The advantage of having notes on cards is that you can shuffle them as you wish until you find the organization that suits you best. If you have limited each card to one subject, you will not have the problem of overlapping.

When your cards are arranged correctly, the outline almost writes itself. By the way, don't try to get by without making a final ouline. A good outline is like a candle in the dark – it will guide you on your way surely and safely.

Writing the paper

As suggested in Unit 41, no one expects to write a finished paper or an article on the first try. You should, therefore, prepare a rough draft, using a combination of Notehand and longhand (by this time, you'll probably write most of the material in Notehand). From this rough draft you can make a typewritten copy. You may find that even this is not exactly what you want as final copy. If so, edit and polish it carefully and make another typewritten copy.

When you are finished, lay the paper aside for a few days (assuming you have given yourself a little time before the paper is due!) to allow your report to "age." Then read it again. You'll probably be glad you did—for it is only when you put your paper completely out of mind that you can approach it with a clear and fresh perspective. You'll be surprised to find even at this late stage that your paper contains errors in punctuation, grammar, sentence structure, and perhaps even organization. Thus a delayed final trip through the manuscript will often pay big dividends.

Form of the paper

The final form of your paper will depend upon the preferences of your instructor. Before you reach this stage you should, of course, have found out exactly the required form. Most instructors provide some kind of style sheet for guidance in preparing research papers. Some general suggestions can be given, however.

1 The typewritten paper should be double-spaced, with a minimum of one-inch margins all around. The only things that are single-spaced in the body of the paper are the verbatim quotations.

2 Provide a bibliography at the end, that is, a list of all the reference sources you have used. Include books, magazines, newspapers, pamphlets, and so on. If you have done a good job on your bibliography cards, you merely have to arrange them alphabetically and copy the information for your paper. If the bibliography is long, you may wish to group the cards by books, magazines, and pamphlets.

3 Be generous with white space. Leave plenty of space around major headings, tables, and other displayed material.

4 Use side headings liberally. The report will be much easier to read if you break up long paragraphs with apt, well-worded side headings. Be sure all headings of the same value within a section are parallel. Here is an example of nonparallelism and the same headings in parallel form:

Nonparallel: Grant as a Soldier
Grant Is Elected President

Parallel: Grant as a Soldier
Grant as a President

5 Prepare a title page. This usually includes the following:

- **a** The title of the paper (most prominent)
- **b** Your name
- **c** The course for which the paper is submitted
- **d** The name of the instructor
- **e** The date

6 A table of contents is usually in order. It need not be detailed—a listing of the major headings and their page numbers is enough.

7 Bind the report in an art-paper cover, which can be purchased at almost any school bookstore. Paste a label on the outside, giving the title of the paper and your name.

To think about and discuss

1 In what order should your note cards be arranged when you are ready to write your paper?

2 Should a final outline be made before you begin to write your report, even though you have made complete notes on cards?

3 For what kind of material is it permissible to single-space on the typewriter in your final paper?

4 Why use side headings liberally in your final report?

5 Are these side headings parallel?

- **a** Addition and Subtraction of Polynomials
- **b** Dividing Polynomials

PRINCIPLES OF NOTE**HAND**

124 **Compounds.** It is often possible to join the two parts of a compound word. Sometimes, however, it is more convenient to write the two parts of the word separately but close together.

-body

everybody **anybody** **somebody**

-thing

everything anything something

-ever

however whenever whatever

-where

everywhere anywhere somewhere

With-

within withstand without

Reading and writing practice

HE LIKED EVERYBODY

125 Intersection. Intersection, or the writing of one character through another, is sometimes useful for special phrases. Before you apply this principle, however, be sure that the expression to which you apply it occurs frequently in the writing you do.

a.m.		chamber of commerce	
p.m.		school board	
vice versa		Associated Press	

Reading and writing practice

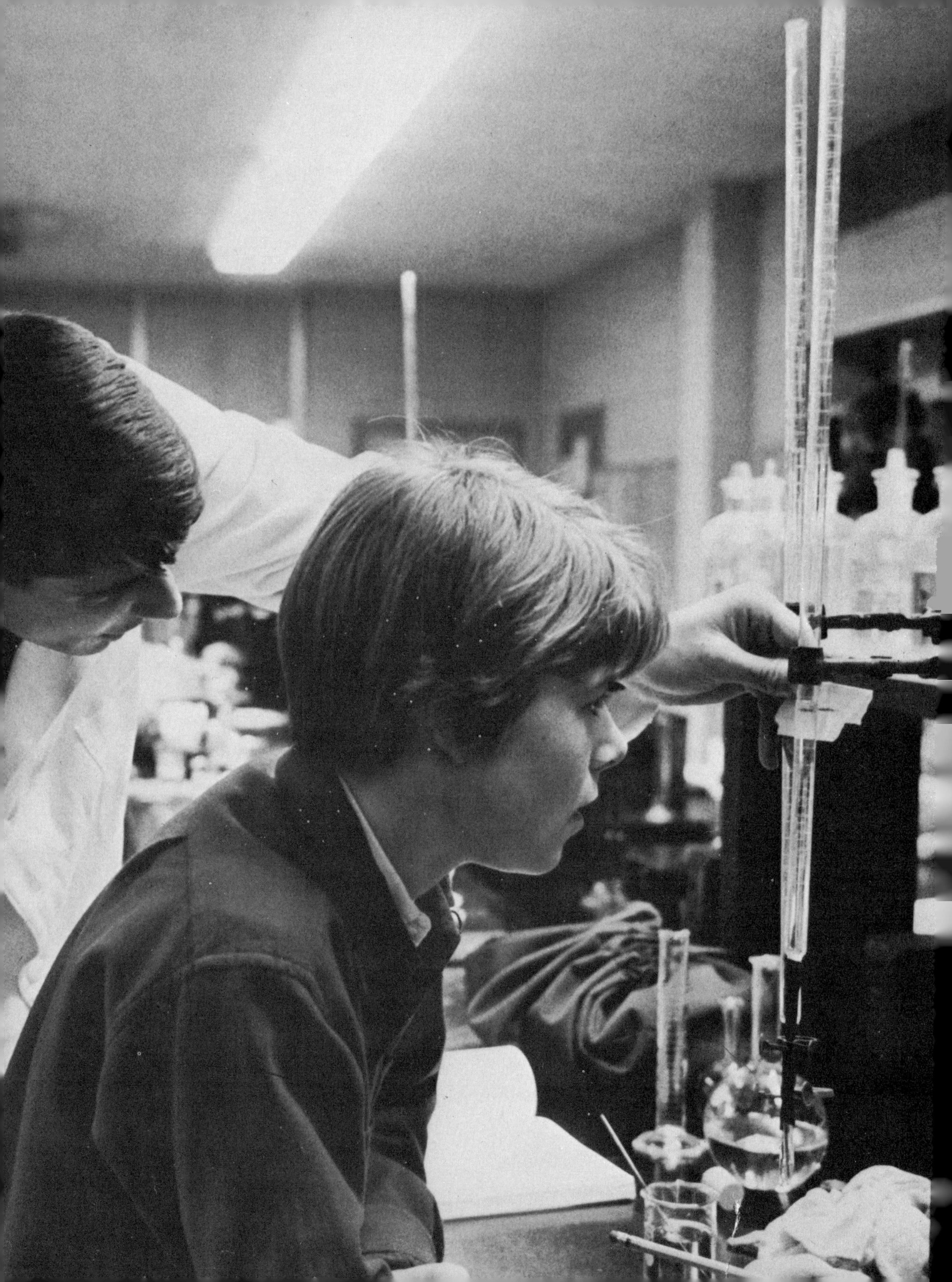

Unit 48

PRINCIPLES OF NOTEHAND

RECALL

Through the chart and Reading and Writing Practice in this unit, you will review every character and abbreviating device (except brief forms) in Notehand.

126 Recall chart. Can you read the 108 items in this chart in 7 minutes or less?

Words

1						
2						
3						
4						
5						
6						
7						
8						
9						
10						
11						
12						
13						
14						

15

16

17

18

127

Reading and writing practice

NEVER SATISFIED!

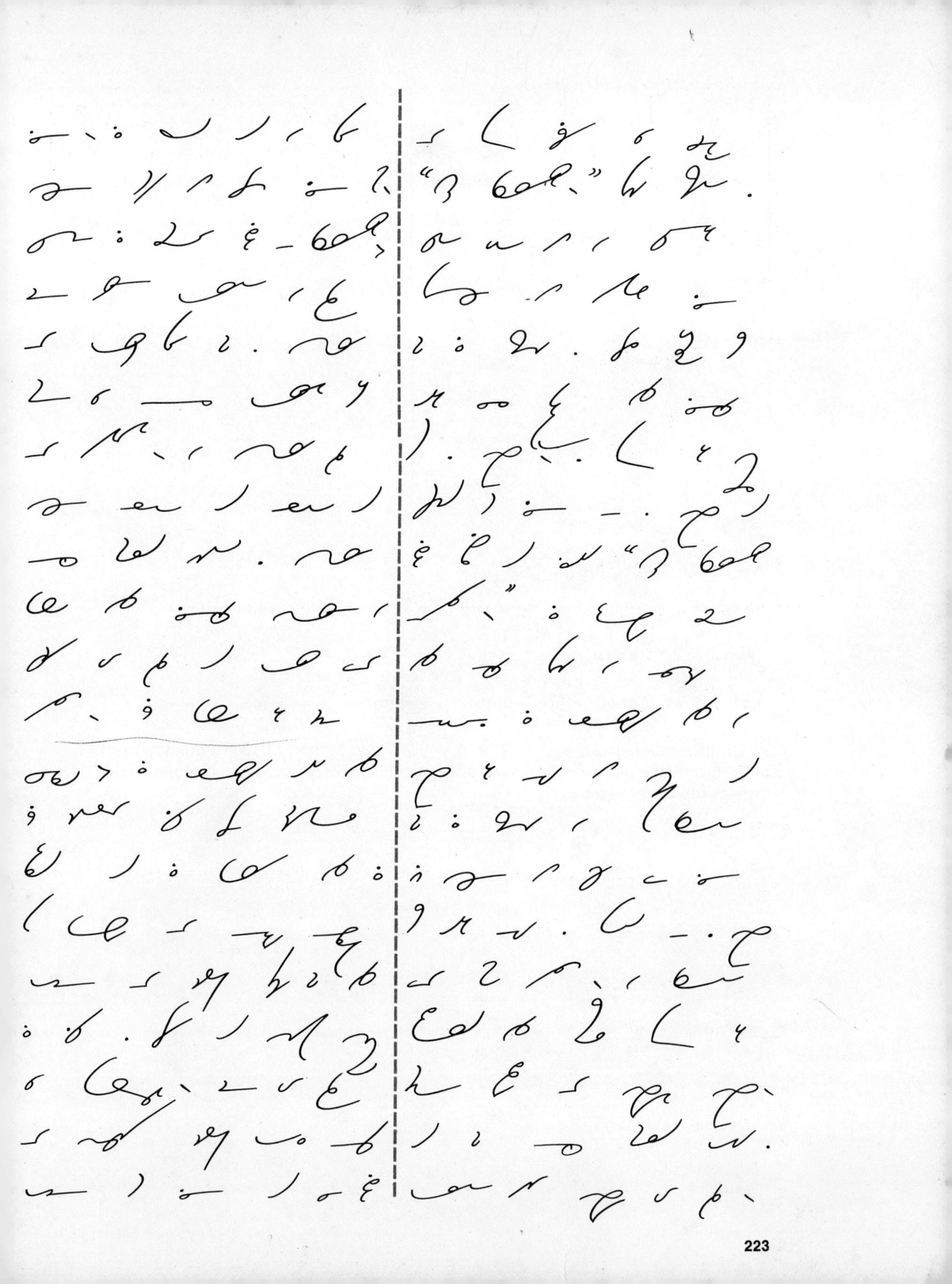

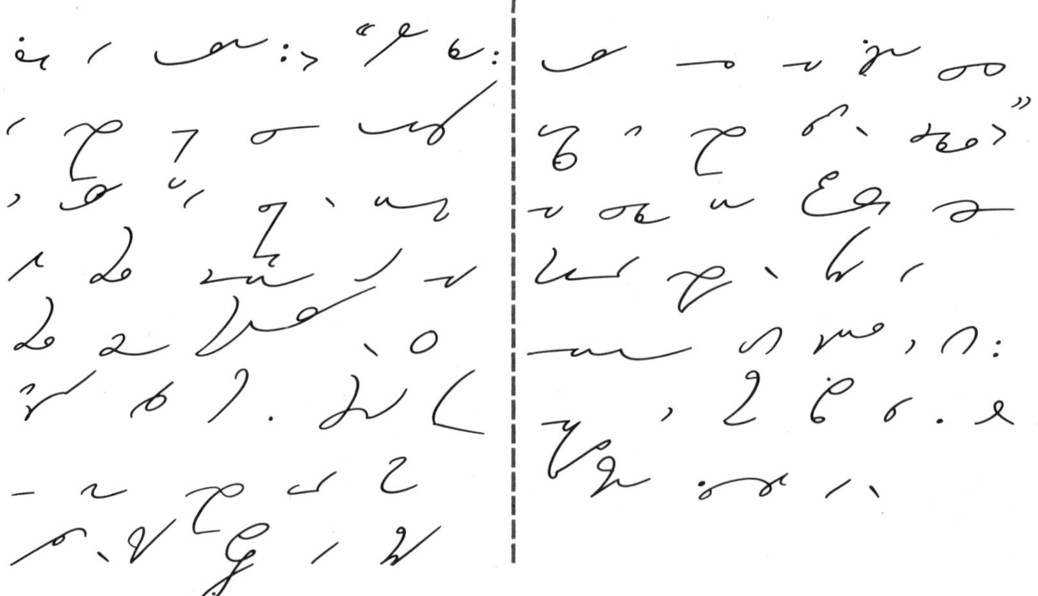

Most-used Gregg Notehand forms

Here is the final group of ten Notehand forms for frequently used words.

glad — know, no — give — go — wish

got — good — day — may — or

On the back end paper of this book you will find a chart of 100 frequently used words. From this point on turn to the chart occasionally and read through those words as rapidly as you can.

Unit 49

PRINCIPLES OF NOTEMAKING

Reviewing and preparing for examinations

Notes are virtually indispensable in reviewing and preparing for examinations. An even more permanent value of notes is that they serve as a "memory storehouse" for you. They are always available to refresh your thinking, your recall, your memory.

Using your notes in reviewing

Reviewing is an essential process in learning. We tend to forget what we learn, and reviewing is an effective means of relearning. In addition, through reviewing we often learn things that were not learned—or only partially learned—the first time.

Notes are an invaluable source of material for reviewing, whether they were made from reading a book, from a discussion, or from listening to a lecture.

Review your notes promptly

By reviewing notes promptly, you need less time to relearn and to fix previous learning. Also, notes can be "filled in," if need be, with pertinent bits of information, comments, facts, or ideas that were omitted when the notes were first made. Reviewing promptly also gives you an opportunity to change the content or organization of your notes while they are still fresh in mind. For example, a point made in the latter part of a lecture may have significant bearing on a point made in the early part of the lecture.

Reviewing promptly also helps you plan further reading and studying. A review of your notes may reveal a point on which you need additional information or a theory or a problem that you do not fully understand. You can then do something about it while there is still time.

Review your notes more than once

How often you review notes depends on the subject, how difficult it is for you, and how well you are learning it. How often you review your notes also depends on the lecturer or instructor—how well he teaches for your purposes, whether he gives unannounced quizzes, and so on. Incidentally, if unannounced quizzes are customary, you will need to review your notes more frequently.

Review your notes as frequently as you need to in order to learn well and do well in a particular learning situation. At any rate, review more than once—the first time shortly after making the notes and again before taking an examination related to the notes. It is far better to review too often than not often enough.

Review for examinations

To be effective, reviewing for examinations should be done well in advance of the examination. All too often, reviewing is put off until the last minute. Delaying review until the eleventh hour tempts you to "cram"—and cramming is never so productive as deliberate reviewing. Last-minute reviewing leads to fears and anxieties, which impair mental and physical efficiency. It interferes with the adequate sleep and rest one should have before an examination. It makes difficult, if not impossible, checking information, obtaining additional facts, and other preparations for the examination.

Recite to yourself as you review

Notes may be reviewed passively or actively. In passive review you simply "spin your wheels" and waste time. If you review notes actively, your time and effort will be productive. To review actively means to think as you review and to recite to yourself the essential information, ideas, events, facts, and formulas. For example, review a relatively short segment at a time —a section, a paragraph, or even a statement in your notes—striving to grasp the essentials, and then recite it back to yourself for fixation and mastery.

If you are reviewing your notes for the first time—which means promptly after making them—read them verbatim. It is also good to read verbatim if you are relatively unfamiliar with them, perhaps because considerable time has elapsed since you last reviewed them.

Notes should also be reviewed by skimming—running through them quickly just to pick up cues, and using the cues to recite to yourself the facts and other information related to the cues. This process will help you to organize the essentials in your own mind and relate them in the notes reviewed. It facilitates fixation and mastery of the material and the recall of what has been learned. Progressing from reviewing through verbatim reading to reviewing through cues is particularly effective in preparing for examinations.

How you review will depend on such things as your purpose, familiarity with the notes, and amount of relearning required. But all review must involve effective reciting back to produce anything in the way of learning results.

To think about and discuss

1 When should notes be reviewed? Why?

2 How many times should notes be reviewed? On what factors should your answer be based?

3 Is it best to put off reviewing notes for examinations until the evening before the examination?

4 Should notes ever be read verbatim when reviewing? If so, when?

Application

Prepare notes in informal outline form on the following.

THE MONROE DOCTRINE

On December 2, 1823, in his annual message to Congress, President Monroe announced a new foreign policy of the United States. It included these points: No European government is to establish any new colonies on the American continents. The United States will take no part in European politics and European wars except when its rights are in danger. The United States will not interfere with existing European colonies in America. But it will not permit any European country to attack a former colony that has won independence.

The foreign policy stated by Monroe is known as the Monroe Doctrine. The United States could not have enforced this policy in 1823 if England had supported the other European countries, but England stood back of the United States; as a result, the Monroe Doctrine was rarely challenged.

The Monroe Doctrine expressed a policy of independence for the Americas. In effect, it built a fence around the New World and said to the Old World: "Keep out! America is no longer an unsettled wilderness in which to plant colonies. America is free and independent. You have your own systems of kings and emperors and eternal wars. We want none of it. We have our own system of free republics that wish to live together in peace. The two systems cannot mix. We shall keep out of European affairs unless you deny us the right to trade. You, in turn, will keep out of American affairs."

NOTEHAND SKILL BUILDING

128 Word endings

-ical

1

-ful

2

-ings

3

-ingly

4

KEY

1 Periodical, physical, medical, surgical, typical, radical.
2 Painful, harmful, thoughtful, grateful, helpful, dreadful.
3 Feelings, sayings, savings, holdings, winnings, earnings, meetings.
4 Decreasingly, increasingly, exceedingly, surprisingly, willingly, knowingly.

129

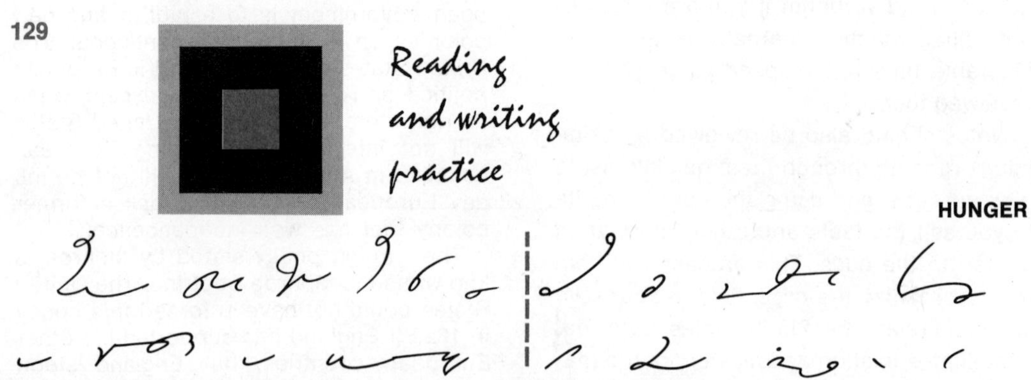

Hunger pangs

Hunger is

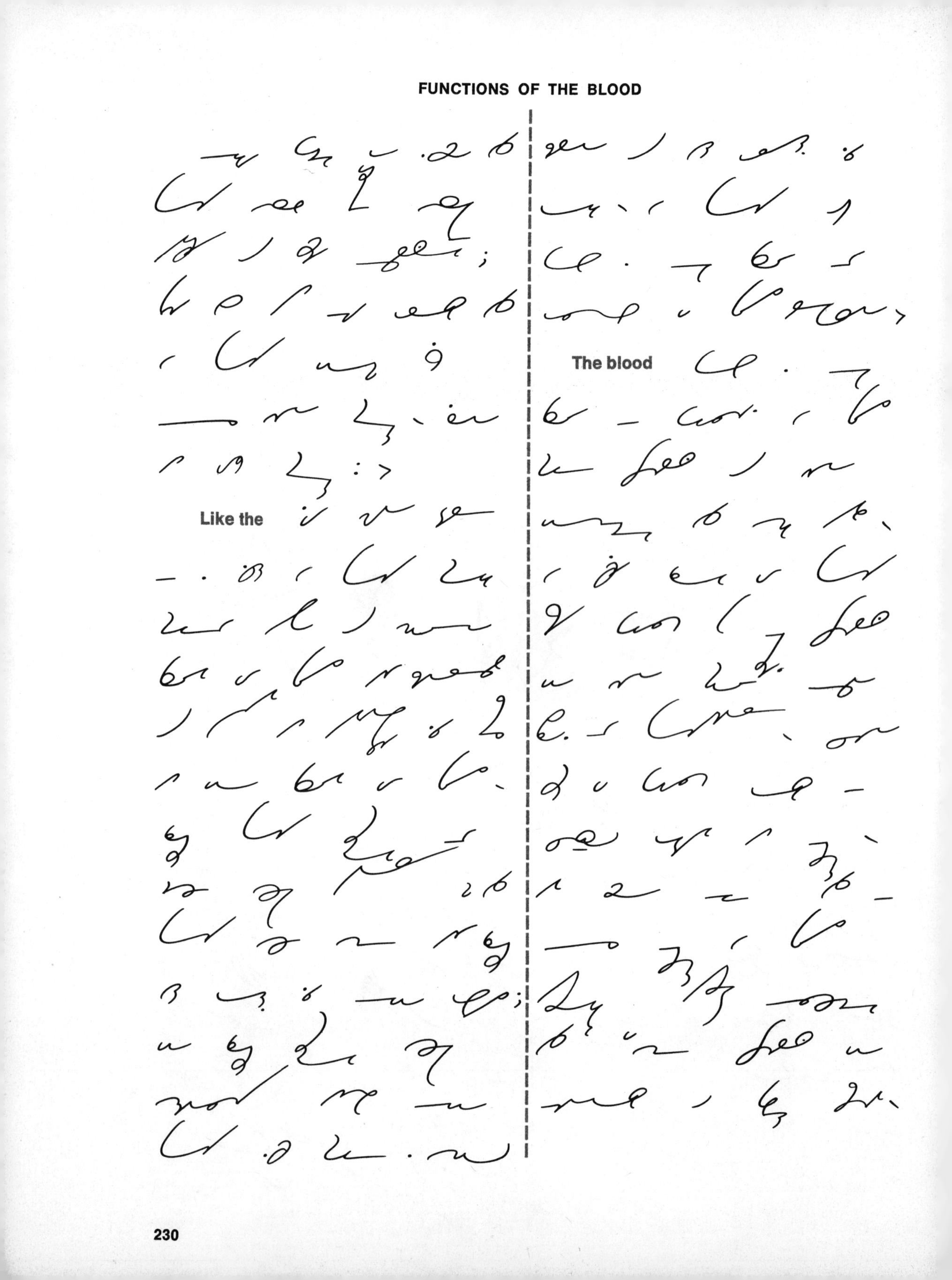

FUNCTIONS OF THE BLOOD

Like the

The blood

U.S.
CONFIDENTIAL

Unit 50

PRINCIPLES OF NOTEMAKING

Making derived notes

Making "derived" notes is a helpful technique in reviewing notes and in relearning. Derived notes are simply revised notes made from original notes. They are, in effect, condensations and summaries of notes; in some cases, they may be a reorganization of notes as well. Derived notes may bring together notes from several sources, such as notes from lectures, from textbook reading, from discussions, and from supplementary reading—all on the same topic.

The purpose of derived notes is to make original notes more useful. For example, suppose you have made a set of notes in biology and you wish to use your original notes to prepare a table comparing all the major divisions of the animal kingdom (the phyla). Your derived notes might resemble the example shown on page 233.

Or suppose you are taking a course in American history, and your instructor does not discuss the events of a particular episode or period in chronological order. You might make derived notes from your original notes by preparing a table or a list of the events in chronological order.

Derived notes can be helpful in reviewing as well as in preparing new notes. Preparing derived notes is, in effect, a reviewing process. In addition, derived notes themselves provide a source of material for reviewing. They are condensations and summaries of cues or reorganizations of cues.

Derived notes may be used effectively in recalling and reciting to yourself the more detailed essentials that appear in the original notes. If you cannot readily recall the details, however, be sure to review the original notes.

The quality of derived notes depends almost entirely on the quality of the original notes. If the original notes were carefully recorded, many good derived notes can be made.

Special notes for reviewing

Some subjects lend themselves to special kinds or forms of notes for review and recall. An example of such special notes are vocabulary cards for a foreign language. To prepare a vocabulary card, simply write the foreign word or phrase on one side and the translation in English on the other. You can then use these cards easily and in different sequence for review and recall. Look at the word on one side of the card and try to remember the translation of the word. Check yourself for accuracy by reversing the card if necessary.

This special form of notes can be applied to chemical formulas, structures, names, dates, laws, and so on.

To think about and discuss

1 What are derived notes? What is their purpose?

2 On what does the quality of derived notes primarily depend?

3 For what subjects are "vocabulary-type" cards used?

Application

Assume that you have made rough notes on the federal court system as follows. Organize the information on a large card (or half a sheet of note paper) in such a way that you can use it for quick review.

There are 9 types of courts in the federal court system. In the order of importance, they are:
Supreme Court. There is only 1 Supreme Court and there are 9 judges. Its principal duty is to hear final appeals of major cases only.
Courts of Appeals. Formerly called circuit courts. There are 11 such courts with 75 judges. Their principal duties are to take care of routine appeals from lower federal courts and administrative tribunals.
District Courts. This is the principal trial court in cases of federal jurisdiction. There are 91 district courts with 311 judges.
Tax Court. This court tries cases involving disputes on taxes owed the United States. There's only 1, but it has 16 judges.
Military Court of Appeals. There is 1 such court (3 judges) and it hears appeals from general courts-martial.
Territorial Courts. These are located in American territories. There are 4 of them with 4 judges. They are trial courts.
Claims Courts. There is just 1, and it handles claims for damages against the United States. There are 5 judges.
Customs and Patent Appeals Court. This court (1) hears appeals on customs and patents disputes. It has 5 judges.
Customs Court. This court tries cases involving customs duties only (9 judges).

Hint: Head your card "The Federal Court System" and provide four columns: *Court, Number, Judges, Principal Duties.*

Major Divisions c Animal Kingdom

Phylum (kind c animal)	Germ Layers	Digestive System	Other Characteristics
Protozoa	Doesn't Co (single cell)	Within cell	Single celled organisms
Porifera	2 layers	Special cells (within cell)	Canal s—
Coelenterata	2 layers	Cavity	Radial symmetry
Ctenophora	3 layers	Cavity	Biradial symmetry

NOTEHAND SKILL BUILDING

130 **Blends**

Ses

1

Ted

2

Tain

3

Ten

4

Md

5

KEY

1 Systems, cases, forces, offenses, consists, offices, courses, resources.
2 Committed, adopted, created, treated, stated, permitted.
3 Retained, maintained, contained, ascertained, detained, pertained.
4 Extend, intend, continent, sentences, contents, intense, tender.
5 Armed, blamed, framed, claimed, exclaimed.

131

Reading and writing practice

MILITARY JUSTICE

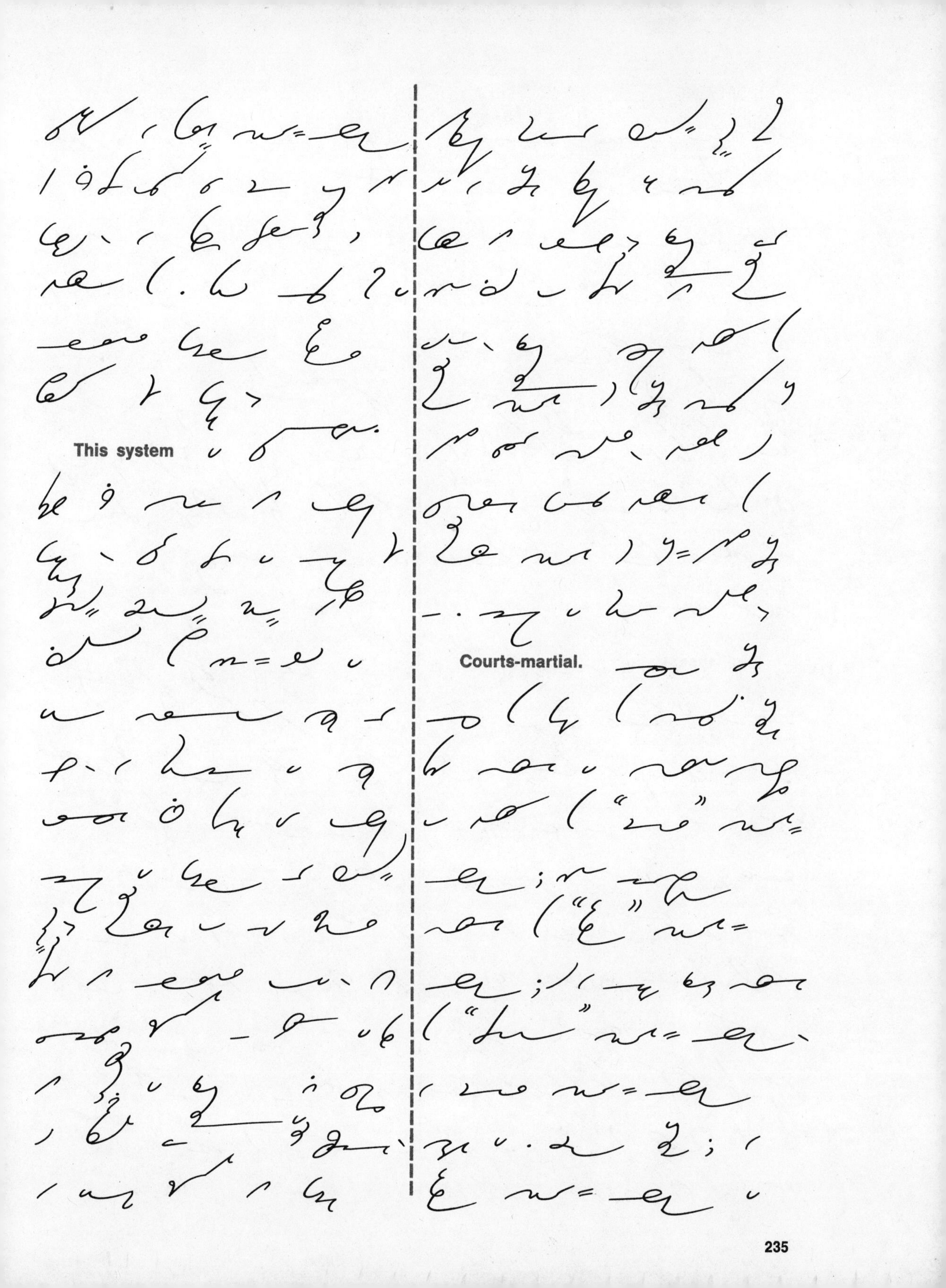

This system

Courts-martial.

Final appeal

The bulk

Unit 51

PRINCIPLES OF NOTEMAKING

Making notes of class discussions

Most class meetings include discussions during which class members exchange facts, ideas, and opinions about the subject under consideration. Many advanced courses are in the form of seminars or workshops in which there is no formal lecture. Instead, the class consists entirely of a free exchange of information and opinions gathered from reading, observation, and research.

In class discussions your primary concern is to pay close attention to what is going on and to participate actively in the discussion. In addition to participating, you should also make notes on the major points covered.

Participation is so important that if you find it impossible to make notes and take part in the discussion at the same time, you should let the notes go. Actually, however, if you are fairly skillful in Gregg Notehand and observe the rules for good notemaking, you won't find it too difficult to do both.

When you are participating in a general discussion and making notes at the same time, your notes will usually be of two types: (1) notes about what others are saying and (2) notes to yourself. For example, someone may make a statement that you do not agree with, that you believe to be incorrect, or that you wish to enlarge on later. While you are making notes from the participant's remarks, you are also making brief notes to yourself to remind you what you want to say when he has finished. Suppose you are engaged in a discussion of federal aid to education. On page 238 is an example of how your notes might appear.

Notice in the example that the notemaker has allowed a very wide left margin for notes to himself. For such notes you might use a different color from that of your regular notes, as in the illustration.

The notes in the illustration are summary statements of the remarks of the participants. In a typical class discussion, it is difficult—if not impossible—to make your notes in true outline form, since the subjects, the points of view, and the appropriateness of the remarks vary widely. It is best, therefore, to organize your notes according to the identity of the participants, as in the illustration. Of course, sometimes their remarks may lend themselves to an outline form. Observe in the illustration, for example, the notes made from Mary L's remarks.

If you will study carefully the notes illustrated, you will see that some of the most important aspects of the subject of federal

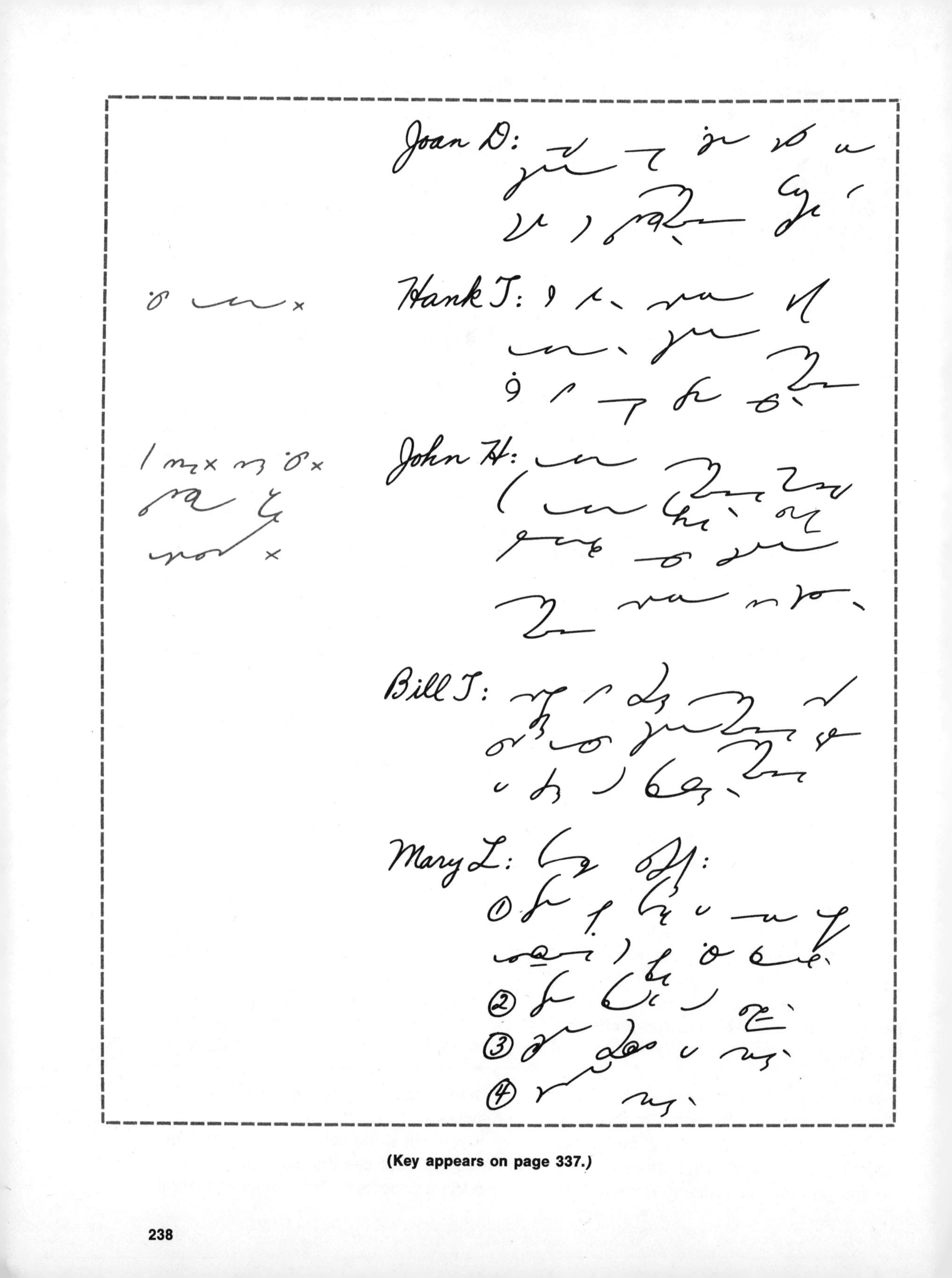

Joan D:

Hank T:

John H:

Bill T:

Mary L:

(1)

(2)

(3)

(4)

(Key appears on page 337.)

aid to education are covered. Ideas do not have to come from textbooks or from a lecture to be important!

This is only one form, of course, in which discussion notes may be made. The form isn't too important. What is important is that notes of some type be made.

Using your notes

You should review notes made from discussion as promptly as possible after the discussion, especially in view of the difficulty of organizing your notes as you make them. If you wait too long, you may not be able to make sense out of your fragmentary jottings, particularly if you are trying to write and participate at the same time. Reorganize your notes as you review, putting them in a form that will be most helpful and usable. Of course, the reorganization should tie in as closely as possible with the notes you have made from lectures or reading to which the class discussion is related. Reorganizing discussion notes is a valuable learning experience in itself. Your reorganized notes on the discussion of federal aid to education might appear as shown below.

To think about and discuss

1 If you find that you are not able to participate in a class discussion and take notes at the same time, which should take precedence?

2 What two types of notes are made in general class discussions?

```
                 F E D E R A L   A I D   T O   E D U C A T I O N
ADVANTAGES

     1. Would provide more nearly equal opportunity for all pupils,
        regardless of individual community wealth
     2. Would probably result in better education
          a. Better facilities
          b. Better teaching
               (1) Higher salaries for teachers
               (2) More rigid teaching requirements
          c. Standardized courses for pupils as well as for teacher
             training
             (Questionable as an advantage)
     3. Probably get more for each dollar spent

DISADVANTAGES

     1. Individual communities might lose interest ("let the
        government do it")
     2. Government control encourages bureaucracy -- "red tape"
     3. Might become "political football" (System of checks and
        balances might prevent this)
```

NOTEHAND SKILL BUILDING

132 **Word families**

-ct

1

-ound

2

-or

3

-en

4

KEY

1 Act, fact, tact, exact, contact, contract, attract.
2 Found, sound, pound, ground, round, around, bound.
3 More, store, floor, door, nor, core, tore.
4 Often, even, oven, woven, driven, given, frozen, forgiven, uneven.

133

Reading and writing practice

IMPROVING YOUR VOCABULARY

1 Read.

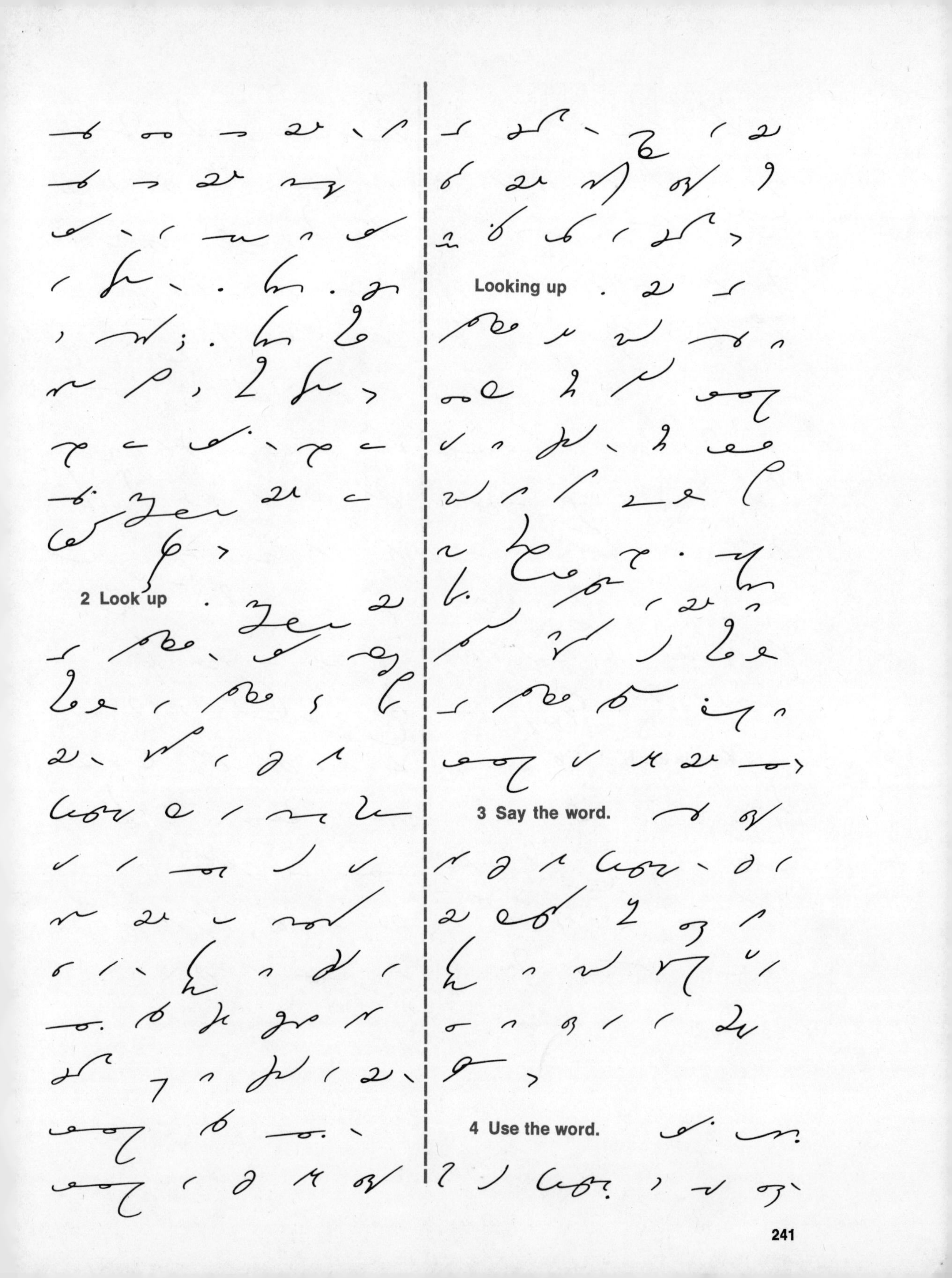

2 Look up

Looking up

3 Say the word.

4 Use the word.

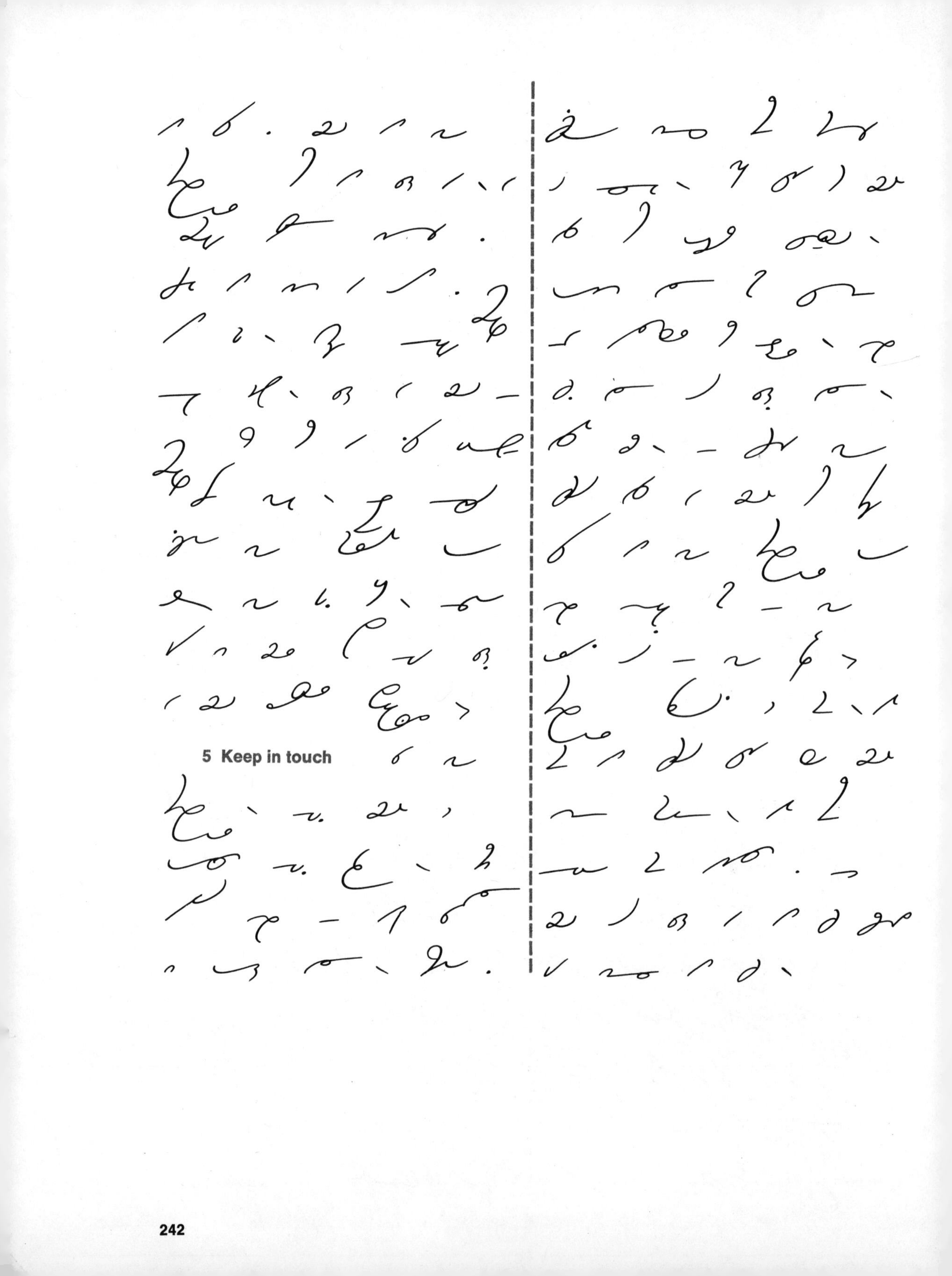

5 Keep in touch

Unit 52

PRINCIPLES OF NOTEMAKING

Making notes of other meetings and discussions

In addition to class discussions, you will attend many other types of meetings in which you can use notemaking to good advantage. If you belong to a club or organization that holds regular meetings, there are frequent discussions of important ideas, suggestions, and business matters. In business you will perhaps be a member of one or more permanent committees—the advertising committee, the research committee, the forms control committee, and so on. Teachers, engineers, doctors, lawyers, and others attend many conferences and committee meetings related to their professions. As an ordinary citizen, you will attend meetings of civic organizations, church groups, parents' committees, and social clubs. Good notemaking skill comes in handy in such meetings and conferences, and the suggestions offered in the previous unit apply here.

If you are recording secretary of any of these groups—in which case your notes must be converted into minutes—notemaking becomes a must.

NOTEHAND SKILL BUILDING

134 Word families

-ther

1

-age

2

Al-

3

Out-

4

-self

5

KEY

1 Whether, other, brother, mother, another, together, either.
2 Cottage, baggage, luggage, storage, marriage, village, message.
3 All, almost, also, already, although, always.
4 Out, output, outside, outlay, outlast, outlet, outline.
5 Self, himself, yourself, myself, herself, itself.

135

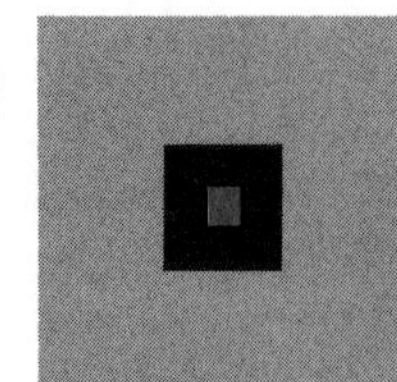

Reading and writing practice

A DISSERTATION UPON ROAST PIG

70,000

Ho-ti

The truth

The upshot

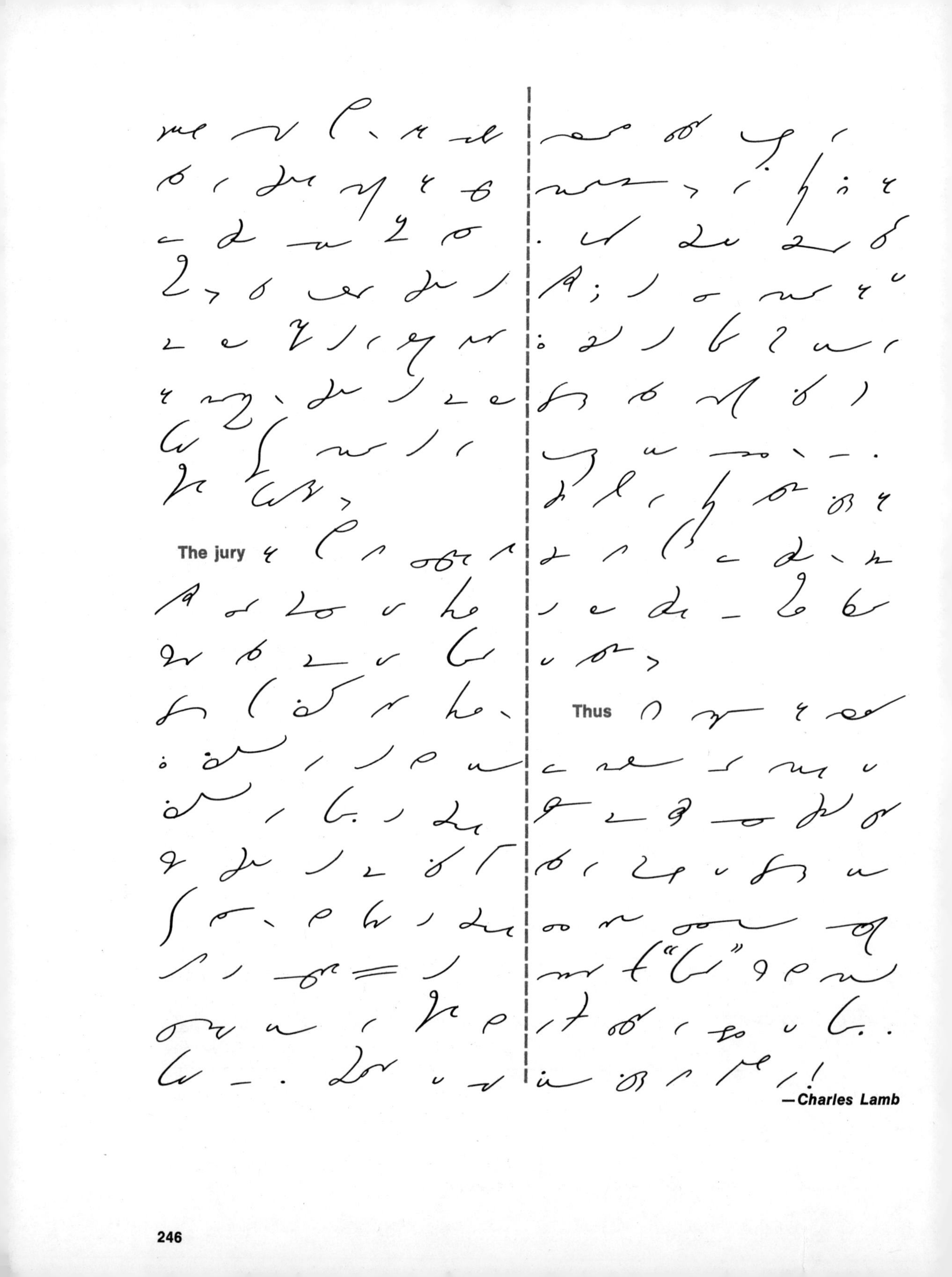

The jury

Thus

—Charles Lamb

Unit 53

PRINCIPLES OF NOTEMAKING

Making notes as a recorder

Notes that will result in official records of your group must accurately interpret the proceedings, sifting the unimportant from the important. Some suggestions for making notes as a recorder are given in the following paragraphs.

Identify the participants

It is usually essential for the recorder to identify the participants in a discussion because in the minutes they are often given credit for their ideas and proposals. Correctly identifying all the participants in a discussion group is simple if the group is small and you know all the members. You can identify each speaker merely by using his initials. If the meeting consists primarily of a report from each individual, you may place his initials at the top of your notes, recording his comments directly underneath, like this:

JRG

Key: 1. Quantity of questionnaire returns not so important as quality. 2. Questionnaire forms should leave plenty of room for personal comments—not merely checking off objective statements.

If, on the other hand, it is a free-for-all discussion where you never know who is going to speak next and when he is going to be interrupted, it is better to place the initials at the side (such as in the example on page 238), as is done in identifying the characters in the script of a play.

Make verbatim notes for motions and resolutions only

Except for motions, resolutions, and similar formal statements, the notemaker should not attempt to record verbatim what is said in discussion meetings. His responsibility is to record the major ideas and proposals discussed. Gregg Notehand is not designed for verbatim recording where ideas fly thick and fast. But it does provide the recorder with an excellent means for noting essential points.

Make use of the agenda

In some cases, an agenda (list of the topics to be discussed) is prepared and distributed to the members a few days before the meeting. This agenda will be an important guide to your notemaking. If the items in the agenda are numbered, your notes can merely refer to the number rather than repeat the subject. Some meetings are tightly run, never deviating from the agenda, and the problem of identifying the subject is solved for the notemaker. In other meetings the agenda is used only as a point of departure, and the meeting is allowed to develop into free-for-all discussions that range far and wide. In this case it is best to repeat the subject matter you are reporting, even though it may appear on the agenda.

Indicate time, place, and other details

Be sure to record the date, time, and place of the meeting. Also, indicate who presided, who was present, who was absent, correct name and title of the speaker (if any), and so on. These details will be needed when you are ready to type up your notes in the form of minutes.

Verify important points

Sometimes the recorder is given an opportunity at the time or later to verify the wording of a particular resolution or motion; if not, he should check his notes with one or more of the other officers after the meeting is over, since he must record such items verbatim.

To think about and discuss

1 In what two ways may participants be identified in your notes in a discussion? Under what conditions is each method used?

2 Under what circumstances are verbatim notes made in a discussion meeting?

3 What is an agenda? How can it be useful in making notes of meetings?

Application

Transcribe the comments on page 249 made at a meeting of the Senior Trip Committee. A McF is in charge of transportation and RW is in charge of housing.

The key to the notes is on page 339.

NOTEHAND SKILL BUILDING

136 Word families

-lize

1

-er

2

a McF	RW
1. etc.	1. Wash $6
2. etc.	2.
3. 7:30	3.
4. Wash	4.

-ory

3

-cated

4

-est

5

KEY

1 Capitalize, realize, analyze, centralize, generalize.
2 Ladder, batter, reader, matter, greater, leader.
3 History, factory, victory, memory, territory, inventory, advisory.
4 Located, educated, complicated, confiscated, dedicated.
5 Nearest, greatest, loudest, hardest, kindest, longest.

137

Reading and writing practice

THE LITTLE THINGS

YESTERDAY AND TOMORROW

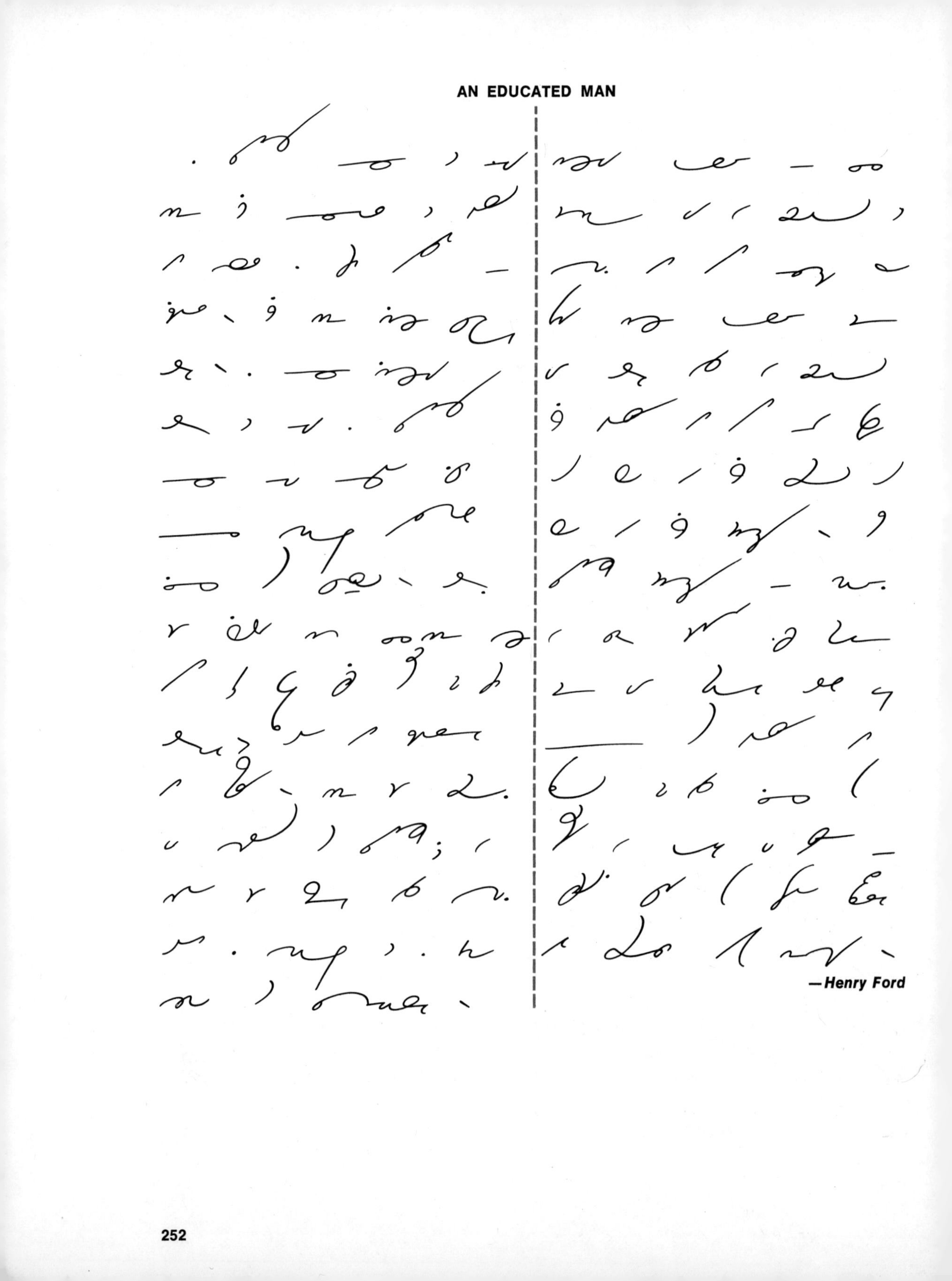

AN EDUCATED MAN

—Henry Ford

Unit 54

PRINCIPLES OF NOTEMAKING

Writing the minutes

The notes of a meeting should be written up as promptly as possible after the meeting ends. The longer you wait, the more difficult it is to make corrections or to decide what is meant by a passage that is difficult to interpret. Read through all of your notes carefully before proceeding to type them; you may even find it desirable to make an outline before you begin to write. Check for any additional facts that are needed for making the report—information that was to be obtained or things that were to be done. Then make a rough draft of your report, using Gregg Notehand (see Unit 41). Finally, type it in final form and distribute it to everyone who should receive a copy.

Do not destroy your notes until the minutes have been approved. This approval is usually given at the next meeting, at which the minutes are read.

An illustration of minutes of a meeting is shown on page 254. Some minutes are much longer, depending on the amount of business transacted. It is a good idea, however, to keep your minutes as short as possible—recording only the essential points and no more.

To think about and discuss

1 When should the notes of a meeting be written up? Why?

2 Describe the steps to be followed in writing up the minutes of a meeting.

3 How long should your notes of a meeting be retained?

NOTEHAND SKILL BUILDING

138 Phrases

The

1

POLITICAL SCIENCE CLUB

MINUTES OF MEETING, APRIL 3, 19--

Time and Place	The regular meeting of the Political Science Club was called to order by the President, John Updyke, on Wednesday, April 3, 19--, in the Chinese Room of the Student Union Building. All 32 members were present.
Minutes	The minutes of the March meeting were read by the Secretary, Mary Jo Juleson, and were approved.
	The report of the Nominating Committee was given by the Chairman, Pauline Glass. A slate of nominees for next year's offices is to be presented at the May meeting.
Committee Reports	The report of the Education Committee was given by the Chairman, Price Logan. News articles about the activities of the club have appeared in three recent issues of the Aggie Daily and the January issue of "Aggievator." The club has been invited to continue its 15-minute radio program next year over WAGI on "Our Political Heritage." This program has received wide attention and has generated a great deal of interest among students in the club's activities.
Old Business	The question of whether dues to the club should be increased was brought up for further discussion. It was moved, seconded, and passed THAT DUES FOR THE COMING YEAR REMAIN THE SAME AS THE CURRENT YEAR AND THAT A SPECIAL ASSESSMENT BE PERMITTED IF NECESSARY.
New Business	After a discussion about the possibility of having a picnic in place of the June meeting (the last of the year), a committee consisting of Harry Longman, Eileen Warren, and Jim Pogue was appointed to report at the next meeting.
	The following resolution was presented and approved:
	WHEREAS, Professor Ralph Thomassen has, for the past three years, been faculty sponsor of the Political Science Club, and whereas Professor Thomassen is leaving to accept an important administrative position in another college, this club desires to incorporate the following resolution in the minutes:
Resolution	RESOLVED, That we recognize the excellent, energetic, and intelligent leadership and service that Professor Thomassen has rendered to the Political Science Club. We feel that the accomplishments of the club have been attained largely because of his earnest efforts and untiring devotion.
	RESOLVED FURTHER, that in recognition of his service to the club, Professor Thomassen be elected Honorary Lifetime Member of the Political Science Club of Midwestern College.

Respectfully submitted,

Mary Jo Juleson

Mary Jo Juleson, Secretary

He

2 [shorthand]

I

3 [shorthand]

To

4 [shorthand]

Should

5 [shorthand]

KEY

1 Of the, in the, at the, on the, from the, with the, for the, is the, as the.
2 He is, he may, he was, he should, he did, he could, he might, he will.
3 I shall, I will, I have, I am, I said, I would, I know, I could.
4 To the, to it, to that, to talk, to go, to try, to take, to you.
5 He should, I should, you should, you should be, I should have, I should like, I should say, he should be.

139

Reading and writing practice

PROFIT

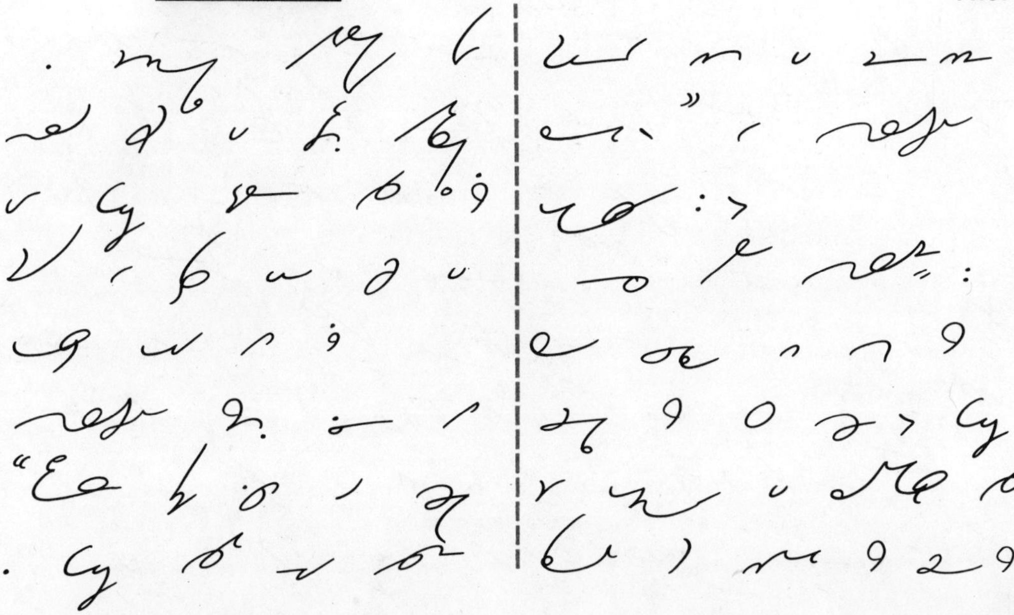

[shorthand]

Our primitive

He will

50

This 100th

The enterpriser

(Concluded in Paragraph 141)

Unit 55

PRINCIPLES OF NOTEMAKING

Indexing your notes

The careful student may want to make an index to his notebooks. Sometimes a partial table of contents, showing the more important items, will be as useful as an index, and it has the advantage of being quicker and easier to make. A helpful table of contents may be made during the making of the notes—even with lecture notes.

If you plan to have a table of contents or an index for your notes, leave a few blank pages at the beginning of each subject. As the course proceeds, you will gradually establish some headings in the table of contents or index on these blank pages. If it is to be a partial index, you will want to spread the entries out to permit the insertion of subheadings under the main headings and to permit the addition of new main headings in alphabetical order.

For instance, if the course is on the Elizabethan period of English history, your index would have main headings for Essex, Burleigh, Drake, and so on (as illustrated on page 259). As important facts about any of these people appear in the lectures, appropriate subheadings would be added. During the lecture you might have time only to insert the page number on which the material appears in the notes, leaving the remainder of the line blank in the index, to be filled in later. Usually, however, there will be time for a hasty Gregg Notehand indication of the nature of the material on the page indicated. For example, under the main heading Essex, the last entry might be simply the page number and one word in Gregg Notehand, *execution.*

With the help of even the simplest index of this kind, you could find in a matter of seconds your notes on the execution of Essex—even if you have a hundred pages of notes. Otherwise, you might have to spend five or ten minutes rummaging through the notes.

A table of contents is even less trouble to prepare, although it is somewhat less helpful than the simplest index. For the table of contents, you need only put the date of each lecture and the page reference on the next blank line of the page left for that purpose at the beginning of your notebook. Then, during or after the lecture, you can write a brief note in Gregg Notehand under the date. Then, instead of rummaging through many pages of notes, you need only run quickly through the table of contents to find the reference to the numbered page in the body of the notes.

259

Table of Contents

Oct.		page
5	Henry 8 Edward 6	4
7	Mary	6
9		8
12	E	9
14	Mary	12
16	Netherlands	15
19	Mary	17
21	Armada 1588	19
23		23

This is a table of contents for a series of college lectures on Elizabethan history, with lectures three times a week.

260

Index

Burleigh
8
Mary's

Drake
18 Cadiz
20 Armada

Elizabeth
6 accession
8
9
12 Mary
15 Netherlands
19 Armada

Essex
24 Irish expedition
29

Leicester
9
18 Netherlands

Mary Eng
5

This is the first page of a running index for the same course in Elizabethan history for which the table of contents above was made. If the next entry were for Frobisher's search for the Northwest Passage, the entry would be made between the present entry for Essex and Leicester, to preserve the alphabetical order.

To think about and discuss

1 Of what value is an index to your notes?

2 Which is preferable—an index or a table of contents to notes? How do they differ?

Application

Study the table of contents and index on page 259. (The key for these pages is on 341.)

NOTEHAND SKILL BUILDING

140 Word families

-tive

1 [shorthand]

-ser, -cer

2 [shorthand]

-vent

3 [shorthand]

Out-

4 [shorthand]

KEY

1 Relative, primitive, active, positive, incentive, creative, effective.
2 Enterpriser, miser, tracer, eraser, closer, grocer, dancer.
3 Vent, event, prevent, invent, convent, solvent, insolvent, eventual.
4 Outlay, outline, output, outside, outward, outright, without.

141

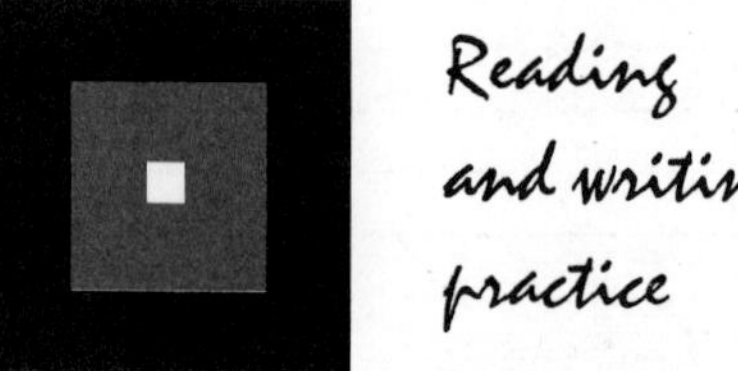

Reading and writing practice

PROFIT (*Concluded*)

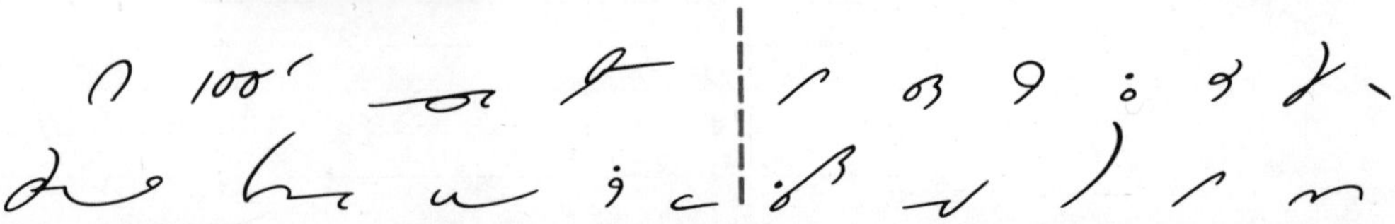

[shorthand]

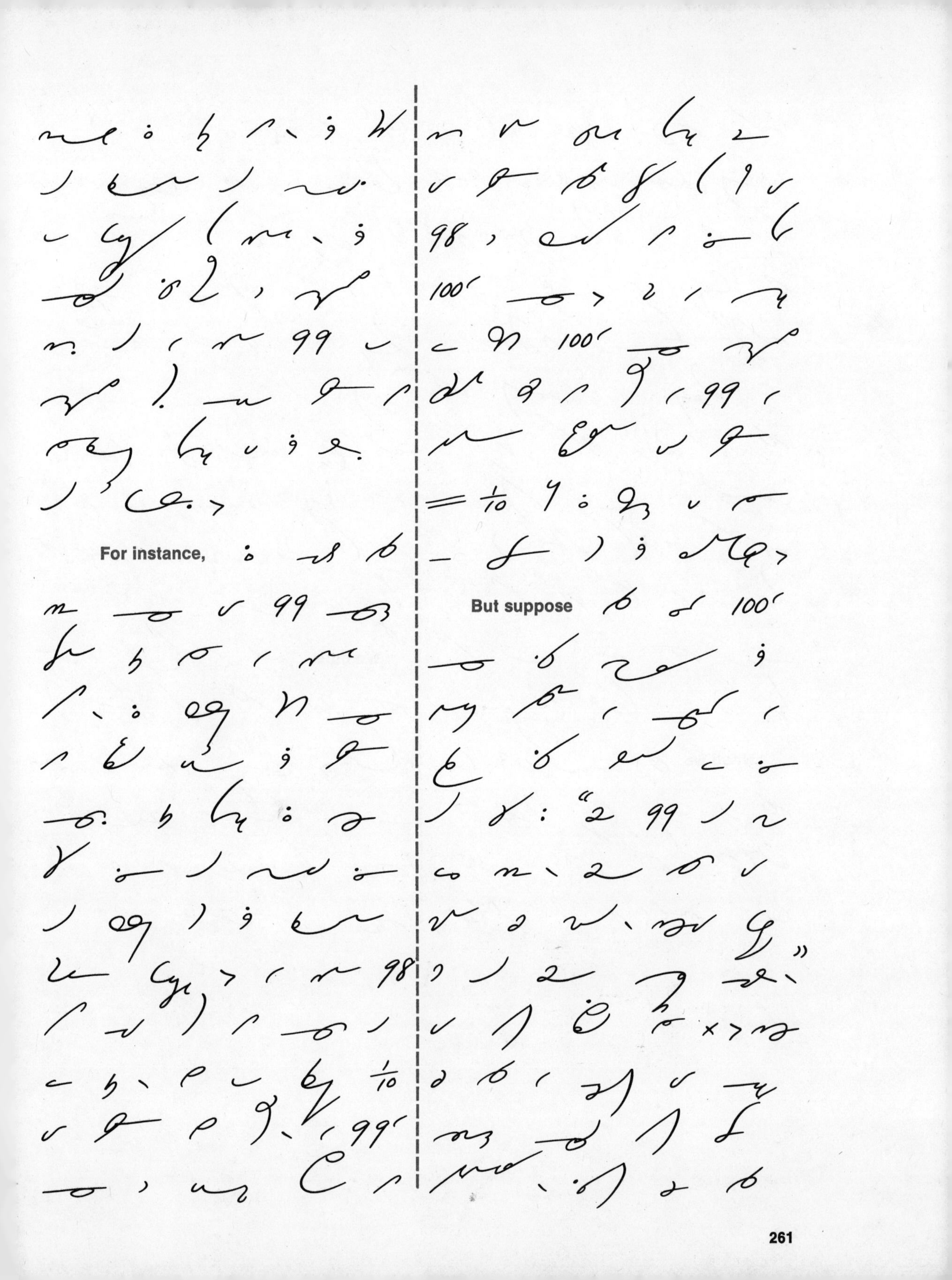

For instance,

But suppose

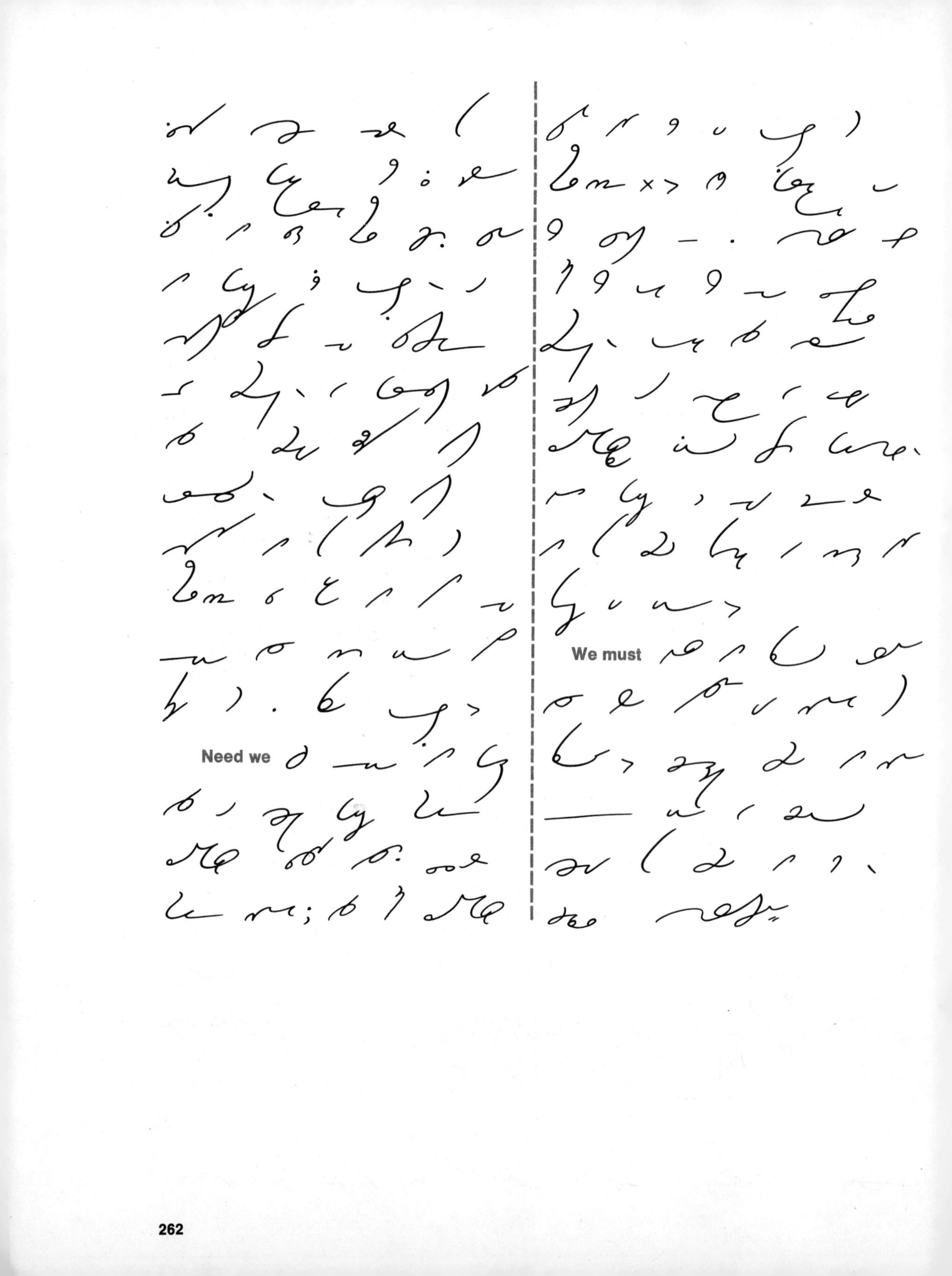

Need we

We must

Unit 56

PRINCIPLES OF NOTEMAKING

Disposition of your notes

Whether you should keep or discard your notes after they have served their immediate purpose, such as completing a course, depends upon what the notes cover, how complete they are, how important they are, how likely it is that you may want them in the future, how difficult it would be to replace them, and so on. It is a good policy to keep notes for a reasonable period of time. You may wish to refer to them soon after they have served your immediate purposes. They may contain information that would be helpful to you—information that would otherwise be difficult to obtain.

In doing advanced work you will find it helpful to be able to refer to previous notes for information and explanations. Courses in science and mathematics are examples of subjects that involve a progressive sequence of subject matter. Sometimes the lapse of time between one course and another may be considerable—as, for example, when a graduate student needs to refer to notes he made in undergraduate courses. Thus, notes often have value long after they were made.

Notes should be properly identified (labeled) and stored in a suitable and accessible place, preferably not far from the place where one studies. The notes should be arranged according to the subjects to which they pertain.

To think about and discuss

1 Should notes ever be retained for future use? How might they prove valuable?

2 Where should notes be stored?

3 How should you arrange your notes for future use?

NOTEHAND SKILL BUILDING

142 Disjoined word endings

-cal, -cle

1 [shorthand]

-lity

2

-ings

3

-rity

4

-ward

5

KEY

1 Technical, medical, mechanical, vertical, particle, article.
2 Locality, facility, ability, quality, personality, possibility.
3 Proceedings, meetings, hearings, ratings, mornings, openings, feelings.
4 Sincerity, majority, minority, priority, clarity, authorities, security.
5 Outward, inward, onward, backward, upward, forward, reward, rewarded.

143

Reading and writing practice

JUST-A-LITTLE-LATE CLUB

"Never

Lord Nelson

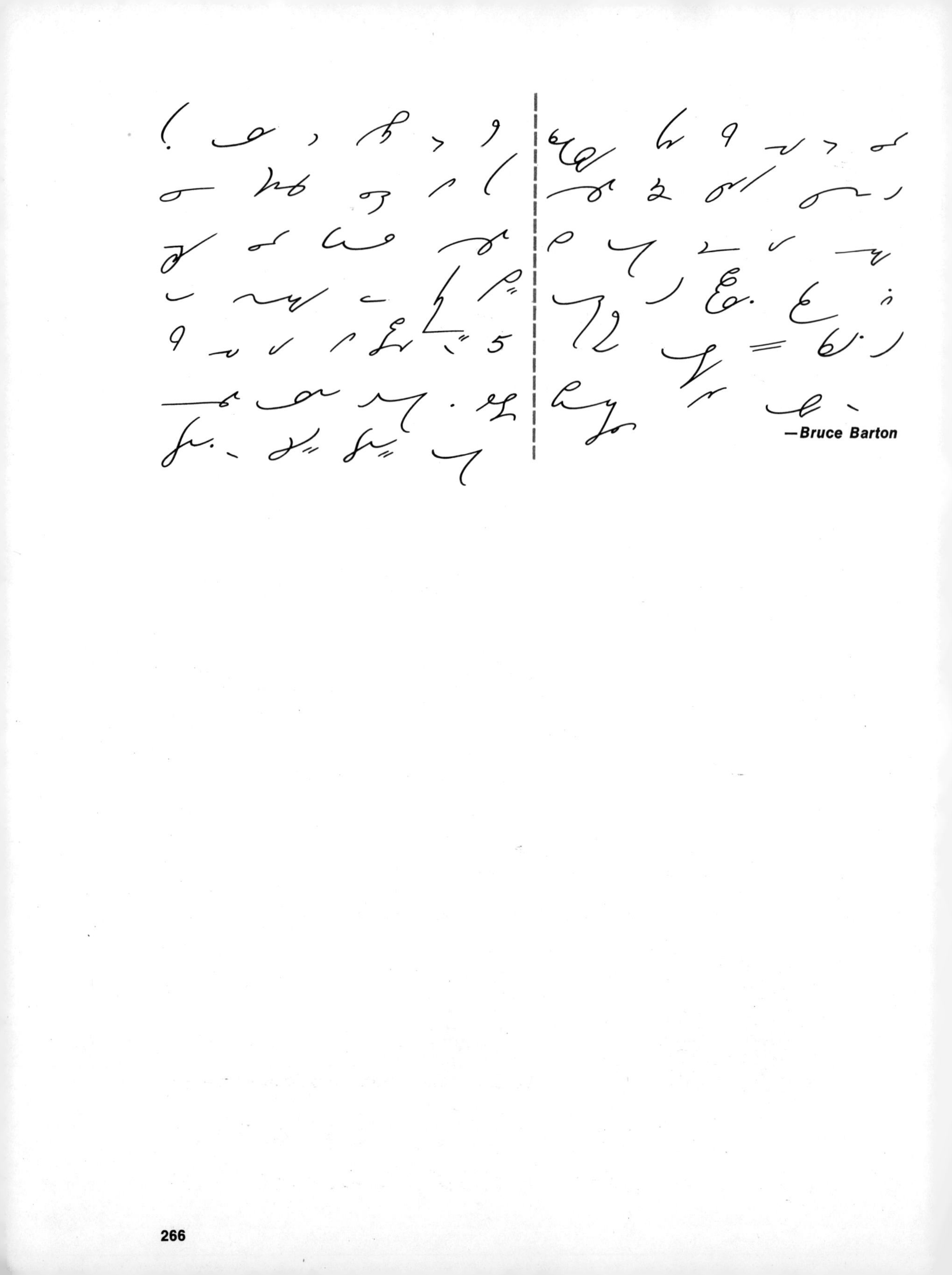

—Bruce Barton

Unit 57

NOTEHAND SKILL BUILDING

144 **Word families**

-long

1

-port

2

-ial

3

-tment

4

KEY

1 Long, belong, along, prolong, lifelong, longer.
2 Import, export, report, comport, deport, support, supported.
3 Industrial, material, editorial, memorial.
4 Adjustment, assortment, investment, readjustment, apartment, department.

145

Reading and writing practice

WESTERN EUROPE AND POSTWAR PROSPERITY

For several

Today,

Competition

British products

Unit 58

NOTEHAND SKILL BUILDING

146 Word families

-ish

1 

-ern

2 

-tional

3 

-ulation

4 

KEY

1 British, English, accomplish, finish, abolish, punish, astonished.
2 Western, eastern, southern, pattern, turn, modern.
3 Educational, national, vocational, traditional, sectional.
4 Circulation, population, stimulation, tabulation, stipulation.

147 *Reading and writing practice*

THE ENGLISH LANGUAGE

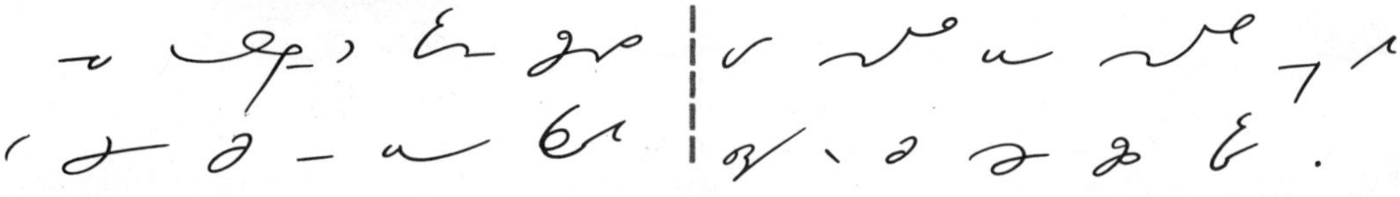

There are

Actually

People's

Many young

Unit 59

NOTEHAND SKILL BUILDING

148 Word families

Per-

1 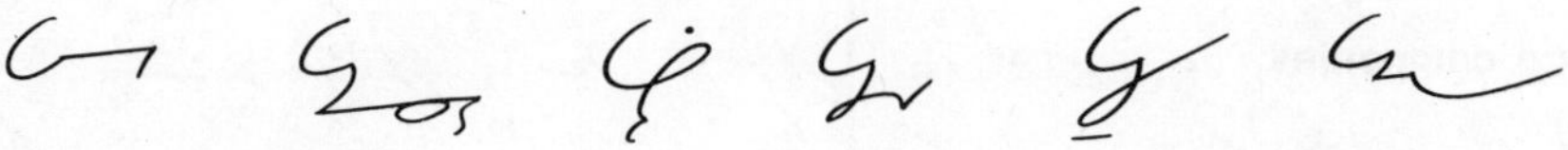

-dent

2 

Be-

3 

Some-

4 

KEY

1 Permission, performances, perhaps, perfect, persuade, personal.
2 Accident, confident, student, incident, evident, president, resident.
3 Between, began, became, betray, because, believe, before.
4 Some, sometime, someone, somewhere, somehow, somebody.

149

Reading and writing practice

WILLIAM SHAKESPEARE

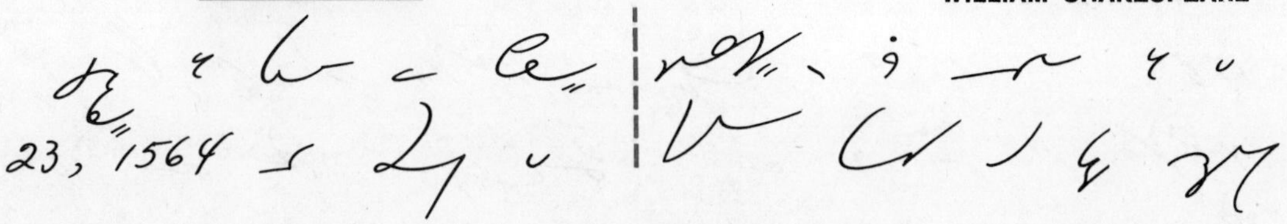

Traveling companies

1578

1585 1587

Burbage

The foundation

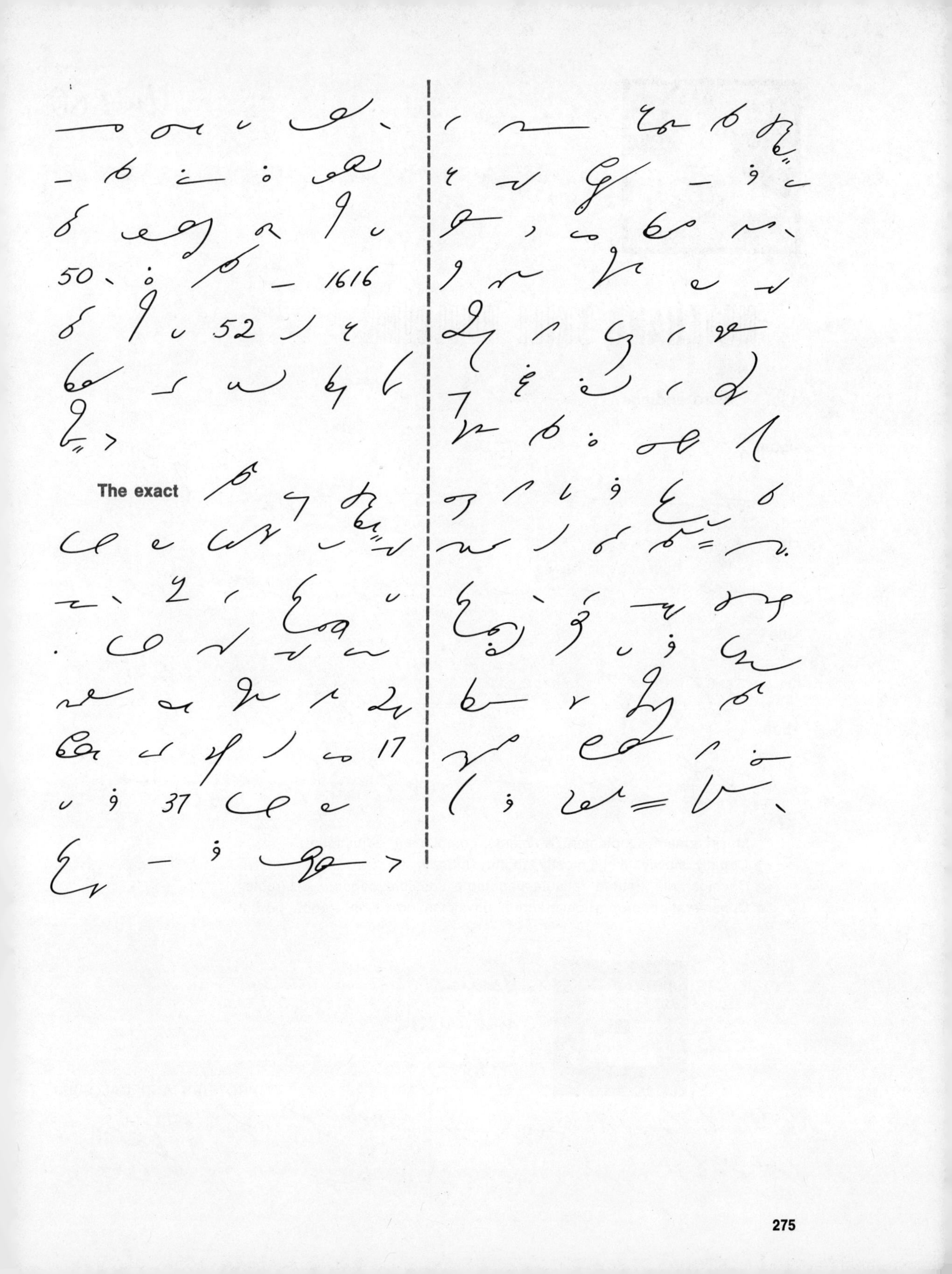

The exact

Unit 60

NOTEHAND SKILL BUILDING

150 Word endings

-ment

1

-ly

2

-ble

3

-tion

4

KEY

1 Measurement, supplement, elements, compliment, adjustment.
2 Rapidly, slowly, likely, mostly, slightly, merely.
3 Considerable, trouble, reliable, vegetable, sensible, capable, desirable.
4 Consideration, proportion, mention, physician, provision, station, portion.

151

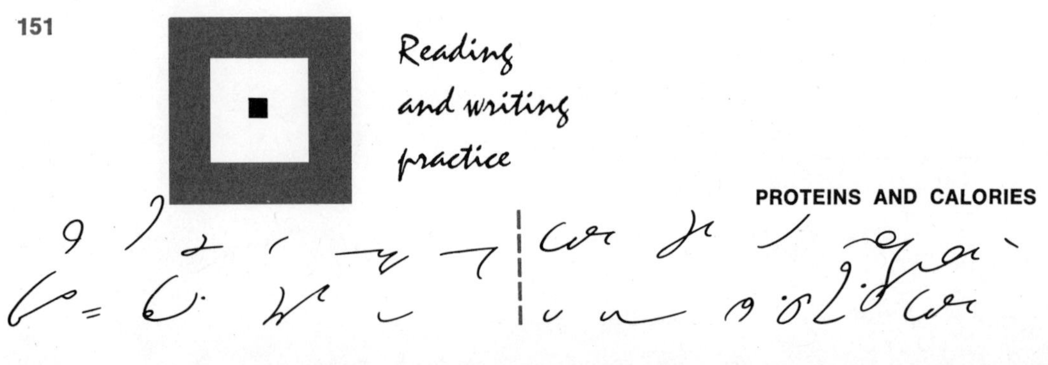

22

12

10

Meats, eggs

10

tryptophan

cysteine

If you find

3,000

4,000

2,500 2,800

We need

Unit 61

NOTEHAND SKILL BUILDING

152 Vowels

Ĭa, Ēa

1

Īa

2

Ī

3

Ow

4

KEY

1 Area, bacteria, variation, created, initiate, negotiate.
2 Diet, variety, dialect, diamond, science, scientist.
3 Climate, widespread, timely, confined, outline, side.
4 Out, down, brown, amount, scouts, aloud.

153 *Reading and writing practice*

CLIMATE

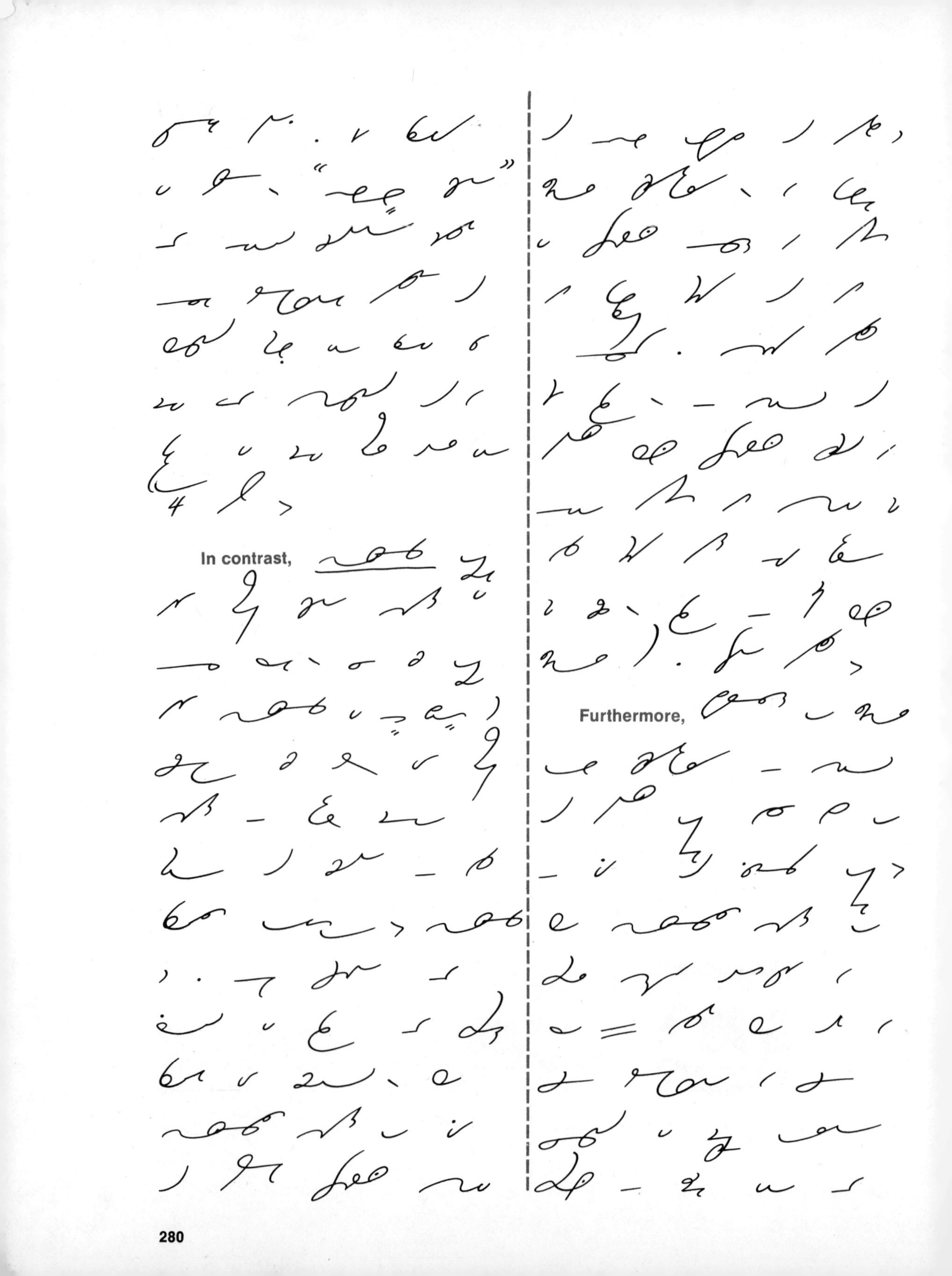

In contrast,

Furthermore,

"mañana"

On the

They need

Unit 62

NOTEHAND SKILL BUILDING

154 Word beginnings

Con-

1

Com-

2

Ex-

3

In-

4

KEY

1 Consider, consisted, contended, confine, concrete, convince, contemplate.
2 Compare, complete, complaint, comply, commodity, community.
3 Expenses, experience, extensive, extreme, example, excite, express.
4 Intense, increase, income, indeed, incapable, install.

155

Reading and writing practice

SMALL AND BIG SOCIETIES

Man's wants

In times

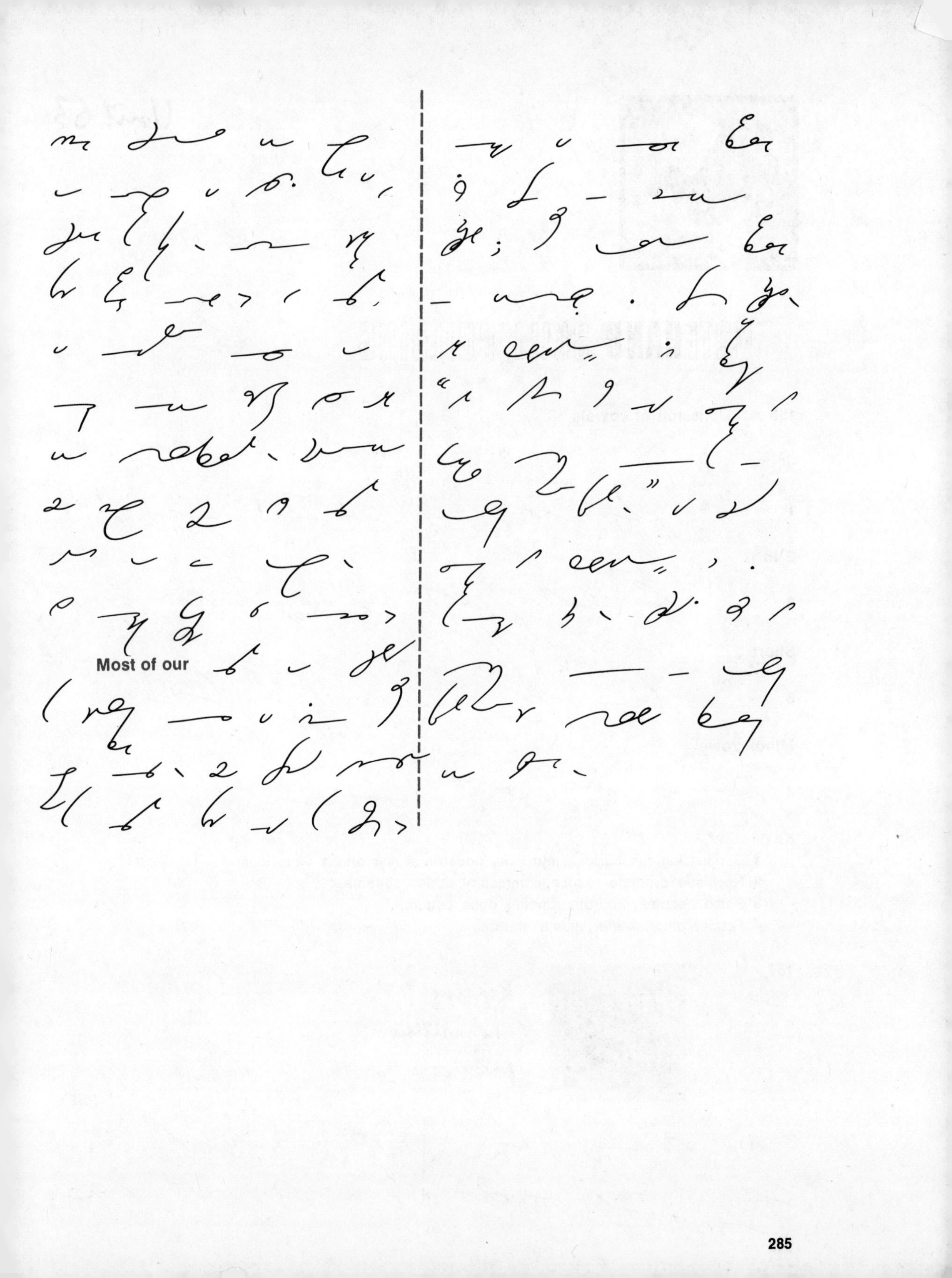

Most of our

Unit 63

NOTEHAND SKILL BUILDING

156 Omission of vowels

-ious

1

E in U

2

Short U

3

Minor vowel

4

KEY

1 Serious, various, curious, injurious, industrious, mysterious, victorious.
2 New, due, produce, reduce, community, duties, suitable.
3 Some, become, confront, running, done, begun.
4 Farmer, other, reader, animal, natural.

157

Reading and writing practice

PESTS

600

There are

In recent

Before the

Unit 64

NOTEHAND SKILL BUILDING

158 Word families

-ological

1 

-ple

2 

-rance

3 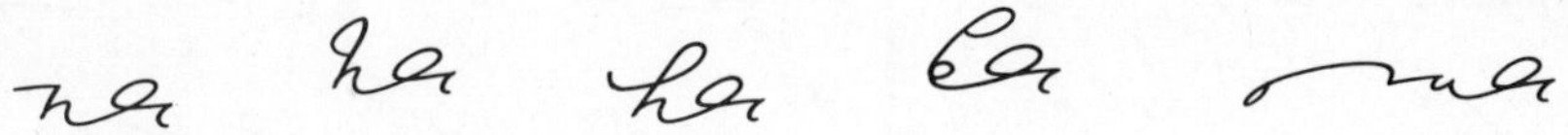

-ral

4 

KEY

1 Psychological, biological, physiological, chronological.
2 People, simple, ample, example, sample.
3 Insurance, assurance, reassurance, appearance, ignorance.
4 General, several, natural, minerals.

159

Reading and writing practice

OUR PSYCHOLOGICAL WANTS

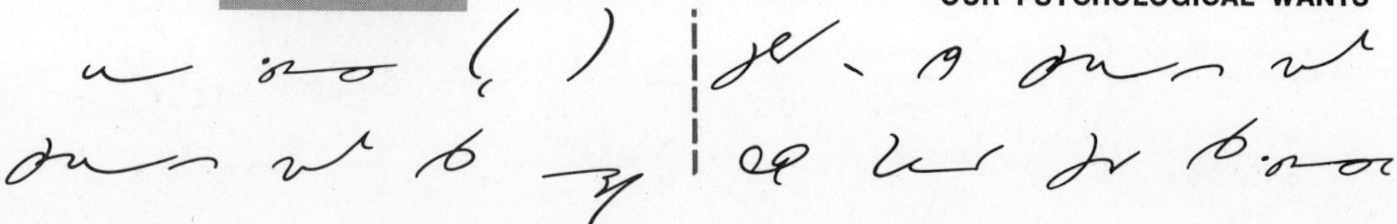

4 To feel respected.

1 To keep alive.

5 To do work we like.

2 To feel safe.

3 To be social.

Related

Some of these

Unit 65

NOTEHAND SKILL BUILDING

160 Word families

-lation

1 

-son

2 

-man

3 

-come

4 

KEY

1 Inflation, deflation, relation, isolation, installation, violation.
2 Son, reason, person, comparison, season, unison, crimson.
3 Man, businessman, salesman, German.
4 Come, income, become, welcome, overcome.

161

Reading and writing practice

INFLATION AND DEFLATION

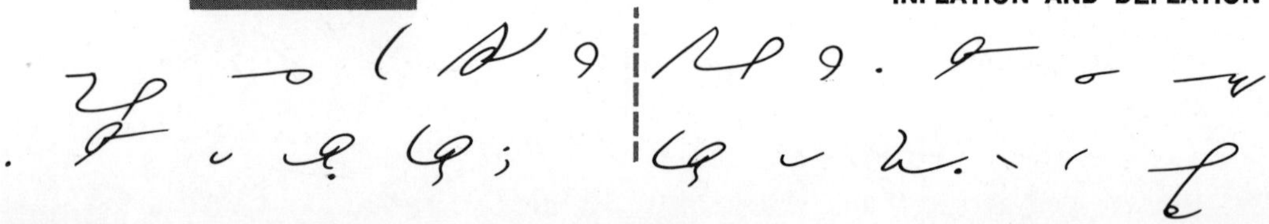

Inflation

$1,000

1920-1923

$75 1944

$100 1954

100 1954

75 1944

However,

If prices

If prices

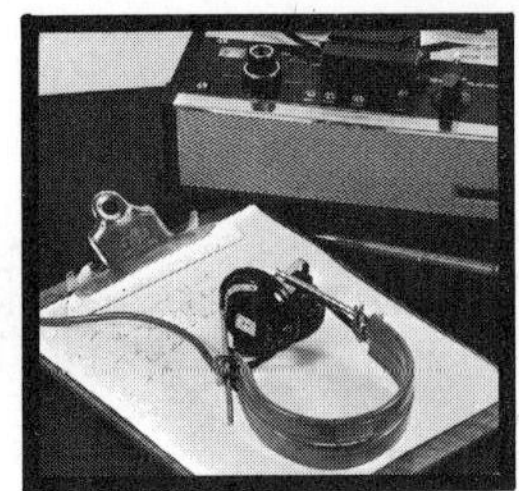

Unit 66

NOTEHAND SKILL BUILDING

162 Blends

Nt

1

Nd

2

Rd

3

Ld

4

KEY

1 Confront, servant, immigrants, century, printing, entirely.
2 Land, island, mainland, Indian, mind, kind.
3 Hard, records, tired, toward, stored, rendered, prepared.
4 Hold, children, world, settled, build, called.

163

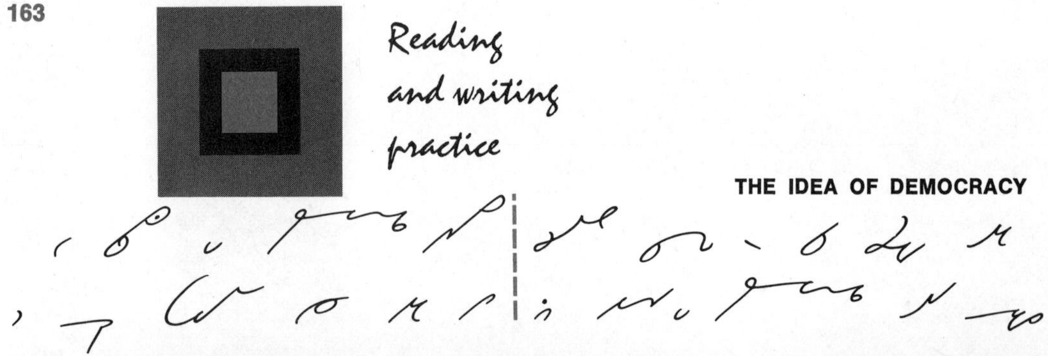

Reading and writing practice

THE IDEA OF DEMOCRACY

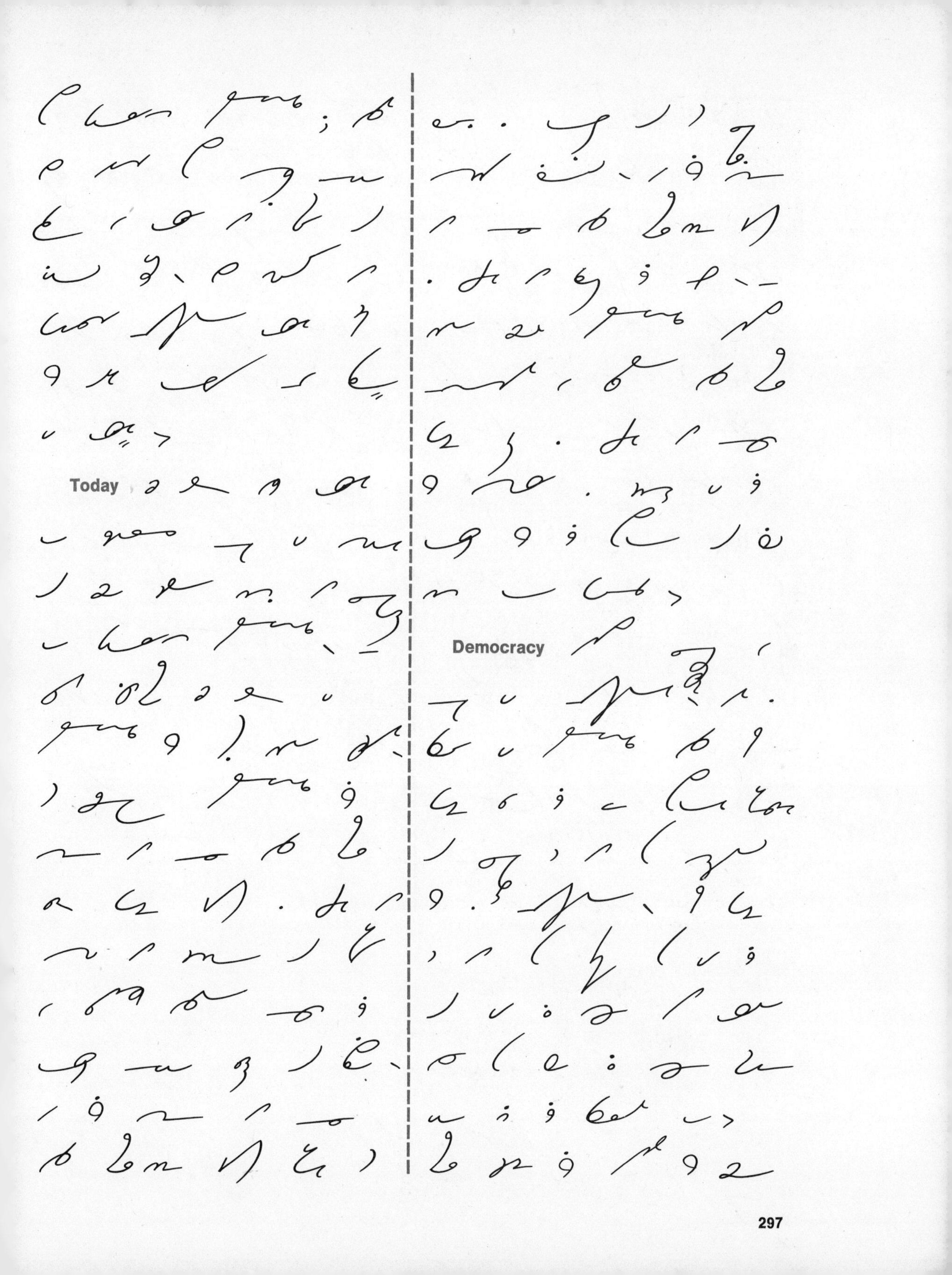

Today

Democracy

He should

He can

Unit 67

NOTEHAND SKILL BUILDING

164 Word families

-quire

1 [shorthand outlines]

-cate

2 [shorthand outlines]

-tive

3 [shorthand outlines]

Pro-

4 [shorthand outlines]

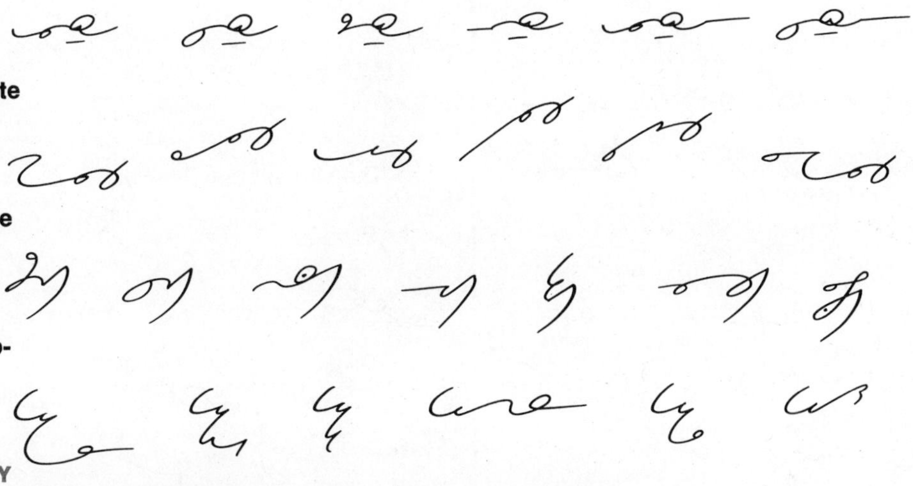

KEY

1 Require, acquire, esquire, inquire, requirement, acquirement.
2 Complicate, indicate, locate, dedicate, educate, implicate.
3 Effective, active, creative, motive, positive, negative, initiative.
4 Problem, proportion, propose, program, properly, produce.

165 Reading and writing practice

MOTIVATION IN LEARNING

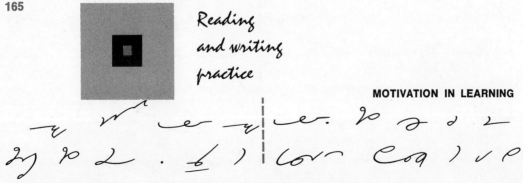

[shorthand text]

Studies of

The student

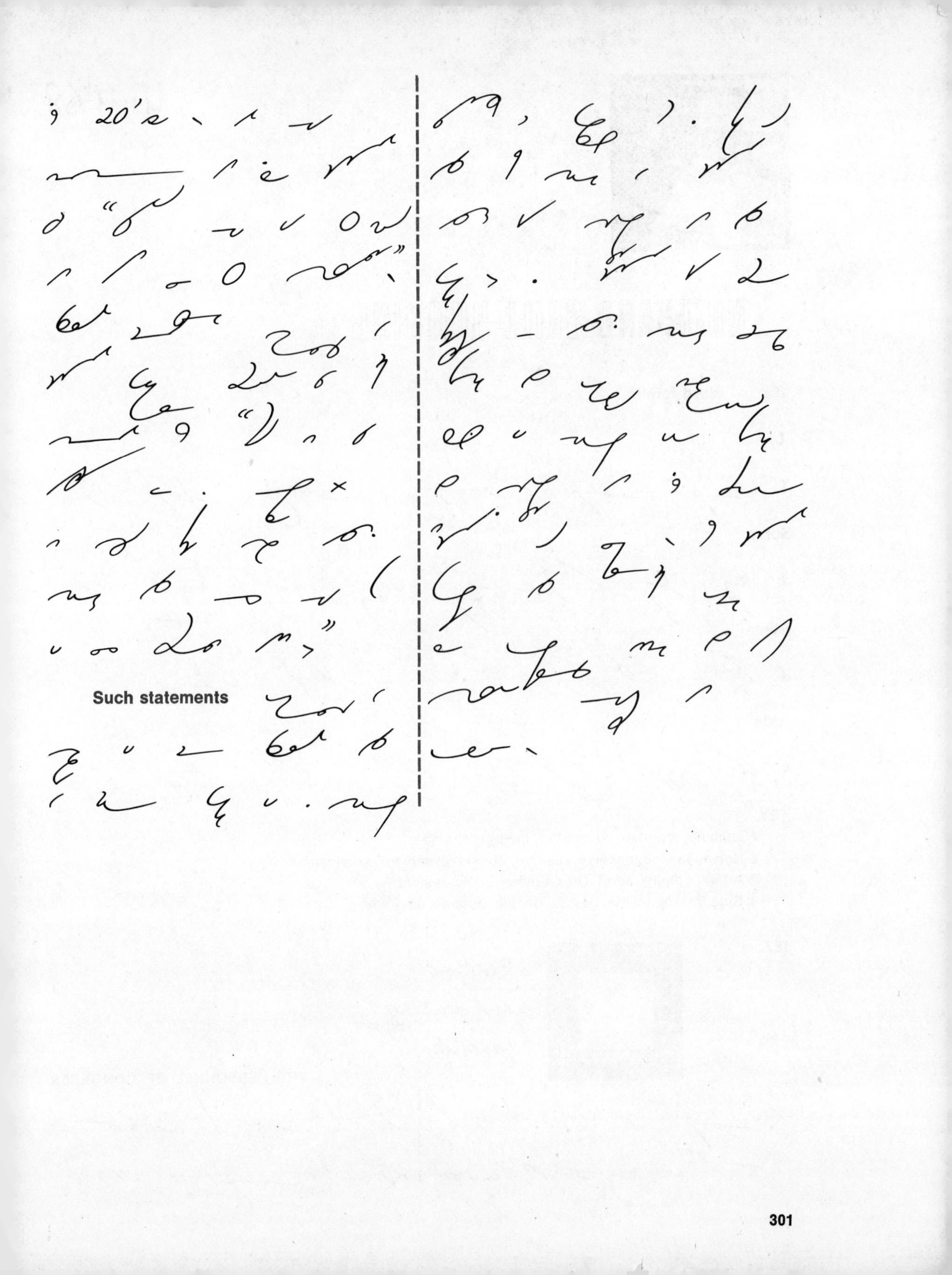

Such statements

Unit 68

NOTEHAND SKILL BUILDING

166 Word families

-br

1

Serve

2

Ad-

3

-side

4

KEY

1 Number, member, remember, lumber, chamber.
2 Serve, service, deserve, reserve, conserve, servant, serviceman.
3 Admit, admire, administer, advise, advancement.
4 Side, reside, inside, beside, decide, outside, coincide.

167 Reading and writing practice

THE PERSONNEL OF CONGRESS

25

60

Vacancies

30

A recent

57

51

Congress

The salary

Unit 69

NOTEHAND SKILL BUILDING

168 Vowels

Ow

1

I

2

Oi

3

U

4

KEY

1 Out, without, found, allow, how, down, proud, house.
2 High, sided, die, rising, tired, excited, like, time.
3 Annoyed, toiled, point, voice, soil, boil, noises.
4 Few, human, value, use, unit, unique, viewed.

169 Reading and writing practice

THE BODY AND REST

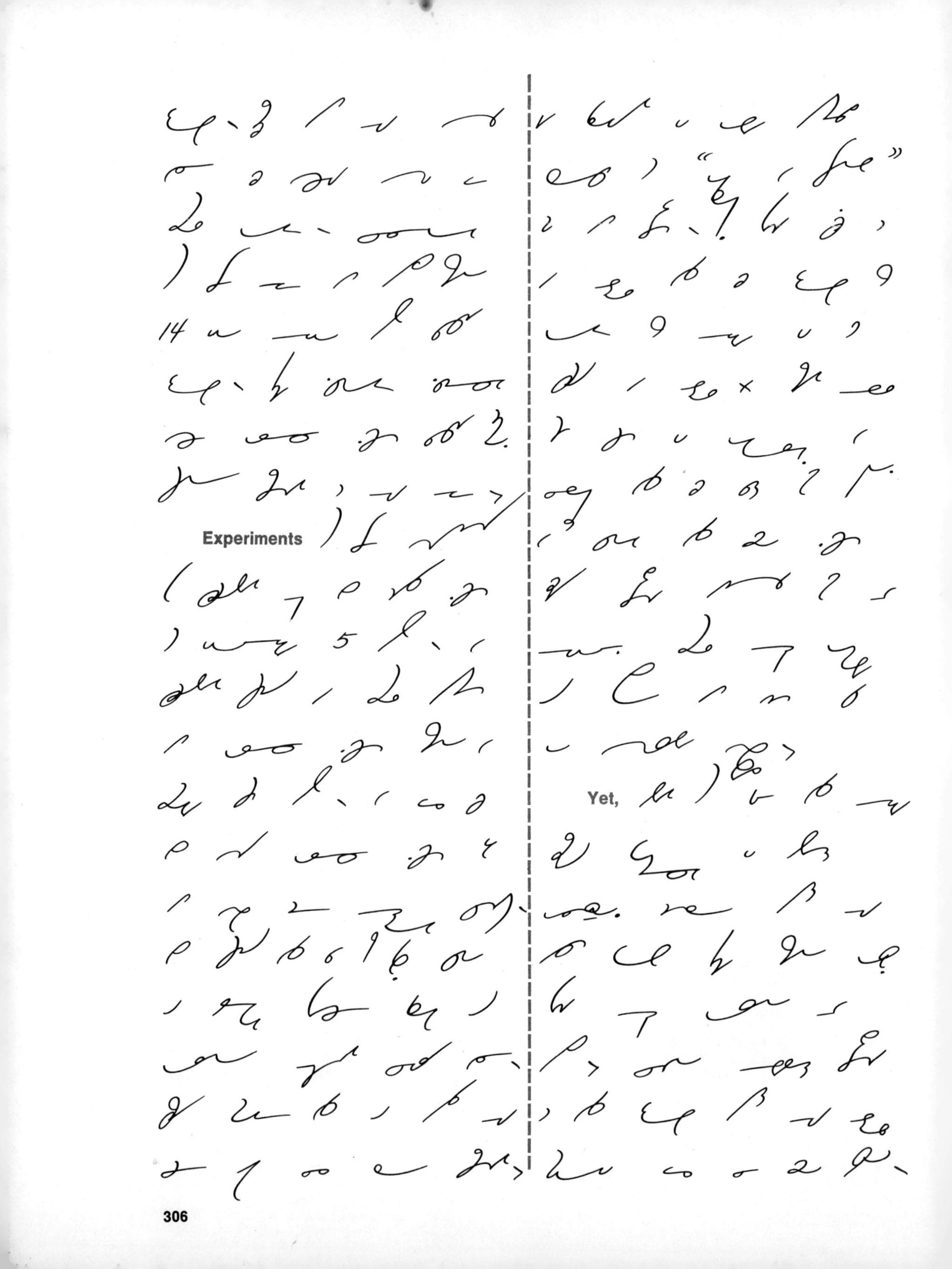

Experiments

Yet,

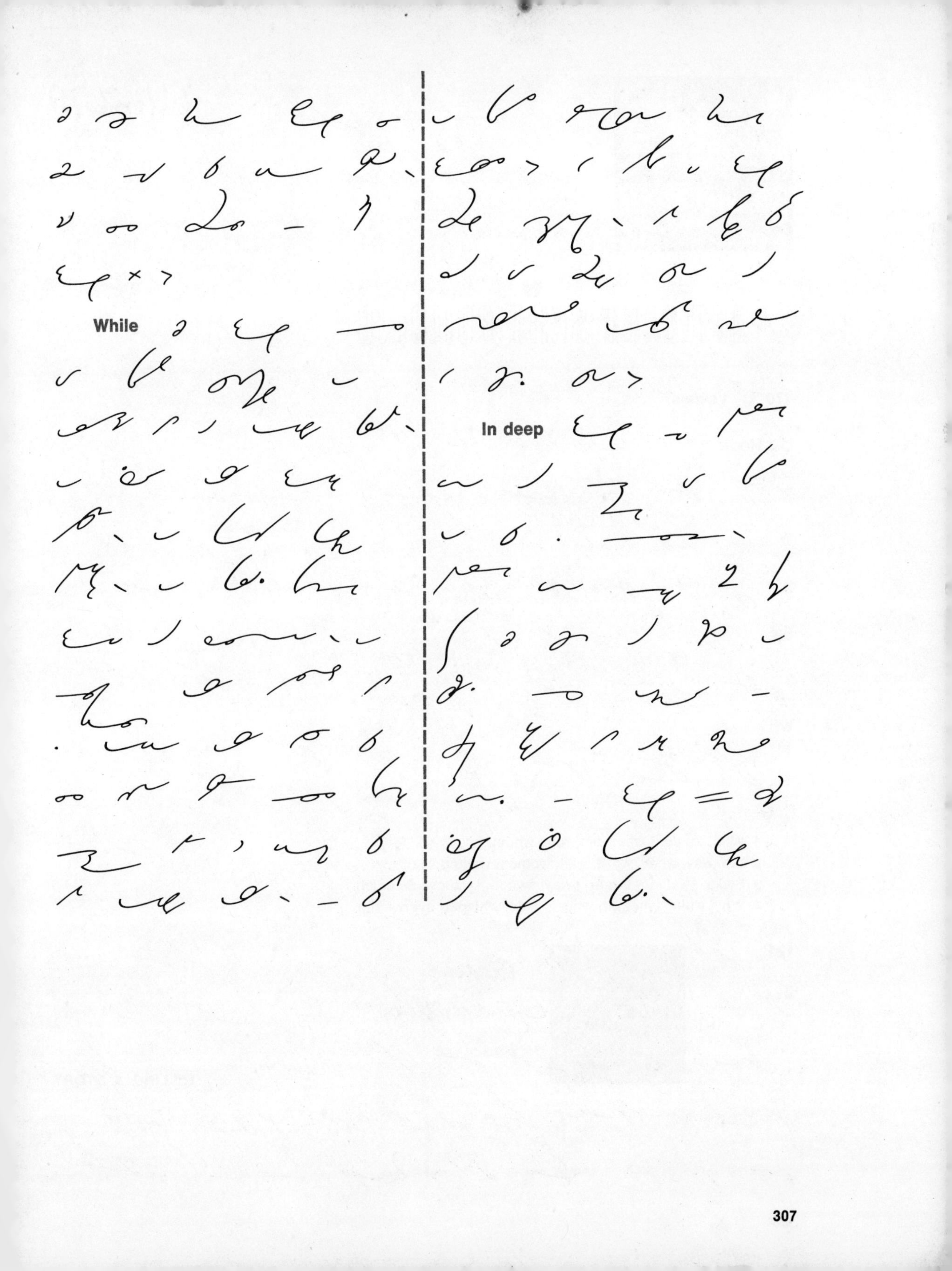

While

In deep

Unit 70

NOTEHAND SKILL BUILDING

170 **Vowels**

OO Hook

1

W

2

Sw

3

Wh

4

KEY

1 Who, to, do, lose, room, rule, whom.
2 We, way, weak, word, wait, women, wasted, wall.
3 Swim, swelling, swear, sway, switch, swallow, Swedish.
4 Why, while, whether, wheel, whip, whisper, overwhelm.

171 Reading and writing practice

TELLING A STORY

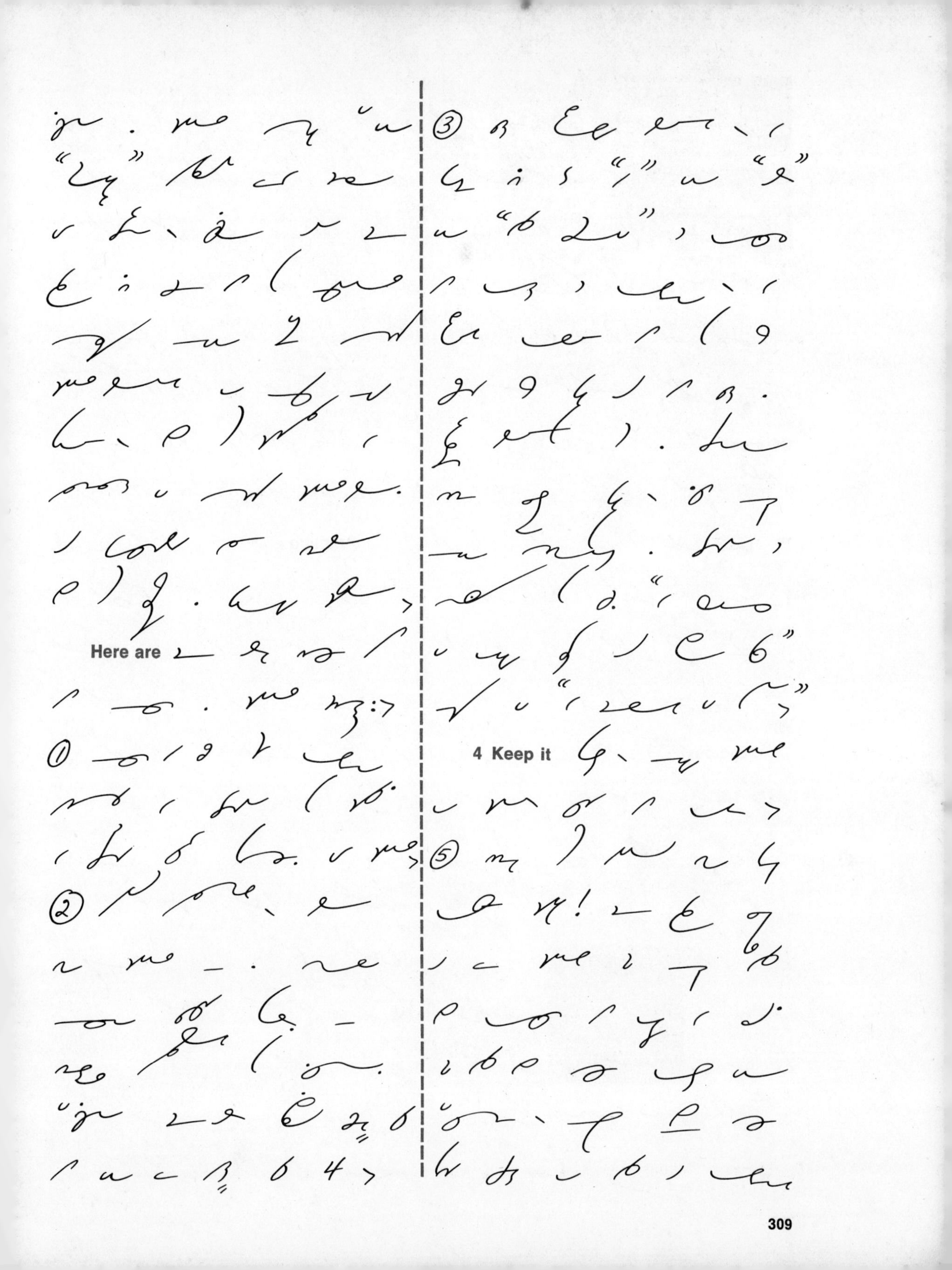

Here are

(1)

(2)

(3)

4 Keep it

(5)

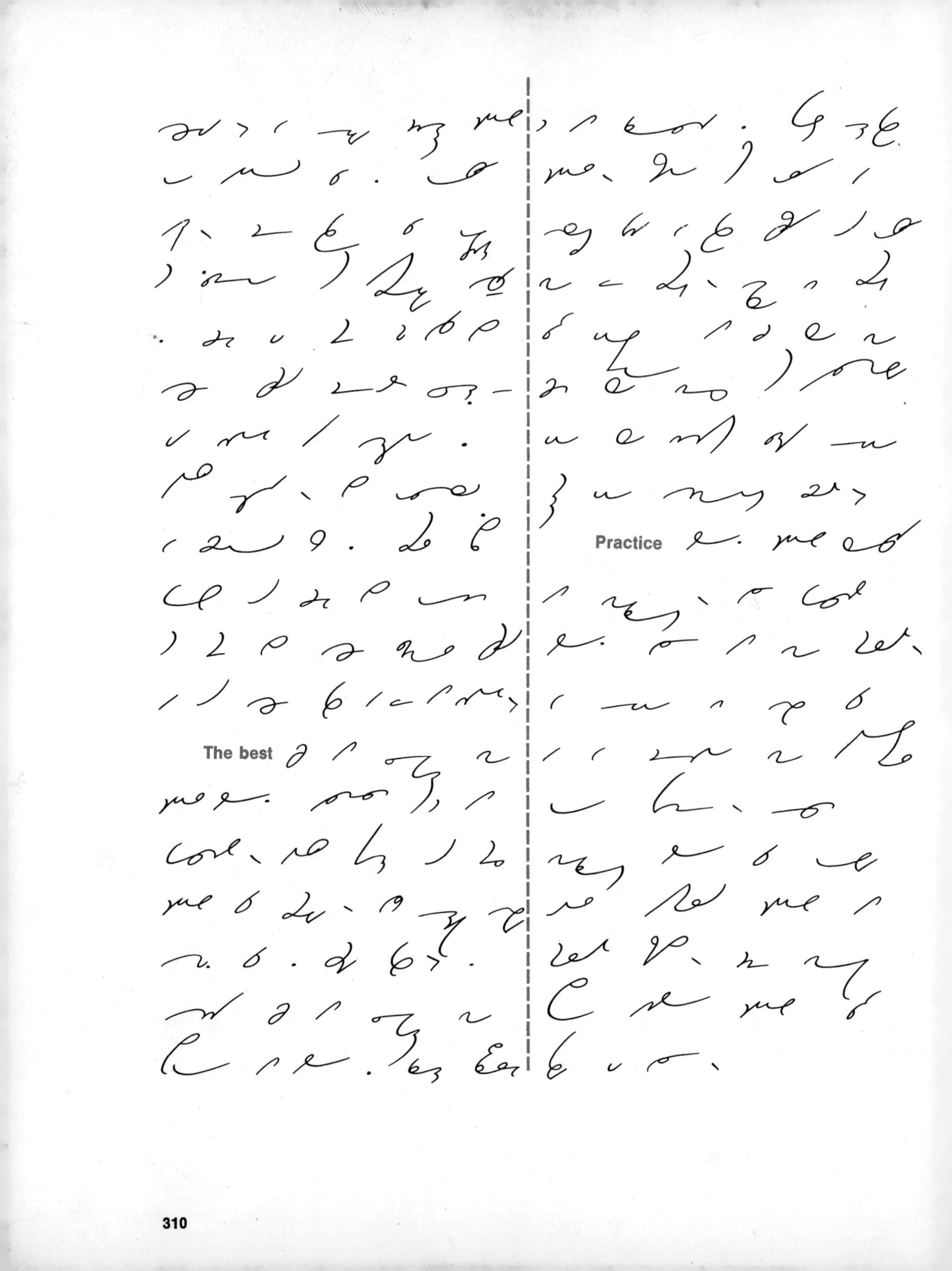

The best

Practice

KEY TO GREGG NOTEHAND

(The number of words is indicated at the end of each group or article.)

PART 1

UNIT 2

3. The letters that would not be written in Notehand because they are not pronounced are: *y* in *day; a* in *mean; a* in *eat; e* in *save; i* in *main; a* in *steam.*

UNIT 3

15. Reading and Writing Practice

1. Dave made the Navy team.
2. Dean made the Navy team the same day.
3. Dave may see me on May 10.
4. Meet me on East Main.
5. Amy made me stay home.
6. May I see your vase?
7. Dave may stay all day.
8. Fay made tea for me.
9. Amy saved the fee.
10. The date is May 12. (41)

UNIT 4

22. Reading and Writing Practice

1. Ray wrote me he leaves for Rome late in May.
2. Is the date May 26 or May 27?
3. I am twenty-one; I may vote.
4. Dear Lee: Monday is a free day for me. I have no classes. May I see you for an hour or so? Ray
5. I am free Friday. Is Ray free?
6. Dave's train is late.
7. I need more seed for the lawn.
8. I made a note to see Lee if he is free.
9. I have made no plans for May.
10. Mary drove me to Dave's store on East Main Street. (74)

UNIT 5

25. Reading and Writing Practice

1. Ray is staying home. He is feeling ill.
2. I need a heater for my store. I may buy a heater later.
3. I am a dealer in motor cars.
4. Ray Taylor made a date with me for Sunday.
5. Dave's train is thirty minutes late.
6. I have purchased a mail meter for our State Street retail store.
7. Do me a favor; leave a note for Lee to phone me Saturday evening at eight.
8. Ray is a homeowner. He bought a home Friday.
9. I hear Lee is leaving Saturday for a rest. He may stay for a week or more.
10. Even though it is snowing, I feel I have to leave for home. (97)

UNIT 6

26. Reading and Writing Practice

1. He eats most meals at home.
2. Ray Macy owns four retail stores on Main Street.

3. Most of the main state roads need paving.
4. Ray fears he may have to leave college.
5. Rose Stevens is sailing for Rome in ten days.
6. I have known Rose for more than a year.
7. I have four seats for Saturday's meet. (46)

27. Reading and Writing Practice

1. Peter paid Mary's plane fare. Please pay him $120.
2. I am postponing our opening meeting for a day or so. I am feeling the heat.
3. Please leave the papers in a safe place.
4. Ray's reading speed is low.
5. I am opening a store for men.
6. Please see that he pays for the papers. He owes me for twenty papers.
7. He is preparing a paper for a sales meeting. (67)

28. Reading and Writing Practice

1. Ray Bates plays first base. He is a fair player.
2. I am opening a boating store on Main Street on Saturday.
3. He placed an order for 1,500 labels, 1,200 postcards, 100 reams of plain paper.
4. Peter's neighbor, Lee Bates, is a paper dealer.
5. Peter's neighbor owns a sailboat. He is a born sailor.
6. He is preparing a brief for me.
7. He is an able labor leader. (72)

UNIT 7

30. Reading and Writing Practice

Group A
1. Most of our players are in shape for the opening of the polo season. It will open May 25.
2. I will trade in our car at the end of the Easter season. The dealer will pay me $450 for it.
3. He is promoting the sale of our mail meters in the East. Our mail meters are retailing for $50.
4. He will pay me $50 for preparing the brief. (71)

Group B
5. I hope most of the people will vote in the election for mayor. I will vote for Lee for mayor.
6. Our phone number is Main 4-1414.
7. Peter is in favor of trading in our car. It is old.
8. The least our neighbor will take for the vase is $10. He feels it is worth more. (51)

Group C
9. He bought a stove for our home. He will pay for it later.
10. Our motorboat is for sale.
11. He wrote me that he will place the deed in our safe. Most of our papers are in the safe.
12. Peter will leave for Spain the end of May. I will see Peter off. (41)

UNIT 8

31. Recall Chart

1. Save, saves, saved, stay, stays, stayed.
2. Free, freeing, freed, place, placing, placed.
3. Trade, trades, trading, open, opens, opening.
4. Deal, dealing, dealer, see, sees, seeing.
5. Heat, heating, heater, face, faced, facing.
6. Read, reading, reader, snow, snows, snowing.
7. Note, notes, noting, vote, votes, voting.
8. Know, knows, knowing, near, nears, nearer.
9. Hope, hopes, hoped, need, needs, needing.
10. Blame, blames, blaming, labor, labors, laborer.
11. Boat, boats, boating, prepare, prepares, preparing.
12. Mail, mails, mailing, mean, means, meaning.
13. Feel, feels, feeling, lease, leased, leasing.
14. Rate, rates, rating, motor, motors, motoring.
15. Is, a-an, for, have, I, am.
16. It, in, of, the, are-our, will.
17. I have, I am, I will, in the, in it, in our.
18. For it, for the, for our, of the, of our, it is.

32. Reading and Writing Practice

Group A

1. Please place the deeds in the safe.
2. The name of our neighbor is Lee Bates.
3. He is a dealer in racing cars.
4. Please leave the mail here.
5. He bought the heater for me wholesale. He saved me $50. (33)

Group B

6. Even though it snowed Monday, the main roads are open.
7. He paid me $100 for the boat. I am pleased.
8. Peter will have to meet me later in the day.
9. The phone is in the living room.
10. I hear he stayed home Saturday. (39)

Group C

11. He made me feel at home.
12. I am in favor of having the meeting later in May.
13. I have a feeling Mary is to blame for the errors.
14. Ray will pay the note in sixty days.
15. He wrote me he needs more paper. (37)

Group D

16. The motorboat is for sale for $180. I feel $180 is a fair price.
17. Is he able to sail the boat? Sailing a boat is an easy job for me.
18. Peter is training for the relay race.
19. I will have the phone placed near the rear door.
20. I will read the mail in the morning. (54)

UNIT 9

33. Reading and Writing Practice

1. Our neighbor's pool is two feet deep.
2. Whom do I see to have our roof repaired?
3. I am moving to Maine soon.
4. Please remove Ray Blue's name from the payroll. It is true that he is leaving.
5. To whom do I have to pay the fee? Do I pay it to Lee, or do I pay it to Ray?
6. Judy will have to leave soon to catch the train.
7. I am leaving soon for a two-day meeting of retail food dealers in the Blue Room of the Hotel Drew. It is a routine meeting. (76)

34. Reading and Writing Practice

1. He will take the claim to court.
2. Our decreasing sales in the East make it hard to raise his pay.
3. He came to speak to the meeting of retail food dealers as a favor to me.
4. He makes a clear case for raising salaries.
5. Please keep our file of local dealers up to date.
6. I will take care of the brakes on our car.
7. In case I am late, please take care of the mail. (61)

35. Reading and Writing Practice

1. He gave me the brief two days ago.
2. The girl is making low grades in the course.
3. If he goes to the game Saturday, he will take me, too. He is the owner of two box seats.
4. Mary Gray is leaving in May. I know an able girl for the vacancy.
5. Please place Miss Gray's name on the payroll.
6. Grace is having two keys made for our safe. (57)

UNIT 10

36. Reading and Writing Practice

1. She showed me a pair of shoes she bought.
2. She gave me five shares of stock for Christmas.
3. Please show Mrs. Baker our line of shades. She will visit our store soon.
4. She will sell twenty shares of steel stock to raise cash to take care of the legal fees.
5. He made it clear that the shoe sale closed on May 10.
6. By making 10,000 sheets of note paper, she will save a great deal. (61)

37. Reading and Writing Practice

1. Mary Chambers teaches a speech course each evening from seven to nine. She wrote a paper on the teaching of speech.
2. The chief feels we will reach our sales goal for May.

3. She came to the store for an easy chair. The easy chairs are on sale.
4. The chief chose Ray Bates to take care of the details of the meeting.
5. I hear the police chief made a speech at the grade school. (61)

38. Reading and Writing Practice

1. The agency is preparing a story for the evening paper.
2. James made two changes in the lease. He made a note of the errors on page 4.
3. She gave her age as twenty-six. She seems at least forty.
4. James Baker owns an agency for Jones Ranges in the East.
5. Please read page 2 of the deed with care. I made a change on page 2.
6. James will leave for Erie in June. (64)

39. Reading and Writing Practice

1. The light in my library is poor.
2. I have tried four times to reach Mary on the phone. Is Mary in town?
3. James Price likes to drive at night. He drove fifty miles two nights ago. Night driving tires most people.
4. I need a file for my private library. May I have a file soon?
5. Please sign my name to the note.
6. Mary's style of writing is like mine.
7. He sells a fine line of dry goods. The price is low. (68)

UNIT 11

40. Reading and Writing Practice

1. He said he enclosed several checks in the letter. The letter and checks will reach you next Friday night.
2. Needless to say, he is very pleased to have the checks.
3. She tells me she is in debt.
4. Ned Price will never settle the case. He feels he has a real grievance.
5. My memory is poor.
6. He made a perfect score on the engineering test.
7. Perry Page takes a test in French next Monday.
8. I am very pleased Mary came home for Easter. (74)

41. Reading and Writing Practice

1. Bill bid $1,500 for the business. His bid is low.
2. Jim Rivers is very busy. His business leaves him no time for fishing.
3. I shipped a special gift to him Friday. Did he get it?
4. James Mix set July 16 as the date for the meeting of our group. Please mail each member of the group a notice of the meeting.
5. The food bill is very big.
6. His grades in history are very low. If he fails, he will have to take the course again.
7. Did Jim pass the test in French? (84)

42. Reading and Writing Practice

1. Miss Gray's firm gave her ten days' pay before letting her go.
2. The firm will close the first of July.
3. He urged her to enroll in the special course for clerks.
4. The date set for the first teachers' meeting is September 8.
5. The June *Journal of Nursing* will reach her Monday.
6. I urged him to take a rest.
7. Dear Dave: I hurt my leg hurrying to the train Wednesday night. My surgeon tells me I will have to stay in bed for five or six days.

Please take care of my mail in my absence. Ted Ellis (82)

43. Reading and Writing Practice

1. He showed me the letter he typed to the mayor of the city.
2. I urged her to visit me the next time she came to New York.
3. Mary baked a cake for James.
4. If the desk is shipped via freight, he will get it Monday.
5. Helen served tea in her home.
6. I searched every room in my home for the missing papers. I did not locate the papers.
7. The teacher checked the test papers with great care. (65)

UNIT 12

45. Reading and Writing Practice

1. Dear Mary: Would you like to have two

seats to the July 15 game? When I purchased the tickets, I did not know my folks were going to visit me.

If you would like to have the tickets, phone or write me by July 12. Jim (39)

2. Dear James: Would it be of help to you when you write the minutes of our June meeting if I were to let you have the notes I made? If so, phone me; I shall be pleased to mail the notes to you. Fred (33)

3. Dear Henry: Will you be able to see Mary Green when she gets to New York Friday? She would like a little help with a term paper she is writing.

If I were here, I would help her myself; but I shall be in Erie Friday for a business meeting. James (45)

4. Dear Dad: I know you will be pleased to see the enclosed list of my midsemester grades. You will notice I made two A's and two B's. I have a B in French, a course I felt I would fail.

You will remember you said you would mail me a check for $10 if my midsemester grades were high. Did I earn the $10? Mary (57)

UNIT 13

46. No Business Runs Itself

Every businessman knows that no business can run itself. The day any business, any factory, any store, is left to run itself, it has passed its prime.

Every business needs a brain in back of it, a brain to supply a rapid stream of plans. A business that is left to take care of itself will soon die. (56)

47. Reading and Writing Practice

Dear Mark: I am having a large party on Saturday, March 10, in my barn for Harry Star. Perhaps you know he has a ten-day leave from the Army starting March 5.

If you can make it, will you drive to the farm? If you do drive, would you pick up Harvey Green, who lives at 415 Parker Road.

Please let me know (1) if you plan to be at the party, (2) if you will be able to pick up Harvey. Jerry (71)

48. Saving With a Purpose

Saving for no special goal can be very dull. It is true that a miser will save dollars so that he can admire them. Most people, though, need more specific goals than that. They have to save for a trip or a car or a home.

Do you have any special goals that you are striving to achieve through saving? If you do, you are in for a real thrill when you achieve those goals. (64)

UNIT 14

49. Recall Chart

1. Who, whom, to, do, night, nights.
2. School, schools, schooling, check, checked, checking.
3. Keep, keeps, kept, tell, tells, teller.
4. Clear, clearer, clears, bill, bills, billing.
5. Go, goes, going, next, fixed, mixed.
6. Grade, grades, grading, urge, urged, urging.
7. Share, shares, sharing, hurry, hurrying, hurried.
8. Shape, shapes, shaped, agree, agreed, agrees.
9. Throw, throws, throwing, mark, marked, marks.
10. Bath, baths, bathing, part, parts, party.
11. Cheer, cheers, cheering, close, closing, closed.
12. Change, changes, changed, take, takes, taken.
13. Leave, leaving, left, grow, grows, growing.
14. Try, tries, tried, gain, gains, gaining.
15. Shall, be-by, you, when, would, were.
16. I shall, I shall have, by the, I would, he would, you would.
17. You are, you will, you will be, I would be, he would be, you would be.
18. For you, to you, have you, you may, he may, I may.

50. Plans for Annual Sales Meeting

Time: It would seem that the best time for our sales meeting is May 10 to May 20. It is a slow season in most territories. Please let me know, though, if you feel a later date would be better for you.

Place: The staff will meet each day from nine to five in the large room on the first floor. If a change of meeting place has to be made, I will post a notice near the elevator. Please try to get to each day's meeting on time.

Expenses: Each man will, of course, be paid his railroad or plane fare. He will be paid $20 a day to take care of his meals and hotel. The members of the staff will be my guests for a night game and a show.

Agenda: Each man will prepare in writing a list of sales helps that he would like for his territory. These lists will be a guide to me in planning our next major sales campaign.

Speakers: Every day we shall have a guest speaker for our morning meeting. After each speaker has finished his speech, you will be at liberty to ask him any questions that you feel relate to the selling of our line of fine papers.

Special Visits: On May 12 the staff will visit our paper mill in James River. You will have a chance to learn how our paper is made. I have arranged for three cars to take the staff to James River. (219)

UNIT 15

51. The Tonic of Praise

I know an official of a large firm who will not often praise a member of his staff for doing a fine job. He is afraid that he will be asked for a raise. The man who adopts that policy is not an asset to any business. He fails to realize a very vital factor—no man lives by bread alone.

Often a man will stay on a low-paying job if he has a boss who makes him feel that he is part of the team. That boss never hesitates to say, "Fine job, Fred," when Fred turns in a fine job. Every man likes praise from his boss even though it is not followed by a raise in salary.

The next time you see a man doing a fine job, pat him on the back! (119)

52. You Can Do It

The head of a large law firm bought a small sign for his desk that read, "You can do it." When he sees himself getting lost in an absorbing problem that he cannot solve, he will glance at his sign. The sign encourages him to try again. More often than not, he will get the answer to his problem from that "one more try."

All sorts of problems are facing our people in these trying times. To help solve these problems, we need more people who will not give up trying. (79)

53. Four Ways to Be a Happier Person

1. Learn early in life to smile readily. The happy man is he who can smile even though things are going badly. The man who can smile only when all is going smoothly is not likely to go far in business or in social life.
2. Have faith in your fellow man. Do not admit even remotely that any man will not treat you fairly, honestly, and sincerely.
3. Do not play favorites. Treat all people alike.
4. Finally, accept setbacks in good spirit. Remember that you cannot be on top all the time. (93)

UNIT 16

55. Tom

In a freshman college class, the teacher was trying to impress on the scholars the need for a large vocabulary. He said, "If you use a word five times, it will be yours for life." Soon I heard the girl in back of me start to mumble. With her eyes closed, this is what she was saying: "Tom, Tom, Tom, Tom, Tom." (53)

Proof

George, it seems, was not happy. About thirty days ago he had let his neighbor have $500 as a loan. He made a mistake, though, by not asking his neighbor for a note or a letter acknowledging this loan. What is more, his neighbor gave no sign that he owed George the $500. Therefore, George was at a loss to know what to do.

Finally, he spoke with his father about the matter.

"That is easy, George," said the father. "This is what you are to do. Write him that you need the $1,000 today."

"You mean the $500," George said.

"No, I do not mean the $500. Write him that you need the $1,000. He will write back to you that he owes you only $500. Then you will have it in writing!" (133)

UNIT 17

56. Reading and Writing Practice

Dear Roy: I had hoped to be able to join your family at Christmas, as I have not seen your two boys since last July. I am afraid, though, that I shall not be able to do this. I was placed in charge of the Troy branch of the Royal Toy Shop. I shall, therefore, have to leave for Troy on December 20. I cannot avoid the trip; I have no choice.

I am today mailing you several toys for your boys. They are marked, "Please do not open till Christmas." I hope the boys enjoy playing with these toys.

Do have a very merry Christmas. I shall call you on the phone when I return from Troy on or about March 15. Sincerely, (110)

57. Reading and Writing Practice

Dear Roy: I will take care of securing the furniture for a lecture hall for our May 15 meeting. So far, I have not been able to procure the right type of projector so that John can show the pictures he made in China. Naturally, I am still trying.

He may have to postpone showing his pictures till the next meeting.

Please let me know if there is any more I can do. Sam (69)

58. Reading and Writing Practice

Dear Samuel: I had a note from John this morning saying that his schedule has been changed; hence, he cannot show his pictures at our annual meeting. Though I would not say it to him, I am actually greatly relieved. After seeing the pictures myself, I feel that they would bore the boys stiff; so lose no more sleep about a projector. Roy (61)

UNIT 18

59. Vacation

If you have not made any provision for your annual vacation, plan to take at least a portion of it in the state of Maine. In Maine, the vacationer can enjoy fishing in the ocean. If he prefers a pretty lake in a natural location for a camping site, Maine offers him a large selection.

After you have been in Maine for even a brief vacation, you will realize that it is a perfect vacation state. (78)

60. Five Principles of Selling

The salesman who hopes to succeed must keep the following five principles ever before him:

1. He will be jealous of his firm's name.
2. He will learn all the selling features of his product.
3. He will not be too unhappy if he occasionally does not succeed in making a sale, but he will keep trying.
4. He will not speak ill of the other fellow's product; but, rather, he will plug the merits of his own.
5. He will follow up every lead he gets. (83)

61. Spare-Time Learners

Spare-time learners are often good learners. Their learning is helped by the fact that they are eager learners.

As an illustration, a boy by the name of Ed Burchell took a job as a full-time janitor in a hospital. He actually did not have a great deal of time for study. He did his cleaning in the lecture halls as the professors gave their lectures. It looked as though he were only cleaning, but as a matter of fact he took in the full lecture. At night, he would write in his notebook the meat of the lecture. Picking up his learning in bits, Burchell made himself a specialist on the structure of the head. Surgeons from all parts of the state looked to him for advice before they tried to do puzzling brain operations.

Burchell is a good illustration of a spare-time learner. (140)

UNIT 19

62. Be Calm

Abraham Lincoln, with all his worries, was a master at keeping calm. When he was faced with a trying problem, he weighed all the facts first, then he took action. The following story illustrates why he was such a great man.

While the war was in its early weeks, no one in the Capitol had the whole story on the way the war was actually going.

Lincoln took one of his cabinet members with him to visit the man who would have the facts—the general in charge of the armies. When the two of them arrived, the general was not at home. They had no choice but to wait. When the general finally arrived, they naturally thought that he would see them at once. But the general just walked past his waiting visitors, going right to his suite on the top floor. (135) *(Concluded in Paragraph 63)*

63. Be Calm *(Concluded)*

The visitors kept on waiting. The cabinet member, who had a quick temper, was quite annoyed. He asked the general's aide to tell the general that he had guests.

The man came back quite embarrassed. The general was already in bed; he would gladly see his visitors the following day. The cabinet member was a picture of rage. He tried to persuade Lincoln to fire the general at once, but he did not succeed in persuading him.

Lincoln said to him: "Let us not fret about the general's bad manners. I will be glad to watch the general's horse for him if he will win victories for us!" Lincoln always thought twice before he took action. (116)

64. Memory

"I am sorry that I did not recall the name of that man who just left. I used to know him when I was in charge of a unit in Mexico City." That was the view that Robert E. Lee took when a man whom he had met once, ages ago, came in to see him.

Lee's memory for faces was quite unusual. Once he saw a human face, he would always remember it. That trait was of great value to him while he was an Army general.

Lee's unique memory won the admiration of his enemies as well as of his allies.

Few will argue with the fact that Robert E. Lee was a great man. Those who were close to him agreed that a part of his greatness might be traced to his unique memory. (126)

UNIT 20

65. Recall Chart

1. Cross, crossed, crossing, cut, cuts, cutting.
2. Shop, shops, shopped, rough, roughly, rougher.
3. Broad, broadly, broader, full, fully, fuller.
4. Talk, talked, talks, book, books, booked.
5. Rarely, fairly, really, swim, swims, swimmer.
6. Annoy, annoyed, annoying, wheel, wheels, wheeling.
7. Toy, toil, soil, equip, equipped, equips.
8. Secure, securely, secures, thick, thicker, thickly.
9. Nature, natural, naturally, human, humans, humanly.
10. Equal, equals, equally, view, viewed, views.
11. Schedule, schedules, scheduling, square, squares, squarely.
12. Ration, rations, rationed, weigh, weight, weighed.
13. Motion, motions, motioned, win, winning, winner.
14. Caution, cautions, cautioned, thrill, thrills, thrilling.
15. What, with, there-their, was, this, about.
16. What is, what are, what will, there is, there are, there will.
17. With the, with these, with this, it was, I was, he was.
18. About it, about that, about this, in this, on this, for this.

66. Follow the Leader

Whether he likes it or not, whether he knows it or not, every man in business is playing the game of "follow the leader." In all that he does, he is either following or leading.

If you look about you, you can quickly tell those who lead from those who follow. If the leader puts up a modern factory, its special features will be copied by others. If each season he dreams up unique ways of improving his business, other firms will have copied his plans before the season is past.

There are firms that follow all their lives; there are others that always lead.

It may be much easier to follow, but it is actually more thrilling to lead. The man who follows has the easier time. He need not take any risks; he need only adopt methods when their value has already been proved. He need not take the risk of giving vital jobs to members of his staff; he can fill those jobs with people who have proved their capacity on the staff of another firm.

But for all this, who would follow if he might be a leader? People who enjoy life look for more than an easy time—they look for a thrill from life. Only the small man with no real ambition will be happy to adopt what others have tried for him. (215)

The Miser

One day a miser who never stopped worrying about the safety of his possessions thought he would sell them all. With the money his possessions brought him, he bought a large piece of silver that he buried next to a wall near his home.

Each day he would dig up the piece of silver to admire it. He dug it up so often that a thief noticed the miser's actions. One day the thief followed the miser to see what he was doing. Of course, he saw the great treasure. Late that night he stole it.

The next day the poor miser saw that his piece of silver had been removed—stolen! He did so much screaming that a number of his neighbors came to see what the noise was all about. After learning the cause, a neighbor said, "Enough of that screaming! Place a stone in the hole; then imagine that it is the piece of silver. It will serve the same purpose as the silver!" The moral of the tale is: The true value of money is not in its possession but in its use.—*Adapted from Aesop's Fables* (166)

UNIT 21

68. Easy Profit

The following is the story of a great senator who was known for his thrift. He never gave his clothes a thought; therefore, he was often shabby in appearance, which annoyed his daughter, who undertook to take care of him. What is more, she never could get him to buy any clothes.

One day, though, she did get him to a clothing store, in which he tried on a few overcoats. The senator liked one of the overcoats very much; in fact, he even asked the price. "$125," said the clerk. The senator dropped the overcoat as though it had been a hot potato.

"I never saw an overcoat in my life for which I would pay that price," he snapped. With that, he left the store.

A little later his daughter came back.

"Here is $90," she said to the clerk. "Please put that overcoat aside. Then in ten days call my father on the phone. Tell him the store is having a sale. Tell him the overcoat he liked is selling for $35. If I know him, he should be here in a hurry!"

The clerk agreed. In ten days he got the senator on the phone. The senator came in on schedule, said it was high time that they charged a fair price for the overcoat, paid the $35, and left.

Back at the nation's Capitol, the overcoat was the natural object of the admiring eyes of his fellow senators.

"That is a mighty fine coat you have there, Jim," said one senator. "It is my size, too."

"I should say it is a fine coat. I bought it at a sale. It was originally $125, but I had an opportunity to get it for $35."

"I'll give you $50 for it," said the senator.

Jim, who could never pass up the opportunity to make a quick dollar, said, "It's a deal." Paying Jim the $50, the senator left with the overcoat under his arm.

It was four or five months before the senator's daughter had the courage to tell her father that his easy profit of $15 had really cost them $75! (359)

UNIT 22

69. Temper

My cousin had without a doubt the worst temper of any girl in our town. In her youth she could always have her own way.

When she married a timid Army officer, we all thought that he would soon be a very henpecked spouse. We were surprised, though, when after several months she was as meek as a mouse. We had an opportunity to ask her about it one day. Blushing a little, she said: "One day after the wedding, there was a pair of trousers over a chair in our bedroom. I was ready to put them in the closet when Joe said, 'Put them on, dear.'

" 'But why should I put them on, honey?' I asked. The trousers were about a foot too big at the waist. He was so firm, though, that I put them on.

" 'Do they fit?' he asked.

" 'Now, sweetheart, of course they do not fit,' I said. As he sat me down on his knee, he said without so much as a smile on his face, 'Then remember which one of us wears the trousers in our house!' " (159)

70. Dither

The cashier of the paper in which the famous writer Henry Watterson ran a column for some time was always in a dither, for each day his cash drawer was out of balance. Whenever Watterson felt the need, he would fill his pockets from the till without telling a soul. One fine day, the treasurer, with the cashier in tow, came to see Watterson. "Henry, it is not that we object to your taking whatever you need—you are welcome to it. But it would help us a great deal if in the future you would jot down on a piece of paper the sum you take. If you will leave that paper in the cash drawer, it will help us keep our books straight." Watterson said that it would be done, though he was not happy about it.

The next morning, just before lunch, the treasurer saw Watterson coming to the cashier's cage. After helping himself from the till, Watterson made a few scratches on a piece of paper. When that was done, he placed the paper in the drawer. As soon as he left the cage, the treasurer made a dash for the cash drawer. In the drawer from which the cash had been taken was a note which said, "I took it all. H. W." (196)

UNIT 23

71. Enrico Caruso

Enrico Caruso was one of the greatest singers that ever sang with the Metropolitan Opera. He had a voice that was not only sweet but so strong that it would "make the rafters ring." In his long singing career, he sang leading roles in dozens of operas. Among these are such famous operas as *Aida, Tosca, Carmen, Rigoletto.*

He was a singer with a very large following. On the nights that he was announced to sing, there would always be a sell-out crowd. A long line of people would wait for hours at the ticket office of the opera house for the chance to buy tickets.

Since Caruso's death in 1921, there has never been a singer with his great drawing power. (125)

72. Abraham Lincoln

Abraham Lincoln was born on February 12, 1809, on a farm in Kentucky. His father was Thomas Lincoln; his mother, Nancy Hanks.

His father was apparently a shiftless person who tried all types of trades but could succeed at nothing. He was frankly a rolling stone. He moved from state to state, from farm to farm.

Very little is known about the Hanks side of his family. Some people think that his mother was the daughter of an aristocrat.

By 1830 Lincoln was a tall, lanky, young man who loved to read. He read every book that he could borrow, often reading until the small hours of the morning by the light of the fireplace.

For a while he was a clerk at a general store in a little town that had a few stores as well as one bank. After a brief time, the owner of the store was bankrupt, leaving Lincoln without a job.

He tried operating his own store; but he, too, was soon bankrupt. It took him a long time to pay off his debts.

About this time Lincoln fell in love with Ann Rutledge, the daughter of an innkeeper. She died of a fever at the age of nineteen.

From all this, you can gather that Lincoln's youth was not a happy one. (210)

UNIT 24

73. The Lark and Her Young Ones

A lark that had her nest of young ones on a wheat farm had to leave them each day to go out to find food for them. As the wheat ripened, the mother warned her young larks to tell her all they learned while she was gone.

One day the man who owned the farm came down to look at the crops. "It is high time," he said to his son, "that the grain should be cut. Tell all our kind friends to come early in the morning to lend us a hand with the reaping."

When the mother lark returned, her young ones anxiously asked her to move them at once to a place of safety. "There is lots of time," she said. "If the farmer waits for his kind friends to help him, there will be no harvesting in the morning."

The following day the farmer came over again. Finding the wheat ripening rapidly, he said to his son, "There is not a second to be lost. We cannot rely on our friends; therefore, we must call in our relatives. Tell them all to be here in the morning to help us with the harvesting." (164) *(Concluded in Paragraph 74)*

74. The Lark and Her Young Ones *(Concluded)*

The larks again asked their mother to move them. "If that is all, don't worry. We have plenty of time. Relatives have their own interests to look after. But I want you to keep listening when I am absent." Eventually, the farmer came back again. Finding the grain almost fully ripe, he said to his son: "We can't wait any longer for our friends or relatives. We must harvest the crop ourselves in the morning." When the mother learned of this, she said: "Then it is high time to be off. If the master has now made up his mind to do the job himself, then the grain will really be cut." So the mother moved her nest to the country. The following morning the farmer came with his sickle to cut the wheat.

Moral: If you want a task done well, do it yourself.—*Adapted from Aesop's Fables* (134)

UNIT 25

75. Study

On finishing college, two boys — one named Brown, the other named Smith — took jobs in business. Both promptly showed that they were going far in business. At twenty-five, both were earning fine salaries. It seemed that both were on their way to the top.

Smith did reach the top. At forty, he had climbed to the position of treasurer of his firm. Brown seemed to mark time when he reached thirty. Why had Smith climbed to the top so rapidly while Brown stood still? The answer is this: Smith never stopped studying. He welcomed every opportunity to better himself through reading or studying.

Brown, on the other hand, claimed that he didn't have time to read or study.

When a person stops studying, it is time to be alarmed. (124)

UNIT 26

76. Recall Chart

1. Vow, vows, vowed, run, runs, runner.
2. Sing, singing, singer, long, longed, longer.
3. Bank, banks, banker, friend, friends, friendly.
4. Come, comes, coming, product, products, production.
5. Bind, binds, bindery, kind, kindly, kindest.
6. Hand, hands, handle, frame, frames, framed.
7. Name, names, named, farm, farmer, farmed.
8. Prompt, promptly, promptness, smooth, smoothly, smoother.
9. Loud, loudly, louder, print, printed, printer.
10. Underneath, undergo, undertake, underground, underpaid, underdone.
11. Overcome, oversee, overpaid, over, overtime, overcoat.
12. Under the, under that, under these, over them, over this, over our.
13. Which is, in which, for which, I could be, he could be, you could be.

14. I should, you should, you should have, he should be, who should, who should have.

77. Farming

We live in the richest food-raising country on the earth. At a time when the people of some nations are going hungry, we are growing enough to feed all our people; still we have a great deal left over.

Our country has several kinds of soil. Some soils are good for farming; others are not. Some soils are good for one kind of crop; others are good for another.

In the cold North, soils are gray in color but are not naturally fertile. In some parts of the North, glaciers scraped the surface of the land, leaving the soils rather stony.

In the humid East-Central part of the country, the soils are gray-brown in color. They are known as brown forest soils. They are not especially fertile, but if they are properly fertilized, they can be effectively farmed.

In the warm, humid Southeast, the soils are red in color. They are not naturally fertile but will grow crops if properly managed.

In the interior of our country, there are two types of soils, both of which are quite fertile. The first of these is the dark brown to black soils; the second, chestnut brown.

In the West, the soils are light in color. They are not good for farming. They are used mainly for grazing, if they are used at all.

There are more farms in the humid East than in any other part of the country. The eastern half of the country also has a better climate for farming than the western half. Rainfall is generally heavy enough in the East for good farming.

In those parts of the country in which the rain, the climate, as well as the soils are good for farming, a great number of crops can be grown. In most parts of the country, though, farmers specialize in one or two crops at the most.

Dairy farming is carried on in the humid parts of the East. Fresh milk spoils easily. Therefore, dairy farms are usually located near large cities in which the milk will be sold. Urban centers provide a large market for milk and cream. (342)

UNIT 27

Woodrow Wilson

Education

1. Early education in the South.
2. Entered Princeton University in 1875.
3. Good debater but not great scholar.
4. Served as professor and later as president of Princeton University.

Politics

1. Democrats elected Wilson Governor of New Jersey in 1910.
2. Democrats elected Wilson President in 1912. His election was made possible by split in Republican Party.

Domestic Policy

1. Democratic campaign called for lower tariff. Wilson proposed and Congress passed Underwood Tariff Act.
2. Wilson proposed and Congress passed Federal Reserve Act.

Foreign Policy

1. Wilson asked for neutrality at start of war in 1914.
2. Wilson's policy approved by people who elected him for second term in 1916 by narrow margin.

79. The Measure of a Man

I suggest that the place to take the true measure of a man is by his fireside, where he puts aside his mask so that you can soon learn what type of man he is. I do not care how important he is in business or what his work may be; I do not care whether people think he is a hero or a villain. If his young ones shrink from him when he gets home at night and if his wife cringes every time she has to ask him for a $5 bill, he is a fraud.

But if his young ones rush up to the door to meet him at night and if love can be seen on the face of his wife every time she hears his footsteps, you can be sure he is pure.

I can overlook much in that man who would rather make a fellow man swear than a woman weep. I cannot but honor a man who cherishes a smile from his wife more than he fears the frown of all his neighbors.

—*W. C. Brann* (149)

Fast Shrinkage

An important businessman we know was overweight, and his wife was alarmed about his health. She suggested that he try to bring his weight down while on his farm. He took the suggestion; and a short time later he walked over to the general store, where he promptly picked out a pair of overalls in which he would take workouts.

As the clerk was wrapping the overalls, the man thought of a fact of importance that he had overlooked. "Wait a bit," he said. "Those overalls fit me now, but shortly I hope to work off a lot of weight. Perhaps I ought to buy a smaller pair."

The clerk shook his head and frowned. "Brother, if you can shrink as fast as these overalls can, you will be doing pretty well!" he said, and went on with the wrapping of the overalls. (131)

UNIT 28

80. Surprise

A doctor out of school just a short time hung up his shingle in a small town, but it was some time before a patient stepped inside his office.

When a man finally came in, the doctor thought it wise to impress him with his importance. Therefore, he picked up the phone and barked, "I have 20 patients on my list today, and I don't believe I can get to the hospital to perform that brain operation before six in the evening." Then he hung up and turned to his visitor with a smile. "Now, what seems to be paining you, my good man?"

"Nothing is paining me," his surprised visitor informed him. "I am here to hook up your phone, sir." (112)

Family Income

One does not have to know very much about the laws of economics to realize the importance of income. I believe that the saying "Clothes make the man" would be more nearly right if it were "Income makes the man." That is to say, if one can know but one fact about a man, a knowledge of his income will prove to be the most informative. Then a rough guess can be made of his politics, his age, and even his life aspirations.

Unless a steady stream of money is in a family's hands every week or every month, that family is sick. All its activities—the things that make life worth living—must suffer—college, travel, and health, to say nothing of food and shelter. (120)

UNIT 29

Stages in Personality Development

1. Stage of Dependence. Everyone starts life completely dependent on others. A few are never weaned fully from this stage. They always lean on others.

2. Stage of Comfort and Eating. A child's interests during the first couple of years of life are bodily comfort and food.

3. Show-Off Stage. Soon after he learns to walk, the child likes to get attention by showing off the things he can do. "Watch me" is a phrase he uses very often.

4. Stage of Low Boiling Point. About the time he is three, his parents start to worry about the mischief he gets into. They are always stopping him just as he is doing the most thrilling things. He doesn't like being stopped and gets angry.

5. Gang Stage. Toward the end of grade school, boys start to organize boys' clubs; girls organize girls' clubs. They start to cooperate as groups.

81. Loyalty

In a city located on the West Coast, there lived a noted lawyer who had a Chinese servant by the name of Sam. The two had lived together for a long time and had great affection for each other.

But one morning, as Sam greeted his master, he hesitated a little and then informed him, "Next week I must leave you. Before I go, I will hire for you a better man." The lawyer waited, thinking that Sam would say more; but Sam just stood silently.

"So you are going to leave me; I do not pay you enough. That Doctor Sanders who visited us last week—he knows what a treasure you are. Don't be a fool, Sam.

Your pay will be adjusted. Say no more." The noted lawyer thought that that would end the matter. Instead, Sam indicated that he was in earnest. "Next week I leave you —I go to China." he said. (144) *(Continued in Paragraph 82)*

82. Loyalty *(Continued)*

"I see," added the lawyer. "You are going back for a wife. All right, bring her home. You can return in two months. I will see that she is provided for. I will also get the papers that are needed." He thought he had Sam persuaded, but he was wrong.

"I go to China next week; no papers are needed. I will never come back," Sam said.

"By heaven, you shall not go!" said the strong-headed lawyer.

"By heaven, I will!" said Sam heatedly.

It was the first time that Sam had spoken that way to his master.

The lawyer pushed his chair back and then added, "Sam, you must forgive me. I spoke without thinking. I do not own you. But," he pleaded, "what have I done? Why do you leave me? You know I need you more than I ever needed you before." (127) *(Continued in Paragraph 83)*

UNIT 30

83. Loyalty *(Continued)*

"I am going to China to die!"

"Nonsense. You can die here. I promised you many months ago that I would ship your body back to China if you die before I do. I meant it."

"I will die in four weeks, two days."

"What!"

"Many weeks ago my brother was tried for a tremendous crime. He is now in prison. He must die. He has a wife who is going to have a baby before many days. In China," he added, "they accept a brother to die in his place. I will go to China. I will give my money to my brother. He will live; I will die."

The lawyer started to speak again but stopped. He thought he understood men, but it took him a long time to grasp the immensity of Sam's sacrifice. (124) *(Concluded in Paragraph 84)*

84. Loyalty *(Concluded)*

The following day, with a minimum of fuss, another Chinese boy by the name of Joe arrived to administer the lawyer's affairs. After some preliminary instructions from Sam, Joe took over. He was just like Sam in many ways. Sam terminated his service to his master without saying goodbye. He went to China, where he was beheaded four weeks and two days almost to the minute from the time he had spoken to his master. His brother was set free after Sam's death and returned to his wife.

The lawyer's house goes along about as usual, save that the master calls for Sam when he should say "Joe." At such times there comes to him a kind of clutch at his heart, but he keeps his thoughts to himself.—*Adapted from Elbert Hubbard's Notebook* (126)

UNIT 31

85. Brief-Form Review

1. A-an, is, for, have, am, I.
2. It, in, of, the, are-our, will.
3. Shall, be-by, you, when, would, were.
4. What, with, their-there, was, this, about.
5. Under, over, should, could, opportunity, which.
6. And, suggest, work, importance-important, short, where.

87. Ten Signs of a Mature Man

1. He can say "No" to himself, even on difficult questions, and make it stick.

2. He can take suggestions in good spirit and profit by them. They do not send him into a rage. He knows that suggestions will probably help him to grow.

3. He has close friends among men and women. His friendships are long-lasting.

4. He can look into a question or a problem with care and thought and make up his mind on what course to follow, but he does not act on impulse alone.

5. He promptly admits a weakness, but at the same time he can realize his strong points without being vain about them.

6. He can put aside his failures of yesterday and look to the future. (117) *(Concluded in Paragraph 88)*

88. Ten Signs of a Mature Man *(Concluded)*

7. He is tolerant. The immature man, who will find success difficult, often criticizes those who do not believe as he does.

8. He thinks for himself. He analyzes. He raises many questions. He does not follow fads or buy on impulse. It is necessary to sell him.

9. He is calm. When necessary, he faces a crisis on an even keel. If the other fellow insists on arguing—probably even loses his temper—he smoothes things out.

10. He follows a long-range plan. He arranges his finances so that he can pay for what he needs. He does not get into debt if he can avoid it. He faces the future; he does not live in the past. (121)

UNIT 32

89. Strictly the Truth

The captain of a certain vessel once wrote the following sentence in his log: "The mate was drunk tonight." When the mate became normal and the sentence was brought to his attention, he was angry. He pleaded with the captain to scratch out the sentence. He said that he had never been drunk before and he never intended to be drunk again. But the captain insisted that the entry must stand. "In this log we write the whole truth," he said.

The following week the mate kept the log, and in it he wrote, "The captain was sober tonight." (94)

90. Time to Forget

Very often we can remember better by remembering less. Some of us have a tendency to try to remember too much.

Suppose that you have to go to the dentist or attend a meeting or a dinner. Make a note in your date book of the time you are to see the dentist or attend the meeting or dinner. Don't try to keep these facts in the front of your mind all day.

Use good sense in what you remember. It is evident that there is no use in trying to remember a phone number you may never call again. It is also evident that there is no use in remembering all the bus or train schedules. Just the part you will use is worth remembering. For your guidance, keep these two facts in mind:

1. Remember that which you will use over and over again.

2. Forget that which you will not use in the near future. (146)

91. Big Business and Small Business

The person who maintains for a moment that our country can survive without small business is lacking in good judgment. Every fact of our economic life tends to prove that big business cannot get along without small business. It is an elementary fact that you cannot add to the stature of a dwarf by cutting off the legs of the big fellow. Our entire business structure is a unit just like a machine. It is made up of an assortment of big parts and little parts, and each part, large or small, does a fundamental job.

Big business needs small business; small business needs big business.—*Abraham Lincoln* (106)

UNIT 33

92. Recall Chart

1. Income, invites, indeed, beneath, because, belonging.
2. Form, inform, informative, acted, waited, visited.
3. Deduct, traded, guided, men, mention, meant.
4. Minute, nominate, minister, addresses, chances, leases.
5. Threaten, attend, attention, maintain, obtains, certain.
6. Sudden, broaden, denied, moment, payment, arrangement.

93. Budgeting

The path to financial peace of mind does not lie in trying to get more and more income but rather in managing income in a way that makes life richer and more pleasant. Budgeting helps us to live within our incomes. Keep in mind, though, that budgeting does not mean living by a plan. Budgeting means planning to live.

A budget need not be elaborate. In fact, the best budget plans are often quite simple. Budgeting books can be purchased that tell the percentage of income that should be spent on food, clothing, and other items. Such model budgets often are fine guides, but the final allocation of income is a personal matter. Families that try to budget their money on the basis of allocations listed in a budget book for the "average family" often give up budgeting because the plan in the book does not work for them. *You* have to make up your mind what *you* want out of life and then plan how you will spend your money.

Why keep a budget? A budget forces you to make up your mind about what you want out of life. We all have a tendency to drift along. A budget forces us to make plans.

A budget can help you eliminate unnecessary spending. One important function of a budget is to show you the leaks through which your money may be draining without making any return for you.

A budget can help you achieve long-range goals. This is an important function of a budget. If you rely on impulse in buying, you may spend so much on one thing that you will be forced to do without basic necessities, such as shoes or clothing or other things that are more important to you. Only by planning can you fit your spending to vital needs and goals. (301)

UNIT 34

94. Hard Work

A hard-working farmer was getting tired and made up his mind to get a hired man to help him. When the hired man came, he set him to work in the garden chopping wood. Toward the middle of the morning, the farmer went down to see how the hired man was getting along. To his amazement, he found the wood in the garden all chopped.

The following day, the farmer asked the hired hand to get the wood stored in the shed. This was a hard job that required a lot of lifting, and the farmer figured that the job would keep the man busy a long time. But by noon the man had the job done and was ready for another task. (106) *(Concluded in Paragraph 95)*

95. Hard Work *(Concluded)*

On the third day, the old farmer, thinking that the hired hand was entitled to a light assignment for a change, called him over and told him to sort out the potatoes in the bin.

"Put the good ones in one pile, those that you are not sure about in another, and throw out the spoiled ones." An hour later the old farmer went back to see how the job was coming. Suddenly he found the hired man stretched out cold in the field, with almost nothing done.

After throwing cold water on the man's face and bringing him to, the old farmer wanted to know what had happened. "The thing that killed me was figuring out which pile each potato should be put in!" answered the hired man. (114)

UNIT 35

First Aid

I. Treatment of Minor Wounds
   A. Break in skin
      1. Clean wound thoroughly with soap and water.
      2. Apply iodine, 2 percent tincture. *Caution:* Never to *deep,* open wounds.
   B. Burns
      1. Clean carefully.
      2. Apply special ointment made for burns.
      3. Cover with sterile dressing.
      4. Extensive burns should be treated by physician.

II. Fainting
   A. Cause: Decrease in the amount of blood in the brain.
   B. Treatment
      1. Have person bend forward and place head down between his knees.
      2. If unconscious, place person flat on back and *lift his feet.*

96. Boiling Water

One day, a capable and reliable young doctor was asked if all those pots of boiling water that the country doctors always seem to call for in the movies are necessary.

"I wondered about that, because it is a lot of trouble, and all the doctor has to have available is one pot in which to boil a needle," he said. "But one of my old professors in school gave a plausible and acceptable answer. He said: 'If you have to bring a baby into the world in the home, the thing that will give you the most trouble is the father. He will make it impossible for you to work efficiently; therefore, it is advisable to keep him busy. Tell him that it is possible for him to help by getting all the pots obtainable and boiling lots of hot water. Many farmhouses have coal or wood stoves, and keeping the fire hot and the water boiling will get the father out of the way. After it is over and you have patted him on the back, you have part of the ingredients for steaming hot coffee.' " (184)

97. Wasted Time

Every morning you are handed twenty-four beautiful hours. They are one of the few useful things in life you get free of charge, whether you want them or not. Your schooling must be paid for, and even your health costs money to achieve or regain. But these twenty-four wonderful hours do not cost you a penny. If you were the most powerful man in the world, it would not be possible for you to buy another hour. If you were the poorest beggar, not a single minute could be taken from you.

What do you do with this wonderful treasure? Do you use it gainfully? Remember, you must use it at once; you cannot save it up for your old age.

Wasted time is a greater tragedy than wasted money or wasted health. Either of these you may regain with thoughtful effort, but time wasted is gone for good.

Be grateful for the time that is given to you. (151)

UNIT 36

98. On the Alert

Waiting in the conference room of a steamship office to be interviewed for a job as a wireless operator, a number of applicants filled the room with such a confusion of conversation that they were not conscious of the constant flow of dots and dashes that were coming over a loudspeaker. About that time, another man entered and was content to sit by himself in one corner. All of a sudden he snapped to attention, walked confidently into the private office of the president, and soon came out with a cheerful smile on his face.

"Say," one of the group called out, "how did you get in before us? We were here first."

"One of you would have had the job if you had been concerned with the announcement coming over the loudspeaker."

"Concerned with what announcement?" they asked in confusion.

"Why, the code," the stranger answered. "It said, 'The man I need must constantly be on the alert. The first man who gets this message and comes into my private office will get a contract as an operator on one of my ships.' " (181)

99. Hearing Aid

An old but competent gentleman often complained about his deafness. He had completed a long and successful business career and had amassed considerable wealth. His physician had tried for a long time to compel him to get a commercial hearing aid, but without success.

The old man learned, though, that one company had just completed a comfortable hearing aid that combined the good features of all the others on the market, and he made up his mind to try it.

Two weeks later he returned to tell us that he could hear conversations with comparative ease, even in the next room. "Your friends and relatives must be happy that you now hear so well," I said.

"I haven't told them," he confessed with a chuckle. "I have been sitting around listening—and do you know what? I have already changed my will twice!" (145)

UNIT 37

100. A Little Late

In the offices of the Memphis Transportation Company, there worked a young, reliable secretary who was quite an efficient transcriber and who would consistently turn out fine transcripts of whatever was dictated to her.

But she was in the habit of coming a few minutes late every day. Her boss had warned her many times and even threatened to have her transferred, but to no avail.

One day, he reached his wit's end and told her that he was going to suspend her for one day without pay and asked her when she wanted to take that day.

She thought it over carefully and then transmitted the following message to him, "If it is all right with you, I think I should like to use it up by coming in a little late every day." (134)

101. A Tooth for a Tooth

Some time ago, a number of business companies made it a practice to mail a person expensive goods that he had not ordered and then bill him for them.

One day, a doctor in Buffalo got such a package with the following letter of transmittal: "We are taking the liberty of sending you three exceptional ties. Because these excellent ties have the approval of thousands of professional men and business executives who are careful dressers, we know that you will like them. Please send us $10."

As you might expect, the doctor was considerably annoyed. He answered: "I am taking the liberty of sending you $10 worth of extra-fine pills. These excellent pills have helped thousands of professional men and business executives, and I am sure that they will help you. Please accept them in payment of the exceptional ties that you sent me." (156)

102. Shock

One morning, a couple that had been married for only a few days had a delightful surprise delivered to them by the mailman — two complimentary tickets to the best show in town. It developed, though, that the donor neglected to give his name.

All day long the couple wondered, "Who could have sent those desirable tickets?" After considerable debate, they decided to use the tickets.

They enjoyed the show, but on their return home they experienced a definite shock. All their wedding presents had been stolen. There was a note fastened directly to one of the pillows in the bedroom that read, "Now you know!" (111)

UNIT 38

103. No Smoking!

I have always had a definite sympathy for those who have the tobacco habit. That is, I have always had it the last nine days since I reformed and gave up smoking myself.The result is that my head has recently been cleared of fumes and my blood of nicotine; therefore, I have been able to review and reflect on the entire problem of smoking. I am happy to report here the results of my reflections and researches.

The average smoker spends $127.50 in twelve months on his habit—enough to buy some 35 good books or a comfortable chair or a restful holiday at some resort. All of this goes up in smoke.

Figuring still further, I uncovered the revealing fact that, if I had never started smoking, I would have saved $3,800 — enough for an excellent car or a transcontinental trip or a first payment on a desirable residence. (169) *(Concluded in Paragraph 104)*

104. No Smoking! *(Concluded)*

I have heard the financial problems of our times discussed and described and explained in many different ways, but I think I have discovered their real cause. In short, if there were no tobacco, the average home would have more than $20 a month extra at its disposal for groceries, rent, or furniture. Our financial troubles would be completely dissolved, dismissed, disposed of!

After nine days of refraining from smoking, I have discovered that civilization is not dying of poverty or war but of tobacco. How can we dispose of our problems and transact our business when our eyes are constantly blinded with smoke?

As I say, it is nine days since I discovered

my mistake. Aside from the fact that I have been miserable the whole time, these have been the happiest days of my life. I am free at last, and as I swore off for one month, I still have twenty-one days of freedom left before I am plunged back into slavery again. I am counting those days! (176)

UNIT 39

105. Recall Chart

1. Attend, attends, attendance, consider, considered, considerable.

2. Threaten, threatens, threatened, complete, completely, completed.

3. Chances, ounces, notices, informed, conformed, performed.

4. Fixes, mixes, gases, transmit, transmits, transmitted.

5. Spend, depend, expend, examine, examines, examined.

6. Procure, procures, procured, excel, excelled, excellent.

7. Hard, harder, hardly, depress, depressed, depression.

8. Bold, bolder, boldly, deserve, deserves, deserving.

9. Equal, equals, equally, repay, repaid, repayment.

10. Equip, equipped, equipment, receipt, receipts, receipted.

11. Ship, shipped, shipment, displace, displaced, displacement.

12. Reason, reasons, reasonable, disappoint, disappointed, disappointment.

13. Desire, desirable, compute, computed, waste, wasted.

14. Thought, thoughtful, sing, sink, transfer, transferred.

106. Medicine Cabinet

Recently a young couple invited me to their home for a weekend. The morning after the weekend, they got up and started for work; but I didn't get up until noon. I had my face completely soaped for shaving when I cut my ear with the razor.

More angry than hurt, I pulled open the medicine cabinet to see if I could find a styptic pencil, and out from the top shelf fell a little paper packet containing nine needles. The packet dropped into the soapy water in the bowl, where it fell apart, leaving nine needles at large in the bowl.

I was, of course, not in the best shape to recover nine needles from a bowl. For a minute or two I groped around in the bowl and soon was successful in getting four of the needles in the palm of one hand and three in the palm of the other. Two of them, I could not find. If I had given some careful thought to the matter, I wouldn't have done that. A man with lather on his face and whose ear is bleeding and who has four needles in one hand and three in the other may be said to have reached what is probably the lowest known point of human efficiency.

I attempted to shift the needles in my right hand to the palm of my left hand, but I couldn't get them off my right hand. Wet needles cling to you. In the end, I wiped the needles off on a bath towel. Hunting for seven needles in a bath towel is the hardest job in which I have ever engaged. I found five of them.

Grave thoughts came to me of what might transpire if a person used the towel.

I sat down on the edge of the tub; and, after considerable thought, I made up my mind that the thing to do was to wrap the towel in paper and take it with me. I also decided to leave a note for my friends, explaining the whole thing to them. I looked in every nook and cranny of the house, but I could not find a pencil.

I then had a sudden inspiration — I could write a message with a lipstick. The wife might have one lying around, and, if so, it might be in the medicine cabinet. I discovered what looked like the metal tip of one, and I got two fingers around it and began to pull — it was under a lot of things. Every item in the medicine cabinet began to slide. Bottles broke in the bowl and on the floor. Red, green, and white liquids spurted over me. It took me about thirty-five minutes to get the mess all together in the middle of the bathroom floor.

I made no attempt to put things back in the cabinet. I felt it would take a steadier hand than mine. Before I got out (with but one side of my face shaved), I left a note saying that I was afraid there were needles in the bathtub and in the bowl and that I had taken their towel and that I would call up and tell them all about it — I wrote it in shoe polish with the end of a toothbrush.

I did not keep my promise. I have not had the courage. I guess my friends believe that I messed up their bathroom and stole their towel on purpose. I don't know for sure, because they did not call me up either! — *James Thurber* (536)

UNIT 40

107. Table Conversation

There is one extremely important detail of conduct at dinners or anniversary parties that I have never seen discussed satisfactorily in etiquette books — what to do when you inconveniently find both the person on your left and the person on your right busily engaged in conversation with somebody else.

You have perhaps turned briefly from Mrs. Jones on your right to take care of some minor matter, and when you turned back, you found her already engaged in conversation with Mr. Smith on her other side.

So you quickly wheel about to your left, only to find yourself confronted by the back of Mrs. Brown. Consequently, you are left looking directly in front of you with a roll in one hand and nothing in particular to do with your face. Should you sit and cry softly to yourself or should you start playing with your knife and fork? (154) *(Continued in Paragraph 108)*

108. Table Conversation *(Continued)*

Of course, the main thing is to be careful not to let your hostess notice that you are not engaged in conversation. If she spots you seemingly looking into space, she will either think that you have insulted Mrs. Jones on your right and Mrs. Brown on your left, or she will feel responsible for you personally and accordingly will start a long-distance conversation that has no particular basis except that of emergency. Consequently, you must spend your time acting convincingly as though you actually are very busy.

You can always make believe that you are engaged in an exceedingly interesting discussion with the person opposite, occasionally changing the expression on your face and laughingly nodding your head knowingly. This may fool your hostess in case her glance happens to fall your way, and it will surely confuse the person sitting opposite you if he happens to catch you in the act. (169) *(Concluded in Paragraph 109)*

109. Table Conversation *(Concluded)*

If you have thought to bring along a bit of charcoal, you can make little drawings on the back on either side of you. These proceedings would, at least, get one of your partners to turn around, even though reluctantly!

As time wears on, you can start juggling your cutlery. If the other guests have any feelings, this ought to attract their attention.

Of course, there is always one last resort, and that is to slide under the table, where you can either crawl about collecting slippers that have been kicked off, growling frighteningly like a dog and scaring the more timid guests, or you might collect your bearings and crawl out from the other side and go home. Perhaps this last would be the best—it would end your evening's difficulties.—*Robert Benchley* (126)

UNIT 41

Jane Austen

One of the bright lights of the nineteenth century was Jane Austen.She exploited brilliantly all the potentials of a very narrow mode of existence. From the start, she limited her writings to the world that she knew so well and the influences that she saw at work.

She was the only daughter of a minister and spent her entire life in a country parish. Her friends included county families, ministers, and naval officers — her brothers were in the Navy.

The chief business of these people, as she saw them, was attention to social duties; their chief interest was matrimony. This is the world that Jane Austenpresents in her writings; she never steps outside of it.

One of her great admirers was Sir Walter Scott. (131)

110. The Value of Reading

Before Morris Fishbein, the brilliant doctor, decided to transfer to a school of medicine, he took a course in shorthand to speed up his notetaking. He was a brilliant scholar, who added to his brilliance by adopting exceedingly efficient working methods. When he was a young doctor, his association made him editor of its magazine, a post he held for more than a decade. He was constantly presenting creative and workable ideas, many of which were the result of his readings in all areas of medicine.

When he retired, the association had to appoint four people to do the work that this speedy reader had been doing alone. (122) *(Continued in Paragraph 111)*

111. The Value of Reading *(Continued)*

Thomas Edison, that quiet man of science who did so much for society, did not have much schooling, but his wide reading made him one of the best informed men in the country. While his deafness was a great trial to him, he says in his diary that it enabled him to concentrate on reading. In his laboratory he built up one of the finest scientific libraries of his time.

"When I want to invent an appliance," he said, "I begin by reading up on all that has been done in that area in prior days. Frankly, that is what all these books are for. I use these books to prevent the waste of time and money in the future by not doing again the things that have already been done and tried out by others." (131) *(Continued in Paragraph 112)*

112. The Value of Reading *(Continued)*

Henry Ford got the idea for his first car from a magazine—*The Science of the World*—which he read while he was away visiting a friend. He lay awake all night reading the magazine and sketching his plan for a gas engine that was far ahead of his time. We are aware, of course, that Ford was a man of action, but the reading that made him a successful man should not be overlooked. Describing his early days, he said, "I devoted every second I could spare to the reading of scientific books." (92) *(Concluded in Paragraph 113)*

UNIT 42

Illustration of Footnote

In most states a corporation comes into existence when a certificate of incorporation is prepared by the persons* who wish to form the corporation.

---

*Three or more persons usually are required as incorporators to form a stock corporation.

The document is signed by each of the incorporators and is sent to the Secretary of State for filing.

Stoppage in Transit

Sometimes a seller learns that the buyer to whom he has shipped goods is insolvent.*

---

*Failure on the part of the buyer to meet a payment is considered to be sufficient evidence of his insolvency to justify the exercise of the right of stoppage in transit by the seller.

He may notify the common carrier that the goods should not be delivered. That is known as stoppage of goods in transit. This occurs only while goods are in the hands of the common carrier.

The seller should keep this in mind, though: He may be held liable for damages if he stops goods in transit without just cause. That liability exists if the buyer is assumed to be insolvent on the basis of facts that are not correct.

113. The Value of Reading *(Concluded)*

Our fast-moving world requires more and more thoughtful reading if we hope to keep up with it. There are hundreds of magazines in the area of business and office methods. Last year there were more than a hundred papers and magazines for farmers on the market. Nearly ten thousand books are published in the United States yearly. Yet, as few people are aware, reading is a recent accomplishment. One hundred fifty years ago not half the people in the country could actually read. Those who could read had been taught by trial-and-error methods that made their reading inefficient. They read too slowly and did not gain enough from their reading. Many older persons are still poor readers.

Yes, extensive reading will yield big dividends. (132)

114. The Traits of Successful People

What combination of traits will you find in the person who has risen to a high station in life? An examination of the traits of 100 people in many different areas who have earned a fine reputation for themselves in recent years reveals that they possess these traits:

1. They are not afraid of hard work. They attack a difficult task without hesitation and stay with it until, in their estimation, the job has been done well. They are self-reliant.

2. They have the patience to sit down and think. Most people find thinking a painful process.

3. They always have a pleasant smile on their faces. In addition, they are aware of the importance of getting along with people in all stations of life.

4. They have the habit of study. They are always eager for information on any and every topic. (150)

UNIT 43

Making a Speech

Appearance

Select your clothing with care. Be sure you look "right." The feeling that you are well dressed promotes self-confidence.

Posture

Place your weight evenly on both feet and lean forward a little. Let your arms hang loosely from the shoulders. For a "change of pace" occasionally place your hands in back of you or put one hand in your pocket.

Platform Manners

As you wait your turn to speak, give your attention to any speakers who may precede you. Do not exceed the time that has been allotted to you. At the end of your speech thank your audience.

Delivery

Adopt the same tone you would use when speaking to friends. Be sure that everyone can hear you. Look at your audience. Do not look at the ceiling or the floor.

115. The Art of Saying "No"

Last year a friend of mine submitted to a feature magazine to which I subscribe a paper he had written on a subject in which he had done substantial research. The editor subsequently returned the paper, together with a letter of explanation saying that the paper did not meet the needs of the magazine.

Usually, getting back a paper that had been submitted for publication is a discouraging experience, but it was not in this instance. The letter that accompanied the returned paper was so gracious and so complimentary of the author's handling of the subject that the author said he would almost rather have it than a substantial check.

The "No" he had received was given in the right manner and was taken in the right manner — which goes to show that we can say "No" and still leave a good taste in the mouth of the person to whom we say it. (161) *(Continued in Paragraph 116)*

116. The Art of Saying "No" *(Continued)*

In the typical business concern, the employer must periodically say "No"—and the person who has learned to say it so that it will be accepted in the right spirit has a practical asset indeed.

A man I know has charge of a "suggestion" committee in a large medical, surgical, and chemical supply firm. He says that when a suggestion is made that is not practical or logical, he does not promptly turn it down. He considers the employee's feelings. He takes the trouble to meet with the person who submitted the suggestion, and the two of them analyze the suggestion critically. The one in charge of suggestions may actually think highly of the other fellow's idea but still know that technically it will not work. By analyzing and then discussing the suggestion critically, the person who made the suggestion can be brought to see it in the same way and accordingly be satisfied to take "No" for an answer. (176) *(Continued in Paragraph 117)*

UNIT 44

117. The Art of Saying "No" *(Continued)*

In business there is always the awkward matter of salary increases. When a person approaches an employer about an increase that cannot be granted, the employer can compliment the man's work and still point out the reasons why he cannot reward the employee further at the present time. The employer can assure the employee, though, that he can look forward to an upward revision of his salary just as soon as conditions permit.

When an employee understands the logical reasons why he cannot have an increase in salary, he holds no grudge afterwards. (106) *(Continued in Paragraph 118)*

118. The Art of Saying "No" *(Continued)*

A very successful and forward-looking personnel man in a transportation company in my locality tries not to say "No" when he is angry or when he is in a hurry. He also has the faculty of facing each problem squarely. He believes in the desirability of dealing with each problem at once to the best of his ability, so that the person with whom he is dealing knows exactly where he stands. It is his belief that the employee who is left in doubt about a matter will not perform so well as the one who may have been told "No" but who, at least, knows without any possibility of misunderstanding where he stands. The members of the staff appreciate this quality in him and give him their loyalty. (137) *(Concluded in Paragraph 119)*

119. The Art of Saying "No" *(Concluded)*

People in authority must often take the responsibility of saying "No" — and this is especially true of parents. The majority of parents must say "No" many times before their children reach maturity. The chances are that long afterwards the child will remember how the "No" was said—whether the parents explained their refusals with sincerity.

The majority of us have to say "No" many times in life. If we are to enjoy popularity and prosperity, we must learn how to say "No" with tact and with sincerity. (101)

UNIT 45

Essentials of a Good Savings Program

- I. Have a definite plan
  - A. A plan will tell you where your money is going.
  - B. Without a plan, you will often neglect providing for emergencies.
- II. Be sure your money is safe
  - A. Some people put money in a hole in the ground.
  - B. There are many safe places:
    1. Savings banks
       - a. No checks but you get interest.
       - b. You may take out money at any time without loss of interest.
       - c. Savings are protected by government.
    2. Government Savings Bonds, Series E
- III. Put your savings where they will earn interest
  - A. In a checking account you have convenience in making checks but receive no interest.
  - B. There are two types of interest:
    1. Simple
    2. Compound
       - a. Most banks pay compound interest.
       - b. Interest is usually compounded quarterly.

120. Dominoes

George Bernard Shaw was having a serious discussion about various matters of importance with a colleague of his at dinner in a restaurant. The orchestra struck up a particularly noisy and tedious piece. When, after the briefest pause, it launched into an even noisier piece, Shaw was obviously annoyed. He called the headwaiter and courteously asked, "Does this orchestra play anything on request?"

"Oh, yes," said the headwaiter with sincerity.

"Excellent," said Shaw seriously. "Kindly tell them to play dominoes!" (99)

121. Press the Button

Three men stood on the third floor of the new Fifth Avenue Music Building, with briefcases under their arms, waiting for an elevator. In due time the elevator came down, passing their floor without stopping. All obviously had failed to press the button. Each thought one of the others had pressed it.

Many things in life are never done because each of us thinks the other fellow will press the button that produces action. Numerous good plans never see the light of day because each of us is expecting the other fellow to put them into action.

Don't wait for the other fellow; it is your duty to press the button yourself. The world needs more button pressers. (119)

UNIT 46

Grant — first term

Weak President. Judgment of men was poor. He was often attracted by wealthy and polished people. Many of his associates were dishonest — Jay Gould, for example.

He rewarded friends and relatives.

Graft and corruption brought morale of government to a new low.

Lorant, The Presidency, page 303.

Grant — second term

Marked by more scandals such as "Whiskey Ring" and graft in Indian affairs. Felt that his friends were being persecuted and made things difficult for investigators. Those friends who were tried and convicted he pardoned. Viewed the investigations of corruption in his administration as political propaganda.

Faulkner, American Political and Social History, page 421.

Grant — the man

Grant probably excellent example of a true extrovert. Rejoiced in his friends and his family. Both he and Mrs. Grant loved to entertain and did so lavishly (thirty-course dinners!).

Mrs. Grant dressed expensively and led the social season dynamically. Probably the entire family loved the good things too much. Had little concern, it seems, for public opinion.

Me

122. Reading and Writing Practice

Dear Fred: The book that we are using in our psychology course is entitled *Modern Psychological Principles,* by the well-known psychologist, James R. Green. The author treats psychology as it applies to business, in which recent technological changes have had a great impact on office and factory personnel. I am finding the course quite exciting.

I wish I could say the same for my courses in biology and sociology! While biology and sociology are interesting studies, the professors I have for those courses are dry as dust. Sincerely, (106)

123. Revenge

One Sunday morning a schoolteacher was issued a ticket for driving through a stop light. She was told to appear in court the following Monday. She went before the judge and explained that school had already started the first week of September and that she had to teach on that Monday; therefore, she wanted her case disposed of at once.

"So you are a schoolteacher," said the judge seriously. "Madam, your presence here fulfills a long-standing ambition of mine. You sit right down at that table and write, 'On Sunday I went through a stop light' 500 times!" (97)

UNIT 47

124. He Liked Everybody

"When I die," Will Rogers once said, "my epitaph, or whatever you call those things on gravestones, is going to read: 'I joked about every big man of my time; however, I never met anybody that I didn't like.' I am so proud of that I can hardly wait to die so that it can be carved on my stone. When you come around to my grave, you will probably find me there proudly reading it."

When they built the memorial to Will Rogers some years ago, someone remembered his wish. Below the bronze bust of the famous humorist appear these words: "I never met anybody I didn't like."

Will Rogers lived up to his epitaph. He met everybody with an open hand and an open heart. (126)

125. Reading and Writing Practice

Mr. Gray: The school board has decided to hold its monthly meeting on Saturday, April 16, in the Chamber of Commerce Building. The meeting will begin at 11 a.m. and run through until about 1 p.m.

I should like to discuss with you something that I plan to bring up before the school board on April 16. Would it be convenient for you to stop at my office on Friday, April 1, about 10 a.m.? The matter I wish to discuss with you will take only a few minutes. John H. Green (91)

UNIT 48

126. Recall Chart

1. Convenient, conveniently, inconvenient, a.m., p.m., chamber of commerce.

2. Exceed, exceeded, exceedingly, long, longer, longingly.

3. Build, builder, buildings, shame, shames, shamed.

4. Begin, beginner, beginnings, chair, chairman, chairmen.

5. Diet, diets, dieted, actual, actually, actuality.

6. Apply, appliance, appliances, figure, figures, figured.

7. Create, created, creation, youth, youths, youthful.

8. Appreciate, appreciated, appreciates, repel, compel, dispel.

9. Awake, awaken, awakened, announce, announces, announcement.

10. Yell, yells, yellow, contain, contained, container.

11. Submit, submission, submitted, transform, transformation, transformed.

12. Chemical, chemicals, chemically, think, thinks, thinking.

13. Forward, backward, outward, dispute, disputes, disputed.

14. Studious, envious, serious, depend, depends, dependable.

15. New, renew, renewed, oil, soil, boil.

16. Majority, minority, sincerity, win, winner, winnings.

17. Possibility, ability, reliability, despair, despairs, despairingly.

18. January, February, September, technical, radical, particle.

127. Never Satisfied!

I met a man recently who was once on a large ocean liner that sank. When the ship took her final plunge, my friend felt himself go down into the waters. When he eventually came to the surface, a great joy possessed his soul. He was alive!

Then there came to him the thought that he could swim for only a little while. The water was very cold. About a hundred feet away, he saw a floating spar; and he felt that if he could only reach that spar it would indeed be paradise. After considerable effort, he reached it, tediously drew himself up, and sat on it. Once more he was grateful. He was alive! But the wind was cold, and he knew he could not physically hold on much longer. Just then he saw a lifeboat about five hundred feet from him. He yelled, and the boat came forward to pick him up. Again, he felt he was in paradise.

Some time later the people in the lifeboat saw a great form, with many lights, off in the distance. The great ship came nearer and nearer, and my friend uttered a great prayer that he might climb the side of the ship and lie on the deck. His prayer was soon answered.

He realized, though, that his strength had been substantially spent, and he prayed that he be placed in the most miserable room in the steerage, just so that he had a bed and could be covered with blankets.

Some of the people in the crowded steerage willingly made room for him, and when he was in the bunk, he said with sincerity, "This is paradise." But after an hour or two, the atmosphere began to depress him, so he asked a petty officer if there was any possibility that he might have a cabin. A bunk was conveniently found for him in a cabin, and he was happy and he thought, "This is paradise indeed." He slept well that night, but the next morning he realized that the cabin was not too comfortable, and so he asked the sailor who came to wait on him if there was not a berth in a cabin on the upper deck. The sailor explained that every bunk was full except in the captain's cabin. And so my friend wrote a letter to the captain of the ship. Here is the letter:

"Dear Sir: The cabin in which I am located is right over the engines. Also, it is very small and not very well ventilated. I understand that you have a vacant bunk in your cabin on the upper deck. I should appreciate it if you would let me know whether I may occupy your cabin with you. Sincerely,"

No answer or explanation came from the captain. But the moral of this story is this: Nobody is ever happy with a thing after he gets it. (456)

PART 2

UNIT 49

129. Hunger

Several hours after we have eaten, when our stomachs are almost empty, we sometimes begin to feel hungry. The feeling that results is difficult to localize, and its origin is not known. As time goes on, hunger pangs develop. They occur in the upper part of the abdomen that we sometimes call the "pit of the stomach." These hunger pangs cause exceedingly unpleasant physical feelings, and they follow one another for some time. They disappear but return periodically until the stomach again receives food.

Hunger pangs are caused by the constrictions of the empty stomach. After three or four hours following a meal, strong peristaltic movements occur in the stomach. These follow one another for about half an hour. We feel hunger pangs after each constriction. Constrictions generally disappear for one-half hour to two hours following a "hunger period." A new period of hunger then begins if no food is eaten. The cause of these constrictions has not yet been identified by the medical profession.

Hunger is a painful feeling inherited by the individual and is not modified by his experience. Appetite, on the other hand, is the desire for food which may accompany hunger, but it is not the same thing. Appetite is a sensation that can be modified by experience and is not inherited. We may still have an appetite for dessert, for example, after we have satisfied our hunger. (272)

Functions of the Blood

Most persons are aware that blood carries oxygen, carbon dioxide, and waste materials; but they do not realize that the blood also has many other functions. Here are two of these functions:

Like the hot water system in a house, the blood flows from the deeper and warmer parts of the body to the extremities and tends to distribute heat evenly to all parts of the body. Surface blood vessels in the skin can be dilated so that blood can come to the surface, thus losing heat more rapidly; or surface vessels can be constricted to keep more blood away from a cold exterior, and thus reducing heat loss. The blood, therefore, plays an important part in the regulation of body temperature.

The blood plays an important part in protecting the body from bacteria and other organisms that cause disease. The white cells of the blood afford protection by ingesting bacteria or other foreign matter appearing in the bloodstream. Another phase of protection lies in acquired resistance to infections. It is well known that in many infections the body develops defensive mechanisms that overcome bacteria or neutralize their poisonous effects. (221)

UNIT 50

131. Military Justice

Military personnel traditionally have been subject to more different systems of justice than have civilians. The British acquired the basis of their system from the Romans. The Second Continental Congress adopted the British court-martial, which has been retained, with some revisions, to the present. The basic pattern is trial by a board made up of military personnel especially appointed for the purpose.

This system of administering justice has grown to large proportions. At the peak of mobilization for the Second World War, it handled about one-third of all criminal cases in the nation. The volume of cases remains high because of the large number of personnel in the Armed Forces.

Civilians are not usually subject to military law. This immunity extends in time of peace to wives of servicemen who accompany their husbands on overseas assignments. It also extends to persons discharged from the Armed Forces, even though the offense charged was committed prior to release.

Servicemen, on the other hand, are subject to civil authority. Servicemen can be tried by civil courts for offenses committed off duty within the country. Treaties and agreements permit trials by civilian courts for off-duty offenses in a number of foreign countries.

Courts-martial. Minor offenses may be punished by commanding officers, but crimes of greater gravity are tried by "summary" courts-martial; other noncapital crimes, by "special" courts-martial; and the most serious crimes, by "general" courts-martial. The summary court-martial consists of a single officer; the special court-martial, of three or more members; and the general court-martial, of five or more members.

Court of Military Appeals. Decisions of courts-martial are first reviewed by the officers who convened them or by boards maintained for the purpose. These boards are somewhat comparable to courts of appeal in the civilian court system.

Final appeal is the Court of Military Appeals, except in those rare cases in which the Supreme Court agrees to rule on questions of law.

The Court of Military Appeals, sometimes called the "GI supreme court," was created in 1950. It consists of three judges appointed by the President from civilian life for fifteen-year terms. This court is without original jurisdiction but has three types of appellate jurisdiction. It has mandatory jurisdiction over all cases in which the death sentence has been given or in which generals or admirals are involved. It is also required to review cases certified to it by the judge advocate general of one of the three services.

The bulk of cases, however, come from petitions for review from defendants who have received adverse decisions lower down the military-justice ladder. The court has full discretion in choosing which of the many petitions for review it will grant. It does not, however, review cases that involve sentences of less than one year. (555)

UNIT 51

Notes on Class Discussion

Joan D: Not important whether state or federal government provides the funds for education.

Hank T: Yes, it is. Control should be local. Federal government has too much power now.

(How local?)

John H: Local governments influenced by local pressures. European democracies make central government control work for them.

(Which ones? Works how? Educational opportunities restricted?)

Bill T: Contributions to various governments could act like federal government's system of checks and balances.

Mary L: Biggest advantages:

1. Better teaching because of more rigid requirements for teachers, higher salaries.
2. Better buildings and equipment.
3. Wider variety of courses.
4. Standard courses.

133. Improving Your Vocabulary

Would you like to increase your mastery of words? If you would, here are five steps that will help you:

1. Read. You cannot build a vocabulary without reading. You cannot make friends if you never meet anybody and stay at home by yourself all the time. In the same way, you cannot build a vocabulary if you never meet any new words. To meet new words, you must read. The more you read, the better. A book a week is good; a book every other day is even better.

Keep on reading. Keep on meeting unfamiliar words on printed pages.

2. Look up an unfamiliar word in the dictionary. Read carefully everything the dictionary says about the word. Study the way it is pronounced, where it comes from, what it means, and what other words are connected with it. Be sure you find the meaning that fits exactly to the sentence in which you found the word. Remember that meaning. Remember the way it was used in the sentence. Compare the word with the words you would have used if *you* had written the sentence.

Looking up a word in the dictionary, though, won't get you anywhere if you don't remember what you found. If you really want to do something about your vocabulary, keep a notebook, jotting down the words you didn't understand and everything in the dictionary that will help you remember what those words mean.

3. Say the word. Get used to the way it is pronounced. Say the word aloud often enough to be sure you won't stumble over it when you use it the first time.

4. Use the word. Reading, looking up, and pronouncing is not enough. To add a word to your vocabulary, you have to use it. The first time you get a chance to work it into a conversation, do so. This is the most important step. Use the word in conversation as if it had always been yours. Never mind whether your friends will think you are showing off. Neither should you worry about not using the word entirely appropriately.

5. Keep in touch with your vocabulary. Knowing words is like knowing people. If you don't keep in touch with them, you lose them. After a while, you may even forget their names. Watch out for words that you have recently acquired. Look them up again in the dictionary if necessary. Keep saying them and using them. That is easy. In fact, you will find that the words you have just added to your vocabulary will keep cropping up in your reading and in your speech.

Vocabulary building is fun. It is fun to find out where words come from. It is even more fun to take a new word and use it to say exactly what you mean to say. (461)

UNIT 52

135. A Dissertation Upon Roast Pig

Mankind, we are told, for the first 70,000 years, ate its meat raw. It seems that the art of roasting was hit upon by accident in the following strange manner:

The Chinese farmer Ho-ti one day left his cottage in the charge of his son, who was very fond of playing with fire. While the son was building a fire, some of the sparks escaped into a pile of straw, and soon the entire cottage had burned down.

The son reached down to feel one of the pigs to see whether there were any signs of life in it. He burned his fingers; and to cool them off, he put them into his mouth.

Some of the crumbs of the burnt skin stuck to his fingers—and for the first time man had tasted crackling! Again he felt the pig. It did not burn so much now; still he licked his fingers from a sort of habit.

The truth broke into a slow understanding that it was the pig that tasted so wonderful—and he tore whole handfuls of the skin with the flesh next to it.

While he was thus enjoying himself, his father entered, armed with a big stick. When he found how affairs stood, he gave the boy a terrible beating, but he could not beat him from his pig until he had almost made an end to it.

The son raked out another pig and pushed it into his father's hands, shouting, "Eat, Father, eat the pig."

The father trembled at every joint as he

held that awful pig, but then he, too, put his fingers in his mouth. He then tasted some of the burnt pig's flavor, which was not at all unpleasant to him.

The upshot was that both father and son raked out the remaining pigs and never left the spot until they had eaten every bit of them.

The father warned his son not to let the secret escape, but strange stories got about. It was noticed that the father's cottage was now on fire more often than ever.

At length, father and son were watched, and the terrible truth was uncovered. Father and son were brought before the court and the evidence produced.

The jury was about to announce its decision when the foreman of the jury asked that some of the burnt pig be handed to the jury. He handled it and they all handled it, burning their fingers as the father and son had done before them. They put their fingers into their mouths—and, against all the evidence, they brought in a verdict of not guilty without leaving the courtroom.

The judge, who was a shrewd fellow, winked at the decision, and when court was over, he went and bought up all the pigs that could be had for love or money. In a few days the judge's town house was seen to be on fire. Soon there were fires in every part of town.

Thus this custom was carried on until, in the course of time, some wise man found out that the flesh of pigs or any other animal might be cooked ("burnt," as they called it) without the necessity of burning a whole house to dress it!—*Charles Lamb* (489)

UNIT 53

Comments on Meeting

(Column 1)

A McF

1. Two buses have been chartered from Empire Transportation Company. They furnish driver plus gasoline, etc.

2. We pay for driver's meals, housing, etc.

3. Buses will pick us up at the high school at 7:30, Monday, May 11.

4. When we get to Washington, the buses will also provide transportation on our various tours.

(Column 2)

RW

1. We have reservations for all at the Hamilton Hotel in Washington at the special rate of $6 each.

2. Everyone must stay at this hotel.

3. No meals are provided by the hotel; everyone is on his own.

4. Jane will pay the entire hotel bill.

137. The Little Things

Most of us forget the fact that it is the little things that count. We have heard often enough that this is true, but because we feel that the big things are more important, we fail to appreciate the value of little things.

The baseball player who bats .250 earns an average salary of perhaps $10,000 a season. The player who bats .350 earns $50,000 or more. The difference is only one more safe hit in every 10 times at bat, and 7 times out of 10, the batter is safe or out at first base by as narrow a margin as 6 inches. Little things make the big difference, and the player must be on the alert to capitalize on them.

How far you climb on the ladder of success depends on how much attention you give to little things. (146)

Yesterday and Tomorrow

There are two days in every week about which we should not worry—two days that should be kept free from any fear or apprehension. One of these days is Yesterday with its mistakes and cares, its aches and pains, its faults and blunders. Yesterday has passed forever beyond our control. All the money in the world cannot bring back Yesterday. We cannot undo a single act we performed. We cannot erase a single word we said. We cannot correct a single mistake. Yesterday has passed beyond our control. Let it go.

The other day we should not worry about is Tomorrow. Tomorrow is also beyond our control. Tomorrow's sun will rise, either in splendor or behind a mass of clouds—but it will rise. Until it does, we have no stake in Tomorrow, because it has not yet arrived.

That leaves us only one day—Today! And every man can fight the battles of just one day! (157)

An Educated Man

An educated man is not one whose memory is trained to carry a few dates in history. He is one who can accomplish things. A man who cannot think is not an educated man, no matter how many college degrees he may have acquired. Thinking is the hardest work anyone can do, which is probably why we have so few thinkers.

There are two extremes to avoid. One is the feeling of contempt for education; the other is the assumption that going through a college is a sure cure for ignorance. You cannot learn in any school what the world is going to do next year, but you can learn some of the things that the world has tried to do in the past and where it has failed and where it has succeeded. If education succeeded in warning the young student away from some of the false theories on which men have tried to build so that he may be saved the loss of time in finding out by bitter experience, its value would be unquestioned.—*Henry Ford* (171)

UNIT 54

139. Profit

A schoolboy, disturbed by the current fashion of speaking disparagingly of the profit system that has formed the basis of our way of life, wrote to his grandfather, asking him to "explain just how there can be a profit that is not taken from the work of someone else." The grandfather replied:

My dear Grandson: I will answer your question as simply as I can.

Profit is the result of enterprise that builds for others as well as for the enterpriser. Let us consider the operation of this fact in a primitive village of perhaps 100 persons who obtain the mere necessities of life by working hard all day long.

Our primitive village, located at the foot of a mountain, must have water. There is no water except at a spring near the top of the mountain. It takes the people one hour to go up, and they do this until at last one of them notices that the water from the spring runs down inside the mountain in the same direction that he goes when he comes down. He conceives the idea of digging a trough in the side of the mountain all the way down to the place where he has his home. He goes to work to build a trough.

Then one day this one hundredth man turns a small part of the water from the spring into his trough, and it runs down the mountain into a basin he has made at the bottom. He then says to the other 99 people that, if they will give him the daily production of 10 minutes of their time, he will give them water from his basin.

He will then receive 990 minutes of the time of the other people each day, which will make it unnecessary for him to work 16 hours a day in order to provide for his necessities. He is making a great profit—but his enterprise has given each of the 99 other people 50 additional minutes each day for himself.

The enterpriser, now having 16 hours a day at his disposal, and being naturally curious, spends part of his time watching the water run down the mountain. He sees that it pushes along stones and pieces of wood. So he develops a water wheel. Then he notices that it has power and finally makes the water wheel run a mill to grind his corn.

This one hundredth man then realizes that he has enough power to grind corn for the other 99. He says to them, "I will permit you to grind your corn in my mill if you will give me one-tenth of the time you save." They agree, and so the enterpriser now makes an additional profit. He uses the time paid him by the other 99 to build a better house for himself. (465) *(Concluded in Paragraph 141)*

UNIT 55

Table of Contents

October	Page
5 Death of Henry VIII and reign of Edward VI	4
7 Reign and death of Mary	6
9 Return to the Protestant Religion	8
12 Proposed marriage of Elizabeth	9
14 Mary, Queens of Scots	12
16 The Netherlands	15
19 Execution of Mary	17
21 Armada 1588	19
23 The great age of English literature	23

Index

(Column 1)

Burleigh
8 Remains in office after Mary's death
Drake
18 Raid on Cadiz
20 Armada
Elizabeth
6 Accession
8 Restores Protestant religion
9 Proposed marriage
12 Mary, Queen of Scots
15 Sends army to the Netherlands
19 Armada

(Column 2)

Essex
24 Irish expedition
29 Execution
Leicester
9 Death of wife
18 Head of the army in the Netherlands
Mary, Queen of England
5 Death

141. Profit *(Concluded)*

This one hundredth man's time finally becomes all his own to use as he sees fit. He does not have to work unless he chooses to. His food and shelter and clothing are provided by others. His mind, however, is constantly working, and the other 99 are constantly having more time to themselves because of his thinking and planning.

For instance, he notices that one man of the 99 makes better shoes than the others do. He arranges for this man to spend all his time making shoes, because he can feed him and clothe him and arrange for his shelter from profits.

The other 98 do not have to make their own shoes. They are charged one-tenth of the time they save. The ninety-ninth man is also able to work shorter hours, because some of the time that is paid by each of the 98 is allotted to him by the one hundredth man.

So it goes on as this one hundredth man constantly finds ways to save the 99 the total expenditure of their time—one-tenth of which he asks of them in payment for his enterprise.

But suppose that, when the one hundredth man had completed his trough down the mountain, the people had turned on him and said: "We are 99 and you are only one. We will take what water we want. You cannot prevent us, and we will give you nothing." What would have happened then?

You can see that the incentive of the most curious mind would have been destroyed. He would have seen that he could gain nothing by solving problems if he still had to use every waking hour to provide his living. There could have been no advancement in the village. The primitive state that first existed would have remained. Life would have continued to be difficult for everyone, with opportunity to do no more than work all day just for a bare living.

Need we say more to prove that there can be profit from enterprise without taking anything from others; that such enterprise adds to the ease of living for everyone?

These principles are as active in a great nation such as ours as in our imaginary village. Laws that kill incentive and cripple the honest enterpriser hold back progress. True profit is not something to be feared, because it works to the benefit of all.

We must try to build rather than tear down what others have built.

We must be fair to other men, or the world cannot be fair to us. Sincerely, Grandfather (420)

UNIT 56

143. Just-a-Little-Late Club

When I was a commuter, I sometimes went to the station early to watch the other commuters running for the trains. I came to know many of them by sight. There were ladies and old men, occasional visitors to the city, who arrived long before train time. There were businessmen who arrived one minute ahead. And just as the gate was about to slam, there would come piling across the station the members of the Just-a-Little-Late Club.

I used to sympathize with them at first, supposing them to be unfortunates who had missed the bus or had lost their watches, but after two years of watching, I understood the difficulty. They were members of the Just-a-Little-Late Club. The members of the Just-a-Little-Late Club do not change from day to day. Membership is not an accident. I submit that it is a habit and one of the most annoying in the world.

"Never be on time," Mark Twain said. "You waste too much time waiting for the other fellow." He had in mind the members of the Just-a-Little-Late Club.

I was lunching with a friend the other day when a "captain of industry" passed me. "A wonderful fellow," said my friend. "Last year I had a long series of technical meetings with him about the formation of a new company in this locality. It was necessary for us to meet almost every day for nearly three months. In all that time he was late for the proceedings but twice, and then only a few minutes. Each time he sent word to me, telling me that he would be late."

Lord Nelson said, "I owe all my success in life to having been a quarter of an hour before my time."

I hold up these records in the hope that they may do some good. Yet, with all sincerity, I believe the hope is very faint. The habit of being late is tenacious.

If I am fortunate enough to be inside when the pearly gates are closed on Judgment Day, I shall know what to expect. Five minutes later, there will be a terrific battering. Saint Peter will be surprised, but I shall not.

When the gates swing outward again, there they will be, some of the most lovable and exasperating people who ever lived—panting and apologetic to the last.—*Bruce Barton* (386)

UNIT 57

145. Western Europe and Postwar Prosperity

The economy of Western Europe today is bustling. Its farm production is high, its factories are turning out more goods than ever before, trade is at an all-time high. Much of the credit for getting Western Europe on its feet goes to the United States. Our country realized that the economic well-being of the Old World depended upon Europe's recovery.

For several years after the war, we poured millions of dollars of aid into Europe under the Marshall Plan. The countries of Western Europe used our aid wisely; they combined our dollars with good planning, hard work, and self-denial.

Britain has made a readjustment to a changed role in the world. In 1900, Great Britain was at the height of its power. The United States had not yet become an industrial rival. From the great city of London the affairs of nearly one-fourth of the world were guided. Britain's colonies were a reliable source of raw materials and a reliable market for her products. British goods carried in British ships and protected by the British navy were sold all over the world. The small, wealthy North Sea country was the world's greatest power.

Today, optimism is still voiced on the streets of London. But it is a cautious optimism tempered by years of extreme trials for Britain. Britain has dropped from first to third position in the world, behind the United States and Russia. Two world wars drained Britain of manpower and financial resources. To pay for the Second World War, Britain had to sell many of her overseas investments, such as railroads and mines. Income from these investments had formerly made up the difference between imports and exports.

Britain is more dependent on world trade than ever before. She must earn enough from exports to make up for her former income from investments. And she must do this in a market which, with the loss of her colonies, is no longer protected.

Competition from the United States, Germany, Japan, and other countries is keen. The European Common Market is cutting increasingly into British sales abroad. For this reason Britain wants to belong to the Common Market.

But despite competition, British exports are at an all-time high. She has managed this partly by limiting the amount of goods that can be bought at home.

A great part of Britain's current income has had to go into modernizing her industries, such as her coal mines and her textile factories. Only by producing high-quality products at low cost can Britain attract the customers that are so necessary to her survival.

British products and British workmanship have a long-established reputation for excellence. This reputation, carefully encouraged and well deserved, is standing Britain in good stead. She has managed to retain a large share of the trade of her former colonies and to win new markets as well. (520)

UNIT 58

147. The English Language

No language is spoken exactly the same way in all parts of the country or countries in which it is used. We can easily spot an Englishman by the way some of his pronunciations and some of his words are different from ours. We can also often tell from what part of our country a person comes by listening to him talk. Differences in words, pronunciations, phrasing, and in grammatical habits that are commonly used in a section of the country are called regional dialects.

Actually, a dialect is speech that does not attract attention to inhabitants in a region where it is used. Dialects are not peculiar to backward regions; nor are dialects the result of lack of education or social standing. An educated Westerner will speak somewhat differently from a Southerner of a similar degree and quality of education. A dialect may show traits of differing British dialects spoken by early settlers or foreign languages spoken by large numbers of people in the region.

There are fewer differences among the dialects of our country than might be expected in a country of such size—many fewer than exist among the dialects in the much smaller Great Britain. The relative freedom of movement of our people, our educational system, the circulation of books and magazines, and more recently radio and television, all keep people who are thousands of miles apart speaking substantially the same language.

There are three speech areas in our country to be traditionally recognized: eastern, southern, and western. Increased travel, education, and reading are reducing the varieties of dialects in our country. Words peculiar to a local area will probably survive, since they fill a real need. The frequent use of localisms on radio and television and in stories may help make one region more tolerant of the language of others, and it may very well introduce into general use words formerly confined to a particular locality.

People's feelings about the use of localisms vary greatly. Some believe that they should be weeded out; others believe that a person should retain as much as possible of the flavor of his native speech. It is a problem that each person will have to settle for himself. An educated person will tend to shed the more obvious local pronunciations of his youth, and he may have little opportunity to use purely local words. But conscious effort to change his speech to a different pattern will often result in an unhappy combination of elements of both.

Many young people first become conscious of their native speech when they go to school or college. They should study their speech if it attracts attention, but they need not abandon it just because their classmates remark about it. They should try to find what is suitable and effective and what seems to defeat easy communication. It would be a pity if everyone's speech were reduced to the colorless tones of a network announcer! (564)

UNIT 59

149. William Shakespeare

Shakespeare was born on April 23, 1564, in the village of Stratford. His mother was of gentle blood and possessed considerable wealth. His father was a man of great influence in the village, although of lower status than his wife.

Shakespeare attended the Stratford grammar school, where he learned a little Latin and Greek.

Traveling companies of actors often visited Stratford and had to get the permission of Shakespeare's father in order to perform their plays. At their performances, Shakespeare was sometimes present, getting his first exposure to the world of drama.

In about 1578 the fortunes of his father began to decline, and Shakespeare had to leave school. Sometime between 1585 and 1587 he left Stratford to seek his own fortune in London. Outside the walls of London was the oldest of London's playhouses called simply "The Theater." The head of the company was the famous actor, James Burbage. Whether by accident or intent, Shakespeare soon found himself a member of Burbage's company, in which he became an important actor and a reviser of old plays.

The foundation of Shakespeare's great fortune was probably laid by a substantial gift from his friend and patron, the Earl of Southhampton, but it was mainly by his earnings in the theater that he was able to reinstate his parents to their old status in Stratford and to obtain for himself a fine home with many acres of land. In that home he retired at the relatively young age of 50. He died in 1616 at the age of 52 and was buried in the old church by the Avon.

The exact dates on which Shakespeare's plays were produced are not known. Often the publication of a play could not occur until years after its first appearance on the stage, and only seventeen of his thirty-seven plays were published in his lifetime.

The common opinion that Shakespeare was not appreciated in his own time is only partly true. If other evidence were not available to prove the esteem in which he was held, the vast fortune that he amassed would be enough to show his popularity at court and with the theater-going public. The most significant hint we have of his personal charm is the adjective that is constantly applied to him by his friends—gentle. (426)

UNIT 60

151. Proteins and Calories

As you have seen, the most important body-building foods are proteins, fats, and carbohydrates. Of all these, however, proteins are the most essential.

Proteins consist of amino acids, of which twenty-two are known. Your body itself actually produces a sufficient supply of twelve of these acids; the other ten amino acids must come from the proteins you eat.

Meats, eggs, fish, milk, and cheese contain all ten of the amino acids that your body does not supply. That is why they are called "complete proteins." Beans, peas, nuts, and other similar vegetables contain some, but not all, of the essential acids. They are excellent protein foods if you supplement them with animal proteins.

If you omit one or more of these essential acids from your diet for a considerable period of time, you may be endangering your health. For example, if your body is starved for tryptophan, you may develop eye trouble or gradually become bald. If your body gets too little of the acid called cysteine, small cuts and scratches will heal slowly.

If you find yourself gaining weight too rapidly and consult a physician for advice as to what to do about it, he is likely to put you on a diet consisting of a certain number of "calories" a day. What is a calorie? It is simply a measurement of heat in the same way that an inch is a measurement of length and an ounce is a measurement of weight.

How many calories should your daily diet be able to release? This depends on many elements. For example, we need more energy, or calories, when we are working than we need when we are resting.

We need more calories in cold weather than in warm weather. Men need more calories than women. The average boy in high school may need between 3,000 and 4,000 calories a day; the average girl, from 2,500 to 2,800 calories.

Important as a consideration of calories in diet planning is, however, it must not be the only consideration. Every diet must contain in proper proportions foods that contain all the necessary nutrients. A diet must make provision for proteins, carbohydrates, and fats, as well as for vitamins, salt, and other minerals. (417)

UNIT 61

153. Climate

Climate is the *average* of weather conditions for a long period of time. Weather, on the other hand, refers to conditions of the atmosphere during a short period of time. "Christmas weather" in the north central states means temperatures down and around freezing or zero, with snow on the ground and the possibility of snow every three or four days.

In contrast, *climate* refers to the average weather conditions over many years. When we refer to the climate of New York, for example, we think of the average conditions in spring, summer, fall, and winter in that particular locality.

Climate is an important factor in the health of people in the various parts of the world. Where climatic conditions are hot and damp, bacteria grow and increase rapidly, and disease is usually widespread. The presence of bacteria makes it difficult to preserve food and to maintain a good diet for the people. In cold and dry areas, bacteria find it more difficult to grow, so that food does not spoil so easily. People in such areas usually have a better diet.

Furthermore, epidemics are usually less widespread in cold and dry regions than they are in hot and humid regions.

Where climatic conditions are fairly constant throughout the year — that is, where there is the same temperature, the same amount of sunshine, little variation in seasons or in the length of days such as in the tropics — life tends to become monotonous.

People in tropical regions also find it difficult to work at a high rate of speed. Usually they have less energy and are willing to put off work until "mañana."

On the other hand, a variety of weather conditions — from hot to cold — stimulates people to greater activity.

Climatic conditions also influence the ways in which people protect themselves from conditions of the atmosphere. In the rainy tropics the natives are concerned primarily with protecting themselves from rain. They do not have the problem of building warm homes to protect themselves from cold. People who live in, for example, Siberia must not only protect themselves from snow but must also build their homes so that the cold will be kept out as much as possible.

They need to make but little provision for ventilation, while natives of tropical regions need as much ventilation as possible. Their homes are left open, perhaps only screened to prevent the entrance of insects, so that the air may circulate freely. (452)

UNIT 62

155. Small and Big Societies

Up until the nineteenth century, a man's social world consisted of a small community of perhaps a few hundred people. He was aware of a larger social grouping — his nation — but it gave him little and asked little of him. His world of reality revolved around his friends and neighbors in his village. Just about all his needs were provided by those friends and neighbors.

Man's wants in those times were few when compared with the present. Most of them were satisfied by his family. Those that could not be supplied by either the family or the community were such commodities as sugar, coffee, silk, and so on — many of which were considered to be luxuries one could do without.

Money in such a community was not as

important as it is in a modern society. The most important thing was his good standing in the community. If the head of a family became ill, the rest of his family worked a little harder and were able to carry on the farming or other business on which their economic security depended.

In times of crisis, such as harvesting or planting, the neighbors pitched in and helped. Medical expenses were small. Any medical attention that was necessary was provided by a doctor who was a neighbor and friend of the patient and whose fees were modest.

The effect of illness in modern society is quite different. To begin with, illness may mean a complete loss of income. One's family or neighbors are incapable of taking over the father's job. Income stops, but expenses increase.

The needs of modern man are much more extensive than those of our grandparents. Furthermore, we are unable to fill these needs through our own labor. They must be purchased with money.

Most of our needs are satisfied by strangers, many of whom we have never met. We are bound together by needs but not by affection.

Most of man's experience has been in small societies; we have little experience in organizing a big society. It was Aristotle who observed, "It is difficult, if not impossible, to properly govern men in large bodies." What seemed impossible to Aristotle is a must for us. Finding ways to govern men in large bodies is the greatest challenge of our times. (387)

UNIT 63

157. Pests

One of the most serious problems confronting our farmers is that of losses due to insect pests. In this country the losses in one year as a result of the depredations of more than six hundred injurious insect species amount to billions of dollars. The control of these pests is not easy—largely because there are so many kinds of them.

There are more species of insects than there are of all other kinds of animals put together. This variation is accompanied by equally great variation in life habits, so that it is impossible to deal with all insects in the same way. An insecticide that is effective against one species may be totally useless against another, or it may be effective at certain periods in the life cycle and not at others. Furthermore, some insects are beneficial. We do not want to kill them along with pests or do damage to other useful animals and plants.

An insect pest must be studied to discover what kinds of foods it eats, what its natural enemies are, and what types of poisons can control it.

In recent years many new chemicals have been developed as insecticides against these pests as well as against medically important insects. Unfortunately, in the past chemicals have in some cases been applied to insect control without prior and thorough field study of their effects. One serious result of such activity is often the increase of another pest as serious as the first. Attempts to control the larva of the codling moth (the apple worm) with DDT resulted in some areas in an increase of a pest called the two-spotted mite. The codling moth larva ruins the fruit, while the two-spotted mite destroys the foliage.

Before the advent of DDT, codling moths were becoming more and more resistant to other insecticides, although there was no serious problem with the mites. Soon after the DDT was used, codling moths were well under control, but the two-spotted mite had increased to the point where it was an important pest. Apparently, DDT was not only effective in destroying the codling moth, but it was also killing the natural enemies of the mite. A thorough study of the moth and its associates in the apple-tree community might have prevented the occurrence of such an unhappy event. (425)

UNIT 64

159. Our Psychological Wants

All human beings have psychological wants that must be satisfied. These psychological wants arise from the fact that humans are social creatures who grow up and live and work with other people.

There are five classes of psychological wants that have been generally accepted by scientists who study human motivation. These are basic, natural things that people want from life and work—the things people work for.

1. *To keep alive.* Reflexes and biological needs are involved in this. We want to eat, sleep, breathe, rest, fall in love, and marry.

2. *To feel safe.* Expressions of this motivating force are often seen in such human traits as the desire for insurance, religion, protection from criminals, and unfair competition.

3. *To be social.* We wish to be accepted by others so that the crowd seems less lonely. We join groups to be with our friends.

4. *To feel respected.* We want to think well of ourselves and desire others to. We select clothes not merely for bodily comfort but also to give us reassurance and to show our good standing in the community. We buy a more expensive car than we can afford for similar motives.

5. *To do work we like.* The "postman's holiday"—taking a walking trip—is an example. The garage mechanic who spends every spare moment tinkering with an old car at home in his yard is another example. Pride in our work may be due mostly to this want. In this age of mass production and occupational specialization, not all of us can do exactly the work we should like to; consequently, we seek other outlets. Some find the outlet in hobbies. Others go to ball games. As humorist F. P. Dunne said, "Work is work if you are paid to do it, and it is pleasure if you pay to be allowed to do it."

Some of these five psychological wants take priority over others at times. The ones listed first in this discussion usually take precedence over the others in human behavior.

Consider the want to keep alive. Go without food for a few days, and your motivation to be social or feel respected will be overwhelmed by the animal-like struggle for food. The want to feel respected takes priority over the want to do work one likes, as shown by the many who do work that only half interests them in order to be on a job that has prestige in the community.

Related to this is the fact that placing workers on jobs that fit them best may not count so much in the long run as handling them so that their feelings of personal worth are enhanced. These wants may be intangible, but they are all-powerful. (475)

UNIT 65

161. Inflation and Deflation

Inflation may be defined as a time of rising prices; deflation, as a time when most prices are falling. The major cause of inflation and deflation is a change in the total of money spending relative to the flow of goods offered for sale. If the total of purchasing power coming on the market is not matched by a sufficient flow of goods, prices will tend to rise. On the other hand, when total spending declines, prices and production tend to fall.

Inflation tends to favor debtors at the expense of creditors and fixed-income receivers. Deflation has the opposite effect. Suppose you lend a person $1,000 today and are paid back one year from now. If in the meantime prices have doubled, then the debtor will be paying you back only one-half as much real purchasing power as you lent him.

If prices were to increase a trillion-fold, as they did in the German inflation of 1920-1923, then the wealth of creditors would be completely wiped out. Savings bonds bought for $75 in 1944 would have paid off $100 in 1954. But one hundred 1954 dollars had a lower purchasing power than did seventy-five 1944 dollars.

However, a person who invests his money in real estate, in common stocks, or in commodities makes a great profit during inflation. The volume of sales shoots up. Prices rise between the time that businessmen buy and sell their goods. Fixed or overhead costs remain the same; other costs rise but not so rapidly as prices. For all these reasons, profits increase—often faster than does the cost of living.

In time of deflation, the shoe is on the other foot. Creditors and fixed-income receivers tend to gain at the expense of debtors.

If prices fall between the time that a creditor lends money and is repaid, then he gets back more purchasing power than he lent. Between the time that a businessman buys and sells goods, he will have to take a loss.

The widow who withstood the urge to buy common stocks during a boom and instead put her money into Government bonds finds herself better off. A hoarder who earns no interest on the money he hides under his mattress finds the real value of his wealth increasing every day as prices fall.

If prices fall at the rate of 10 percent each year, he is being rewarded for his act of hoarding at a 10 percent rate, while the businessman who is foolish enough to give someone a job may find that he cannot even get back his original outlay, much less earn a profit. (468)

UNIT 66

163. The Idea of Democracy

The idea of democracy today is much broader than it was two centuries ago. At first those who talked of democracy thought mostly about political democracy; that is, they talked about giving more people the right to vote and hold office. They wanted to protect individual rights such as those listed in the Bill of Rights.

Today we think these rights are extremely important, of course, and we are still working to improve our political democracy. In addition, however, we think of democracy as having other sides. For example, democracy has come to mean that every young person should have a chance to go to school and obtain the education that will make his life more useful and happier. It has come to mean that everyone should have opportunities for earning a living and for enjoying good health. It has come to mean that everyone should have a chance to serve his nation. In other words, democracy today includes the ideal that every person shall have a chance to make as great a success of his life as his ability and hard work will permit.

Democracy today emphasizes the importance of individuals. It is a part of democracy that each person, with his own abilities, opinions, and ambitions, is to be considered as an individual. Each person is to be judged by what he is and what he can do rather than by where he came from or who his parents are.

Every citizen has duties as well as rights, however. If he does not perform his duties, he will not long enjoy his rights. He obviously has the duty to vote, though too many citizens fail to do so. But a citizen's duty only begins with voting.

He should make his views known by expressing them to friends and by writing them to newspapers and to public officials. Best of all, he can become a working member of the political party of his choice.

The private citizen can contribute to the continued progress of democracy by supporting education.

He can serve as a member of the local board of education, attend meetings of parent-teacher groups, and keep up to date with changes in educational methods.

He can also strengthen democracy by encouraging the organizations to which he belongs to follow democratic practices. When another citizen's personal rights are being threatened, he can stand up and speak for democracy. (444)

UNIT 67

165. Motivation in Learning

Most students learn most effectively if they feel a *need* for learning, if they can see some practical application for what they are learning. Unfortunately, much of the information that the student is asked to absorb in an academic program is remote from his immediate concerns. Some studies may be helpful to the student's attainment of his long-range goals, if he has any—a course in chemistry for a pre-med student, for example. Some required courses, however, appear to have little bearing on the student's goals.

Studies of motivation indicate that learning will occur in proportion to the student's desire to master the material to be studied and his interest in it. Therefore, the student who knows what he wants to do and can see the relationship between his goals and his present activities has a positive advantage over the one who has no immediate or long-term goals.

Unfortunately, from the student's standpoint, many of the courses that he is required to take represent simply a necessary evil in his pursuit of a degree.

The student who consciously attempts to stimulate an interest in the material to be studied and who tries to acquire knowledge for its own sake will learn more effectively and retain more of what he learns than if he approaches his courses as mere means to unrelated ends.

Often the college student is not able to set a goal for himself until he is in his twenty's. It is not uncommon to hear students say, "I don't know what I want to do when I graduate." Parents sometimes complicate the student's problem further with such comments as, "Haven't you yet decided on a major? You can't just keep taking courses that may not be of any value to you."

Such statements reflect the concept of some parents that the sole purpose of a college education is preparation for a job and that each course the student takes should contribute to that purpose.

A student should feel justified in taking courses simply because they represent unexplored areas of knowledge or because they contribute to his general understanding and enjoyment. If students believed that such reasons were legitimate ones, they would have greater motivation to learn. (410)

UNIT 68

167. The Personnel of Congress

Members of the House have a short term of service—two years—and a low age requirement—twenty-five. Each member of the House must be a resident of the state from which he is elected and must have been a citizen of the United States for at least seven years. Custom dictates that a member must reside in the district that he represents, but there have been some exceptions.

Vacancies in the House are normally filled by a special election called by the executive authority of the state.

Senators serve long terms—six years—and have a higher age requirement—thirty years of age. A senator must also be a resident of the state he represents. He must have been a citizen nine years prior to election to the upper house. Senate vacancies may be filled by appointment by a governor if state law authorizes it.

Nearly 60 percent of the members of the two houses are attorneys. The second largest occupational group is composed of persons in various branches of business. Farmers, teachers, and newspapermen follow in order.

A recent review of the personnel of Congress revealed that the average age of senators was fifty-seven, while that of members of the House was fifty-one. Nearly all had previous public experience before election to Congress. A large majority had attended college or professional schools.

Privileges of members of Congress include certain immunity from arrest and special freedom of speech. Members can be arrested only for treason, felony, and breach of the peace; they cannot be arrested in civil suits. Members of Congress speak freely in either house without fear of criminal prosecution or civil suits. They cannot be questioned for any speech or debate made on the floor of either house.

The salary of senators and members of the House is $22,500 per year, all of which is subject to income tax; but members may claim business-expense deductions for the extra cost of maintaining a second residence. The speaker of the House and the president of the Senate receive $35,000 each. These salaries are established and altered by law. Each member is allowed 20 cents a mile traveling expenses to and from Washington once each season. Each member is given an allowance for clerk hire. He can send official mail under postal frank free of charge.

Congress has a life of two years. Each Congress since the first (1789-1790) has been numbered consecutively. The Ninetieth Congress was elected in 1966.

A regular session occurs once each year. Each regular session begins on January 3 and adjourns on July 31, unless otherwise provided by Congress. The President has power to call special sessions. (514)

UNIT 69

169. The Body and Rest

After we have toiled hard and long at a task, we want to rest or sleep. There is definite survival value in rest and sleep. If we do not get them, we cannot go on very long. Animals have been known to die after fourteen or more days without sleep. Just how long humans can remain awake without suffering fatal effects is not known.

Experiments have been conducted by scientists in which they stayed awake for almost five days. The scientists found it very difficult to remain awake after the first few days. The only way they could remain awake was to keep some muscles active. They found that with each passing hour their tempers became sharp and little incidents annoyed them. Aside from that, there did not seem to be any ill effects.

Short periods of rest definitely allow for "recharging the batteries," so to speak. But why is it necessary that we sleep as long as most of us find it necessary? If it is merely for the sake of replenishing the energies that we use up during the hours that we are awake, we should expect to get up in the morning very much refreshed and able to work at our greatest capacity.

Yet, tests have shown that most efficient performance of tasks requiring skill does not take place just after rising but much later in the day.

Another mysterious aspect is that sleep does not necessarily follow only when we are tired. We can fall asleep when we are not at all tired. Is there any value in such sleep?

While we sleep, many of the body's activities are reduced to their lowest points. Our heart rate slows down. Our blood pressure drops. Our breathing becomes slow and irregular. Our metabolic rate decreases to a lower rate than at any other time, mainly because muscle tone is also at its lowest rate. In addition, our body temperature falls slightly.

The depth of sleep varies considerably. It is deepest at the end of the first hour and gradually lightens until the waking hour.

In deep sleep no dreams occur, and movements of the body are at a minimum. Dreams occur most often just before we wake and, if they are exciting, may result in changes opposed to those usually occurring in sleep—fast heartbeat, high blood pressure, and rapid breathing. (414)

UNIT 70

171. Telling a Story

Some storytellers can make a simple experience sizzle with excitement, while others kill even the best tale. Whether a story goes over or "flops" depends on the skill of the speaker. While there are some people who seem to be naturally gifted, more often good storytellers are made, not born. They have studied the techniques of good storytelling and practiced them until they have achieved a polished style.

Here are some things you can do to make a story successful:

1. Make it easy for the listener to get the picture by stating the subject at the beginning of the story.

2. Don't digress. Tell your story in a clear manner without bringing in unnecessary details by haggling over whether something happened Wednesday at two or on Tuesday at four.

3. Use explicit terms. The person who says "it" or "thing" or "that fellow" is likely to lose his listener. The experts learn to be as exact as possible and to use a specific term for a general one whenever possible. How much more colorful a picture is created by saying "the aroma of roast beef and apple pie" instead of "the smells of dinner."

4. Keep it brief. Most stories are strung out too long.

5. Once you have told your punch line, stop! Some people enjoy their own stories so much that they like to repeat the ending so that they can laugh all over again. Maybe *they* can, but chances are that their listeners cannot.

The most successful stories are told with a light touch. Some people with reputations for humor have developed quite a sense of fun, so that they can find something amusing in what others would consider a dry incident. They regard the world as a very happy place, and since they look for fun, they can usually find it and can pass it on to others.

The best way to improve your storytelling technique is to practice. Try jokes and funny stories at first. These must be kept going at a fast pace.

A good way to improve your ability to tell a serious experience is to select a brief newspaper story. After you have read it carefully, put the paper aside and write your own version. Compare your version with the original to see where you are weak, where you may have digressed, or where you could have used more forceful or colorful words.

Practice telling stories aloud to yourself. Then practice telling them to your friends. The more you keep at it, the smoother your delivery will become. Make yourself tell at least three different stories to friends each day. Soon you will be able to tell stories with the best of them. (459)

KEY TO CHARTS ON BACK LEFT END PAPER

Brief Forms of Gregg Notehand in Order of Presentation

4. I, is, a-an, have, for, am.
7. It, in, of, are-our, will, the.
12. Shall, be-by, you, when, would, were.
16. With, what, there-their, was, this, about.
21. Under, over, which, opportunity, should, could.
27. And, suggest, short, work, important-importance, where.
31. Question, yesterday, send, probable, difficult, into.

100 Frequently Used Words in Alphabetic Order

1. A-an, about, after, all, also, am, and.
2. Any, are-our, as, at, be-by, been, before,
3. But, can, come, could, date, day, did.
4. Do, find, for, from, get, give, glad.
5. Go, good, had, has, have, he, her-here.
6. Him, his, hope, how, I, if, in.
7. Is, it, just, know, made, make, matter.
8. May, me, more, much, must, my, not.
9. Now, of, on, only, or, other, out.
10. Over, please, same, say, see, send, sent.
11. Shall, she, should, so, some, take, that.
12. The, them, there-their, they, this, time, to.
13. Up, us, very, was, we, well, were.
14. What, when, which, will, wish, with, would.
15. You, your.

INDEX TO GREGG NOTEHAND

The first figure refers to the unit; the second refers to the paragraph.

THE ALPHABET

ā 2, 2
ă 13, 46
ä 13, 47
ah 41, 112
aw 41, 112
aw 15, 52
b 6, 28
ch 10, 37
d 3, 12
ded 29, 82
den 32, 90
ē 2, 8
ĕ 11, 40
ēa 41, 110
f 2, 6
g 9, 35
h 5, 23
ī 10, 39
ĭ 11, 41
īa 41, 111
ĭa 41, 110
j 10, 38
k 9, 34
l 4, 19
ld 34, 95
m 2, 10
md 25, 75
men 30, 83
min 30, 84
mt 25, 75
n 2, 9
nd 24, 73
ng 23, 71
ngk 23, 72
nt 24, 74
ō 4, 17
ŏ 15, 51
obscure vowel 11, 42
oi 17, 56
o͞o 9, 33
o͝o 18, 61
ow 22, 69
p 6, 27
r 4, 18
rd 34, 94
s, comma 2, 1
s, left 6, 26
ses 31, 88
sh 10, 36
sw 19, 62
t 3, 11
tain 32, 89
ted 29, 81
ten 32, 89
th 13, 48
ū 19, 64
ŭ 18, 60
v 2, 7
w 19, 62
w dash 19, 63
wh 19, 62
y 42, 113
z 2, 1; 6, 26

PRINCIPLES

abbreviation 40, 107
capitalization 3, 13
compounds 47, 124
days 46, 123
intersection 47, 125
months 46, 123
omission of ē in ū 45, 121
omission of minor vowel 5, 24
omission of short u 22, 70
omission of vowel in *-ation*, etc. 42, 114
omission of vowel in *-ious*, *-eous* 45, 120
past tense 11, 43
phrasing 4, 21
punctuation 3, 14

WORD BEGINNINGS

be- 28, 80
com- 36, 99
con- 36, 98
de- 37, 102
des- 38, 104
di- 37, 102
dis- 38, 104
ex- 37, 101
for- 28, 80
in- 28, 80
over- 21, 67
re- 38, 103
sub- 43, 115
trans- 37, 100
under- 21, 67

WORD ENDINGS

-ble 35, 96
-cal 43, 116
-cle 43, 116
-ful 35, 97
-ing 5, 23
-ingly 40, 108
-ings 40, 109
-lity 44, 118
-lty 44, 118
-ly 15, 53
-ment 32, 91
-ology 46, 122
-rity 44, 119
-tion 18, 59
-ual 17, 58
-ure 17, 57
-ward 44, 117

BRIEF FORMS

a 4, 20
about 16, 54
am 4, 20
an 4, 20
and 27, 78
are 7, 29
be 12, 44
by 12, 44
could 21, 67
difficult 31, 86
for 4, 20
have 4, 20
I 4, 20
importance 27, 78
important 27, 78
in 7, 29
into 31, 86
is 4, 20
it 7, 29
of 7, 29
opportunity 21, 67
our 7, 29
over 21, 67
probable 31, 86
question 31, 86
send 31, 86
shall 12, 44
short 27, 78
should 21, 67
suggest 27, 78
the 7, 29
their 16, 54
there 16, 54
this 16, 54
under 21, 67
was 16, 54
were 12, 44
what 16, 54
when 12, 44
where 27, 78
which 21, 67
will 7, 29
with 16, 54
work 27, 78
would 12, 44
yesterday 31, 86
you 12, 44

BRIEF FORMS OF GREGG NOTEHAND

IN ORDER OF PRESENTATION

Unit						
4						
7						
12						
16						
21						
27						
31						

100 FREQUENTLY USED WORDS

IN ALPHABETIC ORDER

1							
2							
3							
4							
5							
6							
7							
8							
9							
10							
11							
12							
13							
14							
15							

NOTE: The key to the above charts appears on page 351.